LEARNING
AND KNOWLEDGE

Companion Volumes

The companion volumes in this series are: *Curriculum in Context* edited by Bob Moon and Patricia Murphy, *Learners, Learning and Assessment* edited by Patricia Murphy and *Learners and Pedagogy* edited by J Leach and Bob Moon.

All of these Readers are part of a course, Learning, Curriculum and Assessment, that is itself part of the Open University MA Programme.

The Open University MA in Education

The Open Universiry MA in Education is now firmly established as the most popular postgraduate degree for education professionals in Europe, with over 3,500 students registering each year. The MA in Education is designed particularly for those with experience of teaching, the advisory service, educational administration or allied fields.

Structure of the MA

The MA is a modular degree, and students are therefore free to select from a range of options the programme which best fits in with their interests and professional goals. Specialist lines in management and primary education are also available. Study in the Open University's Advanced Diploma and Certificate Programmes can also be counted towards the MA, and successful study in the MA programme entitles students to apply for entry into the Open University Doctorate in Education programme.

COURSES CURRENTLY AVAILABLE:
- Management
- Child Development
- Primary Education
- Curriculum, Learning and Assessment
- Special Needs
- Language and Literacy
- Mentoring
- Education, Training and Employment
- Gender
- Educational Research
- Science Education
- Adult Learners
- Maths Education

OU supported open learning

The MA in Education programme provides great flexibility. Students study at their own pace, in their own time, anywhere in the European Union. They receive specially prepared study materials, supported by tutorials, thus offering the chance to work with other students.

The Doctorate in Education

The Doctorate in Education is a new part-time doctoral degree, combining taught courses, research methods and a dissertation designed to meet the needs of professionals in education and related areas who are seeking to extend and deepen their knowledge and understanding of contemporary educational issues. It should help them to:

- develop appropriate skills in educational research and enquiry

- carry out research in order to contribute to professional knowledge and practice.

The Doctorate in Education builds upon successful study within the Open University MA in Education programme.

How to apply

If you would like to register for this programme, or simply to find out more information, please write for the *Professional Development in Education* prospectus to the Course Reservations Centre, PO Box 724, The Open University, Walton Hall, Milton Keynes, MK7 6ZS, UK (Telephone 0[044] 1908 653231).

LEARNING
AND KNOWLEDGE

edited by
Robert McCormick and Carrie Paechter
at The Open University

P·C·P
Paul Chapman
Publishing Ltd

Paul Chapman Publishing

in association with

TheOpen
University

The Open University

First published in 1999
© 1999 Compilation, original and editorial material, The Open University
Reprinted 2000

 Paul Chapman Publishing Ltd
SAGE Publications Ltd
6 Bonhill Street
London EC2A 4PU

SAGE Publications Inc.
2455 Teller Road
Thousand Oaks, California 91320

SAGE Publications India Pvt Ltd
32, M-Block Market
Greater Kailash-I
New Delhi 110 048

British Cataloguing in Publication Data

A catalogue record for this book is available from the British Library
ISBN 185396 4263
ISBN 185396 4271 (pbk)

Typeset by Dorwyn Ltd, Rowlands Castle
Printed in Great Britain

Contents

Section 3   Learning in Domains

Series Introduction

Learning, curriculum and assessment are at the core of the educational process. In the politically charged and value laden context of curriculum reform, an understanding of well grounded evidence about learning theories, knowledge and teaching and assessment practice is essential. Policy development and educational practice in a number of countries is being built around aspects of new understanding about the nature of mind; an acknowledgement that knowledge has long outgrown the traditional discipline categorisations of schools and universities and a realisation that learning and assessment is an essentially social process.

This book is one of a series of four readers that gather together recent research and writing around a number of key issues and themes in curriculum. The books, therefore, act as sources from which a number of narratives can be deduced. The broader contexts of curriculum are considered in the first volume of the series, the remaining three books focus us on learning and assessment, knowledge and pedagogy. The selection is a resource for anyone seeking a deeper understanding of the way any curriculum, formal and informal, is constructed, enacted and experienced. The accompanying Open University course (E836 *Learning, Curriculum and Assessment*) sets out to show one interpretation of the relevance of these ideas to practice in schools, colleges and other educational settings.

Jenny Leach
Robert McCormick
Bob Moon
Patricia Murphy
The Open University, Milton Keynes

Acknowledgements

The editors and publishers wish to thank the following for permission to use copyright material:

Academic Press, Inc for material from Steven R. Williams, 'Mathematics (Grades 7–12)' in Gury D. Phye, ed. *Handbook of Academic Learning: Construction of Knowledge* (1997) pp. 343–68;

American Anthropological Association for Sylvia Scribner, 'Knowledge at work', *Anthropology and Education Quarterly,* 16:3 (1985) pp. 199–206;

American Educational Research Association for S. Messick, 'Meaning and values in test validation: the science and ethics of assessment', *Educational Researcher*, 18:2 (1989) pp. 5–11. Copyright © 1989 American Educational Research Association; and material from P. L. Grossman and S. S. Stodolsky, 'Content as context: the role of school subjects in secondary school teaching', *Educational Researcher*, 24:8 (1995) pp. 5–11. Copyright © 1995 American Educational Research Association;

Cambridge University Press for material from J. Lave and E. Wenger, 'Legitimate peripheral participation in communities of practice' in *Situated Learning: Legitimate Peripheral Participation* (1991) pp. 91, 94–117;

Lawrence Erlbaum Associates, Inc for R. Glaser, 'Expert knowledge and processes of thinking' in D. F. Halpern, ed., *Enhancing Thinking Skills in the Sciences and Mathematics* (1990) pp. 63–75; and S. Carey and C. Smith, 'On understanding the nature of scientific knowledge', *Educational Psychologist*, 28:3 (1993) pp. 235–51;

Kluwer Academic Publishers for material from Wolff-Michael Roth, Authentic School Science: Intellectual Traditions' in *Authentic School Science* (1995) pp. 12–19, 26–30;

The National Academy of Education for material from J. G. Greeno, P. D. Pearson and A. H. Schonenfeld, *Implications for the NationalAssessment of Educational Progress of Research on Learning and Cognition* (1997) pp. 161, 162–4, 183–9, 192–200;

Falmer Press for Carrie Paechter, 'Some voices are more equal than others' in *Educating the Other – Gender, Power and Schooling* (1998) Chap. 6;

The University of Chicago Press for material from Israel Scheffler, *Conditions of Knowledge: an Introduction to Epistemology and Education* (1965) pp 1–5.

Every effort has been made to trace the copyright holders but if any have been inadvertently overlooked the publishers will be pleased to make the necessary arrangement at the first opportunity.

The editors would like to express their appreciation to Brenda Jarvis for her work in the electronic preparation of the manuscript, which made our task in editing the manuscript much easier. We would also like to thank Fulden Underwood for her secretarial support in compiling the reader.

Introduction: Learning and Knowledge Construction

Robert McCormick and Carrie Paechter

In using the two words 'learning' and 'knowledge' together we are saying more than that there are connections between them. Along with the other volumes in this series, this reader builds on the idea of the nature of *learning as a knowledge construction process*. The volume *Learners, Learning and Assessment* explores the variety of theories of learning and how they relate to the various views of this construction; here we examine how they in turn view the nature and types of knowledge. Whole books on learning exist that have almost nothing to say about knowledge, except to treat it as the 'content' of the learning process, i.e. something that has no effect on the process and is itself not affected by the process. Yet it is evident that it is impossible to have a view of learning without also implying a view of knowledge.

We examine the relationship of learning and knowledge as intertwined in a constructive process at two levels, drawing on Rogoff (1995). The first is at the level of the interactions that learners have with each other and with those more knowledgeable than themselves (the interactional level). This is traditionally the focus of learning theorists. The second is at the level of the community, which involves the social processes of public formulations of knowledge and mechanisms for arriving at these formulations (journal refereeing, structures of educational institutions, books and libraries etc.). These two levels are interconnected if it is accepted, as we do, that learning is the *social* construction of knowledge. At the interactional level the social processes will be those in the physical vicinity of the learner, but also at the community level in the sense that knowledgeability, which is more than mere idiosyncratic views of the world, is defined in relation to how others see the world. Language is of course the prime illustration of this, where knowing what words mean and communicating only makes sense in relation to others. However, even if we look at the community level, it has become clear through the many studies of knowledge construction in areas such as science (one of the bastions of 'objective' knowledge) that such construction is indeed a social process. The processes by which scientists or historians validate knowledge are not objective in any absolute sense even if they have to relate to so called 'objective' phenomena or events. These phenomena and events are as *affected by* the knowledge that is created to explain or predict them as *they affect* the knowledge that results.

This view of knowledge has important implications that those concerned with the curriculum cannot avoid. First, the process of knowledge construction for learners is of central importance, and viewing it as such a process transforms both *what* we think can be achieved by way of knowledgeability and *how* we think that process should be supported. Second, if learning is the *social* construction of knowledge then this has implications for how we view the *nature* of knowledge and the *context of learning*. We have already alluded to the nature of knowledge losing its objective properties (the idea of absolute truth) when it is seen as the product of social construction, and therefore when learners come to construct their knowledge, they have to be made aware of this. This does not mean that all knowledge is relative and hence any particular formulation valid, nor that learners can create (or recreate) private knowledge, for so to do would not be education. But they need to be made aware of the nature of the knowledge and the processes involved in validating it. The implications for the context of learning, in taking a 'social construction of knowledge' view, is that this context is a social one. The companion volume, *Learners, Learning and Assessment*, explores the social context at the classroom level (e.g. Cobb, 1994) and here we also explore the community level, where ideas on situated learning add the *physical* context to that of the social and historical context.

All these implications take us a long way from the view that knowledge is an object in the head of the teacher, and that her job is to transmit it from her head to that of the learner's. Thus, we end up with not just looking at the interconnections between learning and knowledge, but among learners, learning and knowledge. It is evident that situated theories of cognition, in particular, see an intimate connection between knowledge and activity and hence learning becomes more pervasive, with problem solving being a central process and one that involves learning. The slogan of 'lifelong learning' then takes on quite a different character when viewed through this conception of knowledge and learning. The separation of work and learning diminishes, and the equation of 'learning' and 'courses' (in or out of educational institutions) become less significant in comparison.

The exploration of this complex territory is carried through in each of the three sections of the reader. Traditionally discussions of knowledge are rooted in philosophical considerations, and we start this way with Scheffler, not because we want to explore these considerations, but because there has been an intimate connection between philosophical positions on the nature of knowledge and views of learning. As Bredo (1997) has shown, the developments from functional psychology at the turn of the century, through behaviourism and cognitivism, to the situated learning current today, reflect different philosophical traditions. Thus functionalism, that saw an interaction between thinking and behaving, reflected pragmatism as a philosophical movement; behaviourism that denied explanatory status to thinking, took an empiricist view of knowledge; cognitivism reacted against behaviourism and focused on mind with a rationalist perspective. Situated learning has returned to a functionalist stance in stressing the transaction between thinking and action, though some of its proponents reflect Marxist ideas of dialectic and focus more on the community rather than the individual level, as other chapters in the reader will show.

The nature of knowledge and learning at the interactional level are considered in the first section (Chapter 2, Roth), with an account of how different theories of learning view the nature of knowledge. Lave and Wenger (Chapter 3) return us to the community level by examining how a community of practice is not just the source of knowledge, but that participating in that practice is to be knowledgeable. This shifts from a view of knowledge as an object to something that is not just a process, but as a participatory construction process. Post-modernists have extended the social construction of knowledge, and the role of power, to the extent of arguing that 'texts', including records of historical events, are narratives reflecting readers' and writers' dispositions. The 'facts', in this analysis, have little consequence in the establishment of any particular view of the past. In the area of science there has been a long debate about the nature of scientific knowledge. Driver and her colleagues (Chapter 4) review the way views about this knowledge have changed. These range from views that see theories deriving from observations of the world (an inductive view), and how these theories are established. They move on to a reversal of this inductive view, where what we observe is what we look for, and hence formed by our theories. Later views from sociologists and post-modernists complicate the picture, seeing knowledge in relation to the social process of its construction and the situations and standpoints of those who produce it.

In Chapter 5, Young considers the curriculum as a social construct, drawing on the sociology of knowledge, and how it has important implications for a number of educational issues. In particular this analysis reveals the value judgements that underlie curricular choices and the power relationships that flow from this at both community and interactional levels. The arguments about the nature of knowledge and how it is established are taken up by Spruce in Chapter 6, who shows that the kind of music that is central to the school music curriculum represents not only a particular social group, but a particular culture. This illustrates Young's arguments about the dominance of a particular social class in the selection of curricular knowledge.

If to learn is to become knowledgeable, then the nature of expertise and expert knowledge must be central to any investigation of the relationship between knowledge and learning. In the first of the two articles of Section 2, this is pursued from different perspectives. In Chapter 7 Glaser reports on the findings of cognitive science to show that, contrary to those who advocate a 'process' approach to subjects, expert behaviour is characterised by well structured domain-specific knowledge. Scribner (Chapter 8), drawing on activity theory (that underpins some versions of situated learning), shows that expert knowledge is formed by and forms the activity to which it is related. Thus knowledge is not an object in the head, but something *only* found in action. McCormick (Chapter 9) examines this in trying to establish the nature of knowledge as part of practical action. In doing so, he draws together a number of the arguments from earlier chapters, in particular the central importance of context in determining our knowledge. This strongly situated view of knowledge is explored by Greeno and his colleagues (Chapter 10) through contrasting this stance with a cognitivist stance. Their intention is to create a framework of knowledge that can be used in an assessment system, which is consistent with a situated perspective on learning. Assessment provides an explicit manifestation of how we view knowledge in relation to learning, and Greeno *et al.* attempt to produce a coherent framework for the situative perspective, as they call it. Such a framework forms the basis for the constructs Messick (Chapter 11) argues for in his advocacy for construct validity as central to assessment. A clear theoretical construct, such as that envisaged by Greeno and colleagues for literacy, needs to be tested empirically in the assessment devices and the way students interpret them. This knowledge becomes central to the assessment enterprise; i.e. in judging the learner's knowledgeability.

In the last section of the reader we turn to particular domains that represent different situations for learning, some defined in terms of 'subjects' found in educational institutions, and others as types of knowledge not easily fitting such terms. In doing this Carey and Smith (Chapter 12) examine learners' views of knowledge. The situations in the rest of the section cover medical education (Chapter 13 by Boshuizen), mathematics (Chapter 14 by Williams), and in Chapter 15 (Paechter), physical education and design and technology (a development from craft-based subjects). But of course it is necessary to consider how school or college subjects themselves become a social context, as is implicit in Young's argument in Section 1, and the final chapter by Grossman and Stodolsky examines this through seeing a subject as a sub-culture.

The reader has no single view of the nature and types of knowledge, but there is undoubtedly a situated bias. It tries to underline the connection between knowledge and learning, and to examine the contested nature of knowledge. Any educator faced with making selections for the curriculum, trying to represent knowledge for learning and assessment purposes, or engaging in the teaching and learning process, cannot stand aside from the arguments and issues contained in the reader. Even those who are faced with curricula given from 'on high' cannot abdicate any responsibility for the way they perceive and represent knowledge in the learning process. To do so is itself to take a view of knowledge. This is a difficult stance to justify in the face of the variety of analyses found in the literature and represented in the reader, let alone the view of learning and pedagogy found in the companion volumes to this reader.

References

Bredo, E. (1997) The social construction of learning. In G. D. Phye (ed.) *Handbook of Academic Learning: Construction of Knowledge,* Academic Press, San Diego.

Cobb, P. (1994) Where is the mind? Constructivist and sociocultural perspectives on mathematical development, *Educational Researcher*, 23 (7), 13–20. (This chapter is reproduced in the volume that accompanies this reader, *Learners, Learning and Assessment.*)

Rogoff, B. (1995) Observing sociocultural activity on three planes: participatory appropriation, guided participation and apprenticeship. In J. V. Wertsch, del Río, P. & Alverez, A. (eds.) *Sociocultural Studies of Mind* (pp. 139–164), Cambridge University Press, Cambridge. (This chapter is reproduced in the volume that accompanies this reader, *Learning and Assessment.*)

SECTION 1
THE NATURE OF KNOWLEDGE AND LEARNING

1

Epistemology and Education

Israel Scheffler

The development and transmission of knowledge are fundamental tasks of education, while analysis of its nature and warrant falls to that branch of philosophy known as epistemology, or theory of knowledge. An adequate educational philosophy must not only address itself to epistemological problems in their general form but must also strive to view these problems from the perspective of educational tasks and purposes [. . .].

Three Philosophies of Knowledge

It will be well to survey [. . .] some of the complexities of our subject. For if the task of epistemology can be simply put as the logical analysis of knowledge, knowledge is itself far from simple. First of all, the range of the everyday concept of knowing is very wide, including familiarity with things, places, persons, and subjects, competence in a variety of learned performances, and possession of ostensible truths on matters of fact as well as faith, the fallible items of science and everyday experience as well as the alleged certainties of mathematics and metaphysics.

Secondly, the concept of knowing is related in important ways to other fundamental and difficult ideas. It is, for example, closely associated with notions of understanding and controlling nature so as to sustain and enhance civilized life; it is also associated with ideas of contemplation, absorption, and appreciation, prized for themselves – ends rather than means of civilized life. In educational contexts, the term *knowledge* is frequently intended as embracing both sets of ideas: the accumulated skill and lore pertaining to technological control of the environment, and those intellectual arts and

This chapter has been edited.

experiences whose value is intrinsic to themselves. *Knowledge,* in such contexts, marks the whole content of our intellectual heritage, which education is concerned to pass on to succeeding generations.

Finally, attributions of knowledge are not, in typical cases, simply descriptive of bodies of lore or types of experience; they express our standards, ideals, and tastes as to the scope and proper conduct of the cognitive arts. They reflect, for example, our conceptions of truth and evidence, our estimates of the possibilities of secure belief, our preferences among alternative strategies of investigation. To describe someone as knowing is as much to appraise and approve as it is to report. Correspondingly, education is concerned to transmit not only what we know, but our manner of knowing, that is, our approved standards of competence in performance, in inquiry, and in intellectual criticism.

It is hardly surprising, then, that the concept of knowledge should have given rise to a variety of traditions of full-blown philosophical interpretation. For not only does the mere breadth of the concept lend itself to alternative emphases, but its ultimate association with variable ideals of civilization and with changing technologies and scientific models invites correspondingly varying evaluations. We shall sketch, by way of illustration, three broad philosophical approaches to knowledge, the rationalistic, the empiricistic, and the pragmatic.[1]

For the rationalistic tradition, mathematics is the model science. Mathematical truths are general and necessary, and may be established by deductive chains linking them with self-evident basic truths. Demonstration forges the chains, intuition discloses the basic truths. Intuition, moreover, guarantees each link in the chain of demonstration. Whoever understands a mathematical truth knows it to be necessary and not contingent on facts of nature. A diagram may well be used to *illustrate* a geometrical theorem, but it cannot be construed as *evidence for* the theorem. Should precise measurement of the diagram show that it failed to embody the relations asserted by the theorem, the latter would not be falsified. We should rather say that the physical diagram was only an approximation or a suggestion of the truth embodied in the theorem. Physical points have spread and physical lines have width, but mathematical points and lines are ideal, not physical objects – they can be understood, but not exemplified in the natural world. Natural objects only approximate, to a greater or lesser degree, the ideal objects of mathematics, and to the extent that they do approximate these ideal objects, they also can be understood. Statements, however, which *directly* describe natural objects are only more-or-less in character; they are contingent rather than necessary, dependent on the evidence of observed particulars for their substantiation, and subject to falsification through experience.

Mathematical truths are not dependent on experience, though an awareness of them may be suggested by experience. Mathematicians do not need laboratories or experiments; they conduct no surveys and collect no statistics. They work with pencil and paper only, and yet they arrive at the firmest of all truths, incapable of being overthrown by experience. In Plato's dialogue, *Meno* an untutored slave boy is led, through a skilful series of questions centered around a diagram, to an acknowledgment of the geometrical truth that a double square is the square of the diagonal.[2] Plato, drawing upon such examples, supposes the source of genuine knowledge to be within, and the knowledge itself to be capable of elicitation by questioning and suggestion which merely draw the mind's attention to that which it already possesses. The ideal education, for Plato, is a mathematical education, in which the mind comes to an apprehension of necessary truths concerning ideal forms, and which equips the student to grasp the natural world as an approximate embodiment of these forms.

In the empiricistic tradition, natural science is taken as the basic model. Natural phenomena are revealed by experience; they are not disclosed by intuition, nor are their interrelationships derivable from self-evident axioms. A person deprived of visual experience from birth may be fully rational and in possession of his logical faculties, but he will be unable to intuit or even imagine the color green. Neither this color nor any other elementary phenomenal component is initially present in the mind, to be drawn up by introspection; it must be gained by observation in the course of experience. Furthermore, the relationships among elementary phenomena – their typical clustering and their patterning through time – cannot be inferred by logic from self-evident basic truths; they are natural associations tentatively projected as generalizations from our limited past experience. The mind, in Locke's phrase, is a *tabula rasa* (a blank slate) at birth, and it is dependent upon experience both for the content of its elementary ideas and for their interrelationships.

The mind must, of course, be construed as having the power to compare, combine, analyse, and generalize upon the materials furnished to it by experience, as well as the ability to perform logical operations upon its concepts. Mathematics may be understood to represent either 'internal' logical relationships among concepts, or very abstract, though still empirical, generalizations based upon experience. In any event, all knowledge which reaches beyond the circle of the mind's own concepts and refers to the world must be based upon observation of what lies beyond, of what is not innate in the mind itself. The ideal education suggested by empiricist view is one which supplies abundant and optimally ordered phenomenal experiences to the student so that his powers of observation and association may take hold and enable him to grasp the natural order among events. The ideal education, further, trains the student not only in proper logical habits but in traits requisite for learning from experience – accurate observation, reasonable generalization, willingness to revise or relinquish purported laws which fail to anticipate the actual course of events.

The pragmatic view stresses the experimental character of empirical science, putting great emphasis upon the active phases of experimentation. To learn something significant about the world, we must do more than operate logically upon basic truths that appear to us self-evident, and we must go beyond reasonable generalization of observed phenomenal patterns in our past experience. Experimentation involves active transformation of the environment, in a manner dictated by leading ideas put forward in response to problems and directed toward the resolution of these problems. The problem provides the occasion and enduring focus of experimental inquiry; it supplies the initial questions, furnishes controlling standards of relevance, and defines success in the undertaking. Thought provides hypothetical ideas in response to the problem, ideas which need not mirror past experience so long as they are directed to the questions at stake and are capable of providing *relevant* answers. These hypothetical ideas are tested in action; using them as instruments for controlled operations upon nature, the experimenter finds that not all of them are equally effective. Some raise expectations that are not fulfilled by experimental outcomes, others accurately foretell the responses of nature. In Dewey's words, the process is one of *trying and undergoing* – trying an idea in practice, and learning from the consequences undergone as a result of such trial.[3]

Mathematical knowledge is continuous with logic in the pragmatist's scheme. It is an apparatus useful for elaborating the import of hypothetical ideas, for showing their connections with practical consequences and exhibiting their mutual relationships. It does not itself tell us anything directly about the world, but in bringing order to our array of concepts and in generating their consequences, it serves as a regulative instrument of inquiry. Inquiry itself is action, but action regulated by logic, sparked by theory, and issuing in answers to motivating problems of practice.

The process of learning from experience is thus an active process for the pragmatist. The mind is conceived neither as a deep well of necessary truths nor as a blank slate upon which experience writes. Rather, it is viewed as a capacity for active generation of ideas whose function it is to resolve the problems posed to an organism by its environment. The ideal education is thus one that connects general ideals with real problems and that stresses their practical bearings. It encourages imaginative theorizing by the student but at the same time insists upon control of such theorizing by the outcomes of active experimentation.

Notes

[1]   Each of the three sketches to follow is a composite, but it may be helpful to associate some names with the approaches treated. With rationalism we may associate Plato, Descartes, and Leibniz; with empiricism, Locke, Berkeley, and Hume; with pragmatism, Peirce, James, and Dewey.
[2]   Briefly, the point may be illustrated by this figure.

The problem is to determine what square is twice the area of the shaded square. The boy is led to see that the large square made by doubling the side of the shaded square yields a figure of four times the area, which is itself halved by the internal square made up of the diagonals, since each diagonal cuts its small containing square in half. The conclusion is that the square of the diagonal of the shaded square has double the area of the latter.

3 John Dewey, *Democracy and Education,* New York: The Macmillan Company, 1916, paperbacks edition, 1961, p. 139.

2

Authentic School Science: Intellectual Traditions

Wolff-Michael Roth

In this chapter I present an outline of the intellectual traditions that contributed to the theory embedded in my observations. These also serve as referents for the interpretations of classroom events. The presentation of these intellectual traditions also reflects an intellectual journey in the search for frameworks that were able to deal with the complexity of those phenomena that I encountered as teacher-researcher in everyday classroom life. This journey began with radical constructivism. By way of a socio-historical view of knowing and learning it then led to those social constructivist theories that emerged from science studies and ethnomethodology. In the process, the nature of situated cognition is outlined. [. . .]

Radical Constructivism

Over the past two decades, constructivism has become increasingly accepted as a viable theory of knowledge, and for many it is replacing more traditional philosophical positions that claimed the knowing subject as a pure entity, unaffected by biological, psychological and sociological contingencies. At the core of constructivism is the belief that human beings build up knowledge in a slow process, that begins with simple sensory-motor schema during early childhood and progresses to complex schema without physical referents from the late teens onwards. Some of those who describe themselves as constructivists have not given up the realist foundations of earlier epistemologies. In their view, the cognitive structures that individuals build stand in a one-to-one correspondence with the external world. These cognitive structures are 'true' representations of an observer-independent world which stand in an iconic or otherwise isomorphic relationship between psychological and real-world structures. As such, these forms of constructivism do not break with traditional, objectivist philosophies. A decisive break was brought about by a new kind of constructivism which challenged the basic tenets of objectivist philosophies, and thus became 'radical' (von Glasersfeld, 1985). For radical constructivists the

---

This chapter has been edited.

traditional correspondence or isomorphism between mental structures and the ontological world is severed.

Radical constructivism is variously referred to as a model of knowing and a theory of knowledge or epistemology (von Glasersfeld, 1987a, 1992). At the same time, it is quite clear that radical constructivism is not an ontology, that is, it does not make any statement about the nature of reality. Radical constructivism cannot make any statement about nature as it really is, because our access to nature, or Kant's *Dinge an sich* (things in themselves), is forever elusive. This, however, does not mean that radical constructivism denies reality. Rather, it denies that humans can know reality in any ontological sense, so that all we can know are our models of the world and our social Others (von Glasersfeld, 1989b). This world and the Others are always on 'the other side' of our experiential interface. Even our perceptions are guided by our current knowledge. Our perceptions do not allow a mapping of the world onto some imaginary screen somewhere in our mind because the signals from the perceptual organs are reconstructed in the brain. As a consequence, according to radical constructivism, we live forever in our own, self-constructed worlds; the world cannot ever be described apart from our frames of experience. This understanding is quite consistent with the view that there are as many worlds as there are knowers (Goodman, 1984). Our universe consists of a plenitude of descriptions rather than of an ontological world *per se*. These worlds, however, are not arbitrary but are highly constrained by our experiences in the world. As such, these constraints can be understood in terms of Darwin's theory of evolution.

As Piaget before him, von Glasersfeld uses Spencer's formulation of the theory of evolution as a mechanism for the construction of knowledge. An important notion in this theory is that of 'fitness.' In the environment, an animal or plant species is fit when it is adapted to the environment in such a fashion that its survival is granted. If it is not fit, a species will die out in a short time. The important thing here is that there are no species that are 'fitter' than others. The phrase 'survival of the fittest' is misleading in this context because a species is either fit or not fit. Any qualification that would warrant the use of 'fitter' or 'fittest' must be based on some other criterion. For example, one might want to call that species more fit which exists in larger numbers, or covers more area than others.[1]

In terms of knowledge, we have to make the same qualification. Here, the notion of 'fit' replaces the traditional notion of 'truth' because we can no longer compare knowledge with some ontological reality to establish its truth value (von Glasersfeld, 1983). All we can do is check if our knowledge is confirmed as we interact with the world through our experiences. Now the notion of fit is not exclusive. A number of different conceptions (constructions) may fit the 'same' experiential realm, and be appropriate in predicting experience. A widely known example is the calculation of planetary positions that can be worked out from a neo-Ptolemaic theory based on epicycles, or a Keplerian-Copernican view, or a Newtonian framework. All three (the Keplerian can be derived from Newton's framework) can be used to calculate the position of stars and planets to some sufficient degree (though in the case of Mercury's precession, Einstein's theory of relativity has to be used to account for the deviations in the predictions within the Newtonian framework). Again, if we want to make a selection of one over another, we have to use a different set of criteria to make a distinction as to which model is 'fittest.' In science, such decisions are usually made on the basis of Occam's principle, according to which the most parsimonious theory is the one to be preferred. In mathematics, elegance and rigor are some other criteria for selecting one framework over another. The main difference between the biological evolution of species and the evolution of concepts is that individuals have no way of changing biologically to adapt to an environment, while concepts can and do adapt through the processes of accommodation and assimilation of new experience, triggered by states of disequilibrium.

While we can never construct correspondences between our knowledge and an ontologically independent world, there is a relationship between our conceptions and our world of experience. This relationship has been expressed in the dialectic that exists between knowing and reality: 'Intelligence organizes the world by organizing itself' (Piaget cited in von Glasersfeld, 1987a) or 'Comprehension and creation go on together' (Goodman, 1978, p. 22). Here intelligence (or rather an individual's conceptions of the phenomenological world) and this phenomenological world stand in a dialectical relationship. It takes the conceptions to perceive the experiential world, and the existence of the experiential world is necessary for any conceptions to be built. As classroom teachers we can often observe students watch a specific physical event designed to help them in understanding some concept. But often they do not 'see' the key features that we consider important to developing a certain kind of understanding. Students simply do not see what has become familiar to us as teachers. For this reason, it is unreasonable to expect students to 'discover' the structures of this world before they have the cognitive framework that allows them to see structures in the first place.

The main question to radical constructivists, then, becomes this: how can humans experience a relatively stable and reliable world when they lack an objective reality to which we can ascribe stability, regularity and reliability? Radical constructivism eschews an answer by declaring the question meaningless. Von Glasersfeld (1984) argues, with Vico, that if the world as we experience it was constructed by ourselves, it should not come as a surprise that it is also relatively stable. The 'fact' that conceptions fit experiences in such a way that they are viable for a great range of experiences over considerable amounts of time does not, however, give any indication as to their relationship to some proposed ontic world. It only means that we have *one* viable way of dealing with our experiences.

Radical constructivism also forces us to abandon the traditional distinction between knowledge and beliefs. This distinction only makes sense within an objective-realist view of the world where the relationship between knowledge and the world can be tested and proven empirically, while beliefs are, by definition, not testable. If, however, all knowledge is constructed and idiosyncratic, the traditional distinction between knowledge and these beliefs do not hold anymore. Knowledge and beliefs are of the same nature. Much of this knowledge (and beliefs) does not exist in simple systems of rules, but in terms of narratives and metaphors (Bruner, 1986, 1990, 1991; Davis and Mason, 1989). Both metaphors and stories can encapsule larger meaning units because a variety of experiences are assembled into a coherent framework. In the case of narrative, coherence is achieved by the temporality of the experience encoded, while metaphors achieve coherence in the images they are able to evoke. For example, teachers who view themselves as gardeners have a referent which provides them with guidance as to the interactions with their students for many classroom situations. This referent replaces a great number of rules that would be needed to describe the actions of these teachers in some detail.

Radical constructivism provides us with an account of what we can know from the perspective of individuals who have no apparent connection with each other (von Glasersfeld, 1987b). These individuals structure their worldly activities in terms of inner mental models and rearrange or reconstruct them as a consequence of cognitive imbalance (Shotter, 1992). But an individualistic view is also a major shortfall of radical constructivist theory. There are many classroom situations in which individualistic accounts of knowing and learning in terms of equilibration processes to balance cognitive conflict seem to be inappropriate. Radical constructivism does not make provisions for socio-historical or cultural phenomena in learning. For example, students participate in classroom conversations without necessarily expressing already-existing ideas or putting previously-formulated plans into action. Rather, their talk constitutes practical action through which they respond to the contingencies of the situation. In the process, students build quite complex understandings of phenomena and collaboratively construct new understandings which transcend the sum of what individuals initially brought to the learning situation (Roth and Roychoudhury, 1992). What we must do now is to investigate the world of experience 'with the intent to find out how we come to have the apparently stable world in which, at a certain point in our development, we find ourselves living' (von Glasersfeld, 1989a). Much of this stability is embedded in the cultures into which we grow by participating in them to increasing degrees. It is at this point that social constructivism, and situated cognition, make important contributions to our understanding of knowing and learning.

Social Constructivism

Piaget's developmental theory and von Glasersfeld's radical constructivism focus to a large extent on individual, isolated minds that construct knowledge from experiences in the world. However, there is ample evidence that a theory of knowing and learning as an individualistic enterprise is inappropriate in accounting for many learning situations. Vygotsky's (1978) view of learning, on the other hand, regards individual cognitive development as subject to a dialectical interplay between nature and history, biology and culture, the lone intellect and society. Vygotsky believed that mind is transmitted across history by means of successive mental sharings which pass ideas from those more able or advanced to those who are less so (Bruner, 1986). The media in which these transmissions are effected are language and its cultural products such as literacy, science and technology. Vygotsky considered the growth of the individual to become a functioning member of society as part of the process of societal change. Changes in tools, for example, bring about changes in thinking. These changes in turn are associated with changes in culture. For instance, with the invention of calculus by Newton and Leibniz, natural scientists began looking at and explaining the world in different terms. The changes in the tools which humans used to look at the world, and the changes in the world they saw went hand in hand. In a similar reciprocal relationship, the introduction of mechanical tools like combine harvesters and tractors fundamentally changed agriculture, and a changing agriculture changed the machines used to farm; the introduction of computers and fax machines changed the interactional pattern within post-modern societies, and changes in the interactions changed the communication tools.

What children have to learn first is not about how to manipulate the 'things' in the world, but how to be listeners and speakers, observers, rememberers and imaginers, requesters, or storytellers (Shotter, 1992). That is, children first have to learn the ways how to make sense of others and construct knowledge which allows them to organize and relate Self to circumstances. In this endeavor, words become transparent means through which children make meaningful contact with their surroundings. When there is trouble in this contact, this transparency disappears, and meaning has to be derived through a process of interpretation. As transparent means, words are unproblematical tools to act in the world. When trouble appears, the meaning of these words has to be negotiated and socially constructed. Socio-historic theories of learning begin at this juncture between words as transparent means, and words that have to achieve meaning as children interact with adults. Thus, Vygotsky's theory directs our attention not to the individual that tries to build an understanding independent of others, but instead, to individuals as they become functioning members of communities before they become Selves. Accordingly, the roots of our intellectual functioning are first to be found in our surroundings and through interactions with Others before they appear internally. From this perspective, Vygotsky formulated a general law of development:

> Any function in the child's cultural development appears on the stage twice, or on two planes. First it appears on the social plane and then on the psychological plane. First it appears between people as an interpsychological category, and then within the child as an interpsychological category. This is equally true with

regard to voluntary attention, logical memory, the formation of concepts, and the development of volition (Vygotsky, 1981, p. 163).

At this point then, the central question becomes this: Where does this transformation of cultural knowledge to individual knowledge happen? Vygotsky answered that the translation of development from a cultural to an internal plane happens in the *zone of proximal development.*

According to Vygotsky (1978), the *zone of proximal development* (ZPD) is the difference between a child's independent problem solving activity and the level of problem solving possible under the guidance of an adult or of a more capable peer. That is, the child's actions interact with those of the adult in *ZPD*. It is in joint activities between adult and children that the latter *appropriate* into their own repertoires knowledge and skills that were initially external to them. Once appropriated, children can use this knowledge and these skills to control their own actions. It is in this zone that culture and cognition create each other. Cole (1985) extends the notion of *ZPD* in such a way that it becomes 'the structure of joint activity in any context where there are participants who exercise differential responsibilities by virtue of differential expertise' (p. 155). Ordinarily, the persons with greater expertise are adults, as when parents assist their children in learning their mother tongue, master tailors pass skills on to their apprentices, or when Zinacantecan mothers assist their daughters to become expert weavers. This collaboration on tasks to reach more competent performance is not limited to asymmetrical dyads. Rather, differential expertise can be developed and employed for cognitive growth in collaborating peer groups. Here lies the strength of collaborative learning yet to be utilized in schools. Students can distribute the responsibilities of tasks so that the whole process does not fall on any one individual. In this, they momentarily develop differential expertise which allows students in peer groups to scaffold their abilities to more complex achievement than any one individual would have been able to accomplish. Such scaffolding without continued access to an expert was observed in the learning trajectory of members of computer clubs. Through mutual support of their respective efforts, these members developed high levels of expertise, that they could then appropriate into their personal repertoires (Collins *et al.*, 1989). The activities in the *ZPD* can then be understood as providing the sort of 'scaffolding' which permits functioning at a higher developmental level. Here, the individual has to be involved in some activity in the context of which s/he is inadvertently coaxed to participation.

In Vygotsky's theory, robust understanding and knowledge are socially constructed through collaborative talk and interaction in and around meaningful, whole activities (including their tasks, problems, and tools). Socio-historical approaches to cognitive development are premised on the idea that higher cognitive skills of individuals develop through participation in socially and culturally organized activity. Thus, novices develop cognitive skills, that is they become fully-fledged members, by participating in joint activities with more knowledgeable others. Critical to the development of skills is the engagement in joint activity. *Activity,* then, becomes a central notion in the theories of Vygotsky and his closest associates. It was Leont'ev in particular who had considerable influence in framing present day notions of the concept of *joint activity.* Accordingly,

> Human psychology is concerned with the activity of concrete individuals, which takes place either in a collective – i.e. jointly with other people or in a situation in which the subject deals directly with the surrounding world of objects – e.g., at the potter's wheel or the writer's desk . . . if we removed human activity from the system of social relationships and social life, it would not exist (Leont'ev, 1981, p. 46).

This notion of activity as mediating agent between individual and culture was taken up by cultural anthropologists. Researchers in this field had realized that activities change over time as they are jointly constructed by participants (Cole, 1985). This mediation can be represented as

Individual ↔ Activity ↔ Society/Culture

The Leont'ev quote makes it also quite clear that intellectual activity cannot be distinguished from practical activity. They are conceptually the same and must be treated in the same manner.[2] This notion of mediation between culture and individual through activity immediately leads to the link between the notions of *ZPD* and *apprenticeship.* While apprenticeship and *ZPD* were developed within different perspectives (culture versus individual), they can be yoked by the notion of *joint activity.* In this joint activity, more capable participants guide the interactions with 'novices' in such a way that the latter can participate in authentic practice until they are able to manage the activity on their own. Much of the mediation in joint activity is done by means of language. At this point, activity theory interfaces with more recent conceptions of *ZPD.* Accordingly, *ZPD* is the 'distance between everyday actions of individuals and the historically new form of the societal activity that can be collectively generated as a solution to the double bind potentially embedded in . . . everyday actions' (Engestrom, 1987, p. 174.).

Apprentices' abilities to understand the master does not depend on the sharing of identical cognitive structures or representations of the task but on their ability to engage in whole performances congruently (Schön, 1987). The crucial aspects are to perform, not to talk about performance, and to engage in whole activities rather than partial or substitute ones. In terms of students' learning of science we would say that students should engage in entire research projects (in Dewey's sense) so that they learn what it means to conduct research from the beginning to the end of a project. That is, students need to begin by identifying a problem and then proceed to its resolution. It would be inappropriate to engage in problem solving without also framing and reframing the problem until it is solved – the very way scientists or *JPFs* solve problems in their everyday lives. In the process of a problem solving activity, talk would then be used as a form of social and cultural practice in the service of accomplishing the activity, not as a second order representation. It is clear then that, along with other aspects of the activity, talk has to be configured to fit into the overall matrix of authentic performance. Learning becomes a way of being in the social world and engaging in forms of authentic activity. [. . .]

Vygotsky's theory focuses on the link between communication, social (joint) activity, and cognitive development which we can observe in the above example. This theory supports the idea that the manner in which language is used in culturally organized activity settings interacts with the development of higher mental functions (Ochs, 1988). Acquisition of linguistic knowledge and acquisition of socio-cultural knowledge are interdependent because linguistic knowledge is embedded in and constitutes socio-cultural knowledge. On the other hand, our socio-cultural knowledge and understandings about moral values, beliefs, and structures of knowledge themselves are largely acquired through the use of language in appropriate (i.e., authentic) activity. Meaning is thus embedded in cultural conceptions of context. This entails that the process of acquiring language is also embedded in the process of socialization of knowledge (Ochs, 1988). Thus activity mediates not only between individual and culture but also between linguistic and socio-cultural knowledge:

Linguistic knowledge ↔ Activity ↔ Socio-cultural knowledge

A community's members use linguistic structures to engage in a wide range of practices, and in doing so change their understanding of these linguistic structures. In language, society provides the individual with a tool kit of concepts and ideas to deal with the world, and to move toward higher intellectual ground by appropriating the speech of others. This internalized speech is then used to fashion the individual's own thought processes: 'Inner speech was for [Vygotsky] a regulatory process that, in Dewey's famous words, provided a means for sorting one's thoughts about the world. And in a somewhat Deweyesque fashion, he also saw language as embodying cultural history' (Bruner, 1986, p. 143). Thought and speech are instruments for the planning and carrying out of tasks just as eyes and hands are. In this, Vygotsky achieved a unity of perception, speech and action which leads to the internalization of the sensory field.

Vygotsky's socio-cultural/socio-historic approach integrates cultural and individualistic views of knowing, thereby promoting the integration of psychology and anthropology. Further support for this integration derives from the work of cultural and cognitive anthropologists as seen in research in cognitive psychology (Brown and Palincsar, 1989; Collins *et al.*, 1989; Newman *et al.*, 1989), anthropology (Goodwin and Duranti, 1992; Lave and Wenger, 1991), and sociolinguists (Ochs, 1988; Wertsch, 1985). In all these disciplines, authentic everyday activity was recognized as structuring and being structured by socio-cultural/historical contexts.

Because there is always a body of shared practices available for making and noticing differences, shared actions and reactions usually remain outside of our consciousness and are inaccessible to description. Nevertheless, they mediate everyday activities. [. . .]

Everyday and Scientific Thinking

Problems solved by students in the classroom and 'subjects' in psychological laboratories are relatively well-defined, and constructed such that specific algorithmic solution strategies will lead to the normatively predetermined and correct solution. In these problems, all the information is provided or, presumably, in the head of the examinee; these problems are 'clearly' stated, and have one best answer. The problems found almost everywhere outside schools and psychological laboratories, however, are complex and often ill-structured; they do not provide all the information needed, or provide so much that the problem solver has to make crucial selections about which information to use as a basis for a solution. In addition, out-of-school[3] problems are not set. Out-of-school problems have to be framed as problems before they can be solved. In many cases, there are no prospects to get a 'right' solution. Rather, some choices may be better than others and are determined by a set of constraints defined by the individual. These constraints may include considerations of the costs involved for a solution, the effort needed for its implementation, and the time available to reach it. In many out-of-school situations, individuals might settle for approximations or probabilities which satisfy their needs rather than search for optimal solutions. For example, a grocery shopper may purchase a larger package of the same product rather than trying to calculate the exact price to weight (volume) ratio. The choice of taking a larger package may be driven by considerations such as household size, shelf life of the product, or upcoming food demands related to visits. A 'best buy' is thus determined not necessarily by monetary considerations, but by some other choice from a host of options. In such situations, nonstandard approaches to problem solving are the rule rather than the exception, and tests of general aptitude often fail to predict success (Frederiksen, 1986).

Scribner (1986) used the term *mind in action* to gloss this form of practical thinking and to refer to thought that is embedded in more encompassing everyday activities. An activity's goals may involve mental accomplishments (such as figuring out the best bet on a race track) and/or manual accomplishments (such as fixing a bicycle), but *mind in action* is always instrumental to an achievement. This framing of practical thinking as *mind in action* bridges traditional separations of thinking and action in Western cognitive psychology. It reflects the interplay between thinking and action in the above-mentioned activity theory (Leont'ev, 1981). [. . .] Acting exists in a reflexive relationship with thinking (that is, with members' descriptions of acting). *Activity*, then, seems to be a natural choice as a unit of analysis.

In recent years, a number of studies have been conducted in natural settings in order to analyse *mind in action.* Among the notable ones were studies of out-of-school quantitative and arithmetic practices while people shopped (Lave, 1988), worked in a dairy factory (Scribner, 1984), sold lottery tickets or candy in street markets (Schliemann and Acioly, 1989; Saxe, 1991), or placed racetrack bets (Ceci and Liker, 1986). In all these studies, researchers noted significant discontinuities in the problem solving activities when they asked participants to move from their usual contexts to structurally identical but investigator-framed paper and pencil problems.[4] These investigators also found that skilled practical problem solving was marked by flexibility, and only novices used algorithmic procedures. Experts, on the other hand, varied their problem solving approaches depending on the specific situation. These changes reflected a concern for the *how* of performance and for efficiency and least effort (Scribner, 1986; *see also* Chapter 8 of this volume). Most notably, problems that might be considered by outsiders as structurally identical tasks were nevertheless solved by means of different strategies. This indicated an inextricability of tasks from the setting so that, in effect, problems always changed with the setting and thus became different problems altogether. A central concern in the study of everyday thinking whether by scientists or *JPFs* is the situatedness of all knowing.

Situated Cognition

Cross-cultural psychology, cognitive anthropology, and cognition and AI research converge in their realization that thinking cannot be understood apart from the contexts in which it appears. Moreover, thinking cannot be understood as that which happens in an individual mind plus some of the social and physical surroundings. Rather, thinking seems to lie in the relationship between individual and the environment. Here, I understand environment in a rather encompassing way so that it may include the physical environment, historical, and the cultural surroundings, as well as more internal aspects such as problem solvers' prior beliefs relevant at the moment (Stuckey, 1990). Thus, thinking as well as knowing and remembering are thought to be distributed phenomena rather than residing in the head of individuals. Conceptualizing knowing as situated also provides a valuable link for comparisons of cognition across cultures, as in the studies of Puluwat navigation and navigation on a modern warship (Hutchins, 1983, 1990); and situated cognition provides us with frameworks for comparing the reasoning of shoppers and dairy workers (Lave, 1988; Scribner, 1986) with that of microbiologists or chemists (Knorr-Cetina, 1981; Latour and Woolgar, 1979). This research seems to indicate that there is no difference between scientists' rationality and that of *JPFs.* We find that the cognition of scientists, Western *JPFs,* and members of other societies (often misleadingly labeled as primitive) is very similar when we take the time to study what people *actually* do rather than what they say they do or what analysts think they do (Stuckey, 1990). People from all these groups turn out to be good not only at inventing and using tools but also in the resourceful use they make of their surroundings. In everyday life, logical thinking is purposefully linked to the solution of practical problems, but when this link is not present, thinking can resemble the abstract forms that previously appeared so important to us (Berry and Irvine, 1986).

If we take seriously the notion of cognition as situated and distributed, there are significant implications for research on learning. Rather than investigating decontextualized 'scientific process skills' or 'problem solving' of word problems, we need to come to an understanding of what cognitions learning environments evoke in the students. Important in coming to understand the dynamics within problem-rich learning environments is the notion of community of practice.

Communities of Practice

In recent years, the notion of *community of practice* has gained prominence as an analytic tool for understanding knowing and learning. Communities of practice are characterized by the shared practices, (linguistic) conventions, behavior, standards of ethics, viewpoints, etc. In communities, knowledge can no longer be considered as a property of individuals that can be quantified, assessed, or transferred *ad libidum*. Rather knowledge is distributed, situated in both physical, psychological and social contexts (Brown *et al.* 1989; Lave and Wenger, 1991). This knowledge is collaboratively constructed, meanings are negotiated, and courses of actions negotiated, determined by majority vote, or dictated from someone in power by drawing on the social and material resources available in specific settings. Schools can be understood, and classrooms designed as sites of multiple communities. Thus, the teachers in a school form a community, administrators belong to a different community, and certain classrooms are designed to operate as communities (Cobb *et al.*, 1991; Roth and Bowen, 1995).

From a community of practice perspective, learning is squarely located in the processes of social coparticipation, not in the heads of individuals. Rather than asking what kind of cognitive processes and structures are involved, the situated learning paradigm focuses on the kinds and quality of social engagements needed to provide optimal learning environments. Rather than focusing on discrete bodies of knowledge to be transferred from more knowledgeable members of a community to those less knowledgeable, situated learning emphasizes learning through the engagement in authentic activities. Authentic here means that the activities in which learners engage have a large degree of resemblance with the activities in which core members of a community actually engage. For example, authentic mathematics teaching-learning environments would allow students to construe mathematics in the same way as mathematicians do. In science classrooms that focus on authentic activities, we would expect students to engage in activities that allow students to (1) learn in contexts constituted in part by ill-defined problems; (2) experience uncertainties, ambiguities, and the social nature of scientific work and knowledge; (3) engage in learning (curriculum) which is predicated on, and driven by, their current knowledge state (wherever that might be); (4) experience themselves as part of communities of inquiry in which knowledge, practices, resources, and discourse are shared; and (5) participate in classroom communities, in which they can draw on the expertise of more knowledgeable others, whether those others are peers or advisors.

In classical apprenticeship situations, learners participate with masters in the actual processes of their trade; apprentice tailors learn by becoming part of the manufacturing process in the shop, and midwives learn at the elbow of their sponsors by gradually taking over more and more of the critical tasks. This form of coparticipation which proceeds from the less crucial tasks to the central tasks of the trade has become known as *legitimate peripheral participation* (Lave and Wenger, 1991; see Chapter 3 in this volume). Such participatory learning is not confined to traditional apprenticeships but can also be observed in the enculturation and socialization processes in academia in the form of graduate and post-graduate work (pertaining to physics see Toulmin, 1982 and Traweek, 1988), and in practicum settings for doctors, lawyers, architects, teachers or psychoanalysts. The central element to all of these situations is that meaning, understanding, and learning are all defined relative to actional contexts rather than to self-contained, mental and linguistic structures. As a consequence of this view of knowing and learning, improvisation, actual cases of interaction and emergent processes all play a constitutive role in learning and cannot be reduced to generalized structures (Hanks, in Lave and Wenger, 1991). This view also brings out the actors' productive contributions to the order of interactions through negotiations, strategy, and unpredictable actions. The order that emerges from these interactions is more an outcome than a predetermining factor. [. . .]

Notes

[1] I am grateful to my friend, colleague, and collaborator Michael Bowen (personal communication, July 29, 1993) who pointed out my own misconceptions of Darwin's theory of evolution. Accordingly , the phase 'survival of the fittest' was coined by Herbert Spencer when he was trying to apply Darwinism to his social construct of biological determinism to justify 19th century social structures and the gap between rich and poor. 'Fitness' in a Darwinian, biological sense refers *only* to a single biological factor: the ability to produce viable offspring.

[2] This attempt to see intellectual and practical activity as two sides of the same coin is not new to modern psychology. One of the ultimate goals of any Zen practitioner is to achieve the state in which the dichotomy between thinking and acting disappears. Similarly, interactionists view talk (discursive action) and practical action at the same level. Both serve to achieve goals.

3 I prefer to make a distinction between in-school and out-of-school rather than between school and everyday activities/contexts. The reason is that for students, schools constitute their everyday life.
4 'Structural identity,' of course, was framed as such by the investigators. From the research participants' perspective, structural identity did not exist.

References

Amann, K. and Knorr-Cetina, K. D. (1988) The fixation of (visual) evidence, *Human Studies*, 11, pp. 133–169.

Berry, J. W. and Irvine, S. H. (1986) Bricolage: savages do it daily, in R. J. Sternberg and R. K. Wagner (eds.) *Practical intelligence: Nature and origins of competence in the everyday world,* Cambridge University Press, pp. 271–306.

Brown, J. S., Collins, A. and Duguid, P. (1989) Situated cognition and the culture of learning, *Educational Researcher*, 18 (1), pp. 32–42.

Bruner, J. S. (1986) *Actual minds, possible worlds,* Cambridge, MA: Harvard University Press.

Bruner, J. S. (1990) *Acts of meaning*, Cambridge, MA: Harvard University Press.

Bruner, J. S. (1991) The narrative construction of reality, *Critical Inquiry*, 18, pp. 1–21.

Ceci, S. J. and Liker, J. (1986) Academic and non-academic intelligence: an experimental separation, in R. J. Sternberg and R. K. Wagner (eds.) *Practical intelligence: Nature and origins of competence in the everyday world*, Cambridge: Cambridge University Press, pp. 119–142.

Cobb, P., Wood, T. and Yackel, E. (1991) Analogies from the philosophy and sociology of science for understanding classroom life, *Science Education*, 75, pp. 23–44.

Cole, M. (1985) The zone of proximal development in J. V. Wertsch (ed.) *Culture, communication, and cognition: Vygotskian perspectives*, Cambridge: Cambridge University Press, pp. 146–161.

Collins, A., Brown, J. S. and Newman, S. (1989) Cognitive apprenticeship: Teaching the craft of reading, writing, and mathematics in L. Resnick (ed.) *Cognition and instruction: Issues and agendas*, Hillsdale, NJ: Lawrence Erlbaum Associates, pp. 453–494.

Davis, P. J. and Mason, J. H. (1989) Notes on a radical constructivist epistemethodology applied to didactic situations, *Journal of Structural Learning*, 10, pp. 157–176.

Engeström, Y. (1987) *Learning by Expanding*, Helsinki: Orientation Konsultit Oy.

Feyerabend, P. (1976) *Against method: Outline of an anarchistic theory of knowledge*, London, NLB: Atlantic Highlands, Humanities Press.

Frederiksen, N. (1986) Toward a broader conception of human intelligence, in R. J. Sternberg and R. K. Wagner (eds.) *Practical intelligence: Nature and origins of competence in the everyday world*, Cambridge: Cambridge University Press, pp. 84–116.

Goodman, N. (1978) *Ways of worldmaking*, Indianapolis, IN: Hackett Publishing Co.

Goodman, N. (1984) *Of mind and other matters*, Cambridge, MA: Harvard University Press.

Goodwin, C. and Duranti, A. (1992) Rethinking context: an introduction, in A. Duranti and C. Goodwin (eds.) *Rethinking context: Language as an interactive phenomenon*, Cambridge: Cambridge University Press, pp. 1–42.

Hutchins, E. (1983) Understanding Micronesian navigation, in D. Gentner and A. L. Stevens (eds.) *Mental models*, Hillsdale, NJ: Lawrence Erlbaum Associates, pp. 191–225.

Hutchins, E. (1990) The technology of team navigation, in J. Galegher, R. E. Kraut and C. Egido (eds.) *Intellectual Teamwork: Social and technological foundations of co-operative work*, Hillsdale, NJ: Lawrence Erlbaum Associates, pp. 191–220.

Knorr-Cetina, K. D. (1981) *The manufacture of knowledge: An essay on the constructivist and contextual nature of science*, Oxford: Pergamon Press.

Latour, B. and Woolgar, S. (1979) *Laboratory life: The social construction of scientific facts*, Beverley Hills, CA: Sage Publications.

Lave, J. (1988) *Cognition in practice: Mind, mathematics and culture in everyday life*, Cambridge: Cambridge University Press.

Lave, J. and Wenger, E. (1991) *Situated learning: Legitimate peripheral participation*, Cambridge: Cambridge University Press.

Leont'ev, A. N. (1981) The problem of activity in psychology, in J. V. Wertsch (ed.) *The concept of activity in soviet psychology,* Armonk, NY: M. E. Sharpe, pp. 37–71.

Newman, D., Griffin, P. and Cole, M. (1989) *The construction zone: Working for cognitive change in school*, Cambridge: Cambridge University Press.

Ochs, E. (1988) *Culture and language development: Language acquisition and language socialization in a Samoan village*, Cambridge, Cambridge University Press.

Roth, W.-M. and Bowen, G. M. (1995) Knowing and interacting: A study of culture, practices, and resources in a grade 8 open-inquiry science classroom guided by a cognitive apprenticeship metaphor, *Cognition and Instruction*, 13, pp. 73–128.

Roth, W.-M. and Roychoudhury, A. (1992) The social construction of scientific concepts or The concept map as conscription device and tool for social thinking in high school science, *Science Education*, 76, pp. 531–557.

Saxe, G. B. (1991) *Culture and cognitive development: Studies in mathematical understanding*, Hillsdale, NJ, Lawrence Erlbaum Associates.

Schliemann, A. D. and Acioly, N. M. (1989) Mathematical knowledge developed at work: The contribution of practice versus the contribution of schooling, *Cognition and Instruction*, 6, pp. 185–221.

Schön, D. A. (1987) *Educating the reflective practitioner*, San Francisco: Jossey-Bass.

Scribner, S. (1984) Studying working intelligence, in B. Rogoff and J. Lave (eds.) *Everyday cognition: Its development in social context*, pp. 9–46, Cambridge MA: Harvard University Press.

Scribner, S. (1986) Thinking in action: some characteristics of practical thought, in R. J. Sternberg and R. K. Wagner (eds.) *Practical intelligence: Nature and origins of competence in the everyday world*, Cambridge: Cambridge University Press, pp. 13–30.

Shotter, J. (1992) *In dialogue: Social constructionism and radical constructivism.* Paper presented at the conference on alternative epistemologies in education, Athens, GA.

Stuckey, S. (1990) Situated cognition: A strong hypothesis. A paper presented at the NATO Advanced Research workshop, *Cognitive modelling and interactive environments.*

Toulmin, S. (1982) The construal of reality: Criticism in modern and post-modern science, *Critical Inquiry*, 9, pp. 93–111.

Traweek, S. (1988) *Beamtimes and lifetimes: The world of high energy physicists*, Cambridge, MA, MIT Press.

von Glasersfeld, E. (1983) On the concept of interpretation, *Poetics*, 12, pp. 207–218.

von Glasersfeld, E. (1984) An introduction to radical constructivism, in P. Watzlawick (ed.) *The invented reality*, New York: Norton, pp. 17–40.

von Glasersfeld, E. (1985) Reconstructing the concept of knowledge, *Archives de Psychologie,* 53 pp. 91–101.

von Glasersfeld, E. (1987a) Learning as a constructive activity, in C. Janvier (ed.) *Problems of representation in the teaching and learning of mathematics*, Hillsdale, NJ: Lawrence Erlbaum Associates, pp. 3–17.

von Glasersfeld, E. (1987b) Preliminaries to any theory of representation, in C. Janvier (ed.) *Problems of representation in the teaching and learning of mathematics*, Hillsdale, NJ: Lawrence Erlbaum Associates, pp. 215–225.

von Glasersfeld, E. (1989a) Cognition, construction of knowledge, and teaching, *Synthese*, 80, pp. 121–140.

von Glasersfeld, E. (1989b) Facts and the self from a constructivist point of view, *Poetics*, 18, pp. 435–448.

von Glasersfeld, E. (1992, February) *A constructivist approach to teaching*. Paper presented at the conference on alternative epistemologies in education, Athens, GA.

Vygotsky, L. S. (1978) *Mind in society: The development of higher psychological processes*, Cambridge: Harvard University Press.

Vygotsky, L. S. (1981) The genesis of higher mental functions, in J. V. Wertsch (ed.) *The concept of activity in Soviet psychology*, Armonk, NY: Sharpe, pp. 147–188.

Wertsch, J. V. (ed.) (1985) *Culture, communication, and cognition: Vygotskian perspectives*, Cambridge: Cambridge University Press.

Zenzen, M. and Restivo, S. (1982) The mysterious morphology of immiscible liquids: A study of scientific practice, *Social Science Information*, 21 pp. 447–473.

3

Legitimate Peripheral Participation in Communities of Practice

J. Lave and E. Wenger

Editors' Introduction

In this extract from their book, Lave and Wenger draw on a previous chapter that contains five studies of apprentice learners becoming midwives, tailors, quartermasters, butchers or non-drinking alcoholics (through A. A.: Alcoholics Anonymous). From these studies they elaborate the participation in communities of practice.

In this chapter we recast the central characteristics of these several historical realizations of apprenticeship in terms of legitimate peripheral participation. First, [. . .] we argue that 'transparency' of the sociopolitical organization of practice, of its content and of the artifacts engaged in practice, is a crucial resource for increasing participation. We next examine the relation of newcomers to the discourse of practice. This leads to a discussion of how identity and motivation are generated as newcomers move toward full participation. Finally, we explore contradictions inherent in learning, and the relations of the resulting conflicts to the development of identity and the transformation of practice.

The Place of Knowledge: Participation, Learning Curricula, Communities of Practice

The social relations of apprentices within a community change through their direct involvement in activities; in the process, the apprentices' understanding and knowledgeable skills develop. In the recent past, the only means we have had for understanding the processes by which these changes occur have come from conventional speculations about the nature of 'informal' learning: that is, apprentices are supposed to acquire the 'specifics' of practice through 'observation and imitation.' But this view is in all probability wrong in every particular, or right in particular

---

This chapter has been edited.

circumstances, but for the wrong reasons. We argue instead that the effects of peripheral participation on knowledge-in-practice are not properly understood; and that studies of apprenticeship have presumed too literal a coupling of work processes and learning processes.

To begin with, newcomers' legitimate peripherality provides them with more than an 'observational' lookout post: it crucially involves *participation* as a way of learning – of both absorbing and being absorbed in – the 'culture of practice.' An extended period of legitimate peripherality provides learners with opportunities to make the culture of practice theirs. From a broadly peripheral perspective, apprentices gradually assemble a general idea of what constitutes the practice of the community. This uneven sketch of the enterprise (available if there is legitimate access) might include who is involved; what they do; what everyday life is like; how masters talk, walk, work, and generally conduct their lives; how people who are not part of the community of practice interact with it; what other learners are doing; and what learners need to learn to become full practitioners. It includes an increasing understanding of how, when, and about what old-timers collaborate, collude, and collide, and what they enjoy, dislike, respect, and admire. In particular, it offers exemplars (which are grounds and motivation for learning activity), including masters, finished products, and more advanced apprentices in the process of becoming full practitioners.

Such a general view, however, is not likely to be frozen in initial impressions. Viewpoints from which to understand the practice evolve through changing participation in the division of labor, changing relations to ongoing community practices, and changing social relations in the community. This is as true, in different ways, of reformed alcoholics as they socialize with other A. A. members as it is of quartermasters as they move through different aspects of navigation work. And learners have multiply structured relations with ongoing practice in other ways. Apprenticeship learning is not 'work-driven' in the way stereotypes of informal learning have suggested; the ordering of learning and of everyday practice do not coincide. Production activity-segments must be learned in different sequences than those in which a production process commonly unfolds, if peripheral, less intense, less complex, less vital tasks are learned before more central aspects of practice.

Consider, for instance, the tailors' apprentices, whose involvement starts with both initial preparations for the tailors' daily labor and finishing details on completed garments The apprentices progressively move backward through the production process to cutting jobs. (This kind of progression is quite common across cultures and historical periods.) Under these circumstances, the initial 'circumferential' perspective absorbed in partial, peripheral, apparently trivial activities – running errands, delivering messages, or accompanying others – takes on new significance: it provides a first approximation to an armature of the structure of the community of practice. Things learned, and various and changing viewpoints, can be arranged and interrelated in ways that gradually transform that skeletal understanding.

When directive teaching in the form of prescriptions about proper practice generates one circumscribed form of participation (in school), pre-empting participation in ongoing practice as the legitimate source of learning opportunities, the goal of complying with the requirements specified by teaching engenders a practice different from that intended (Bourdieu, 1977). In such cases, even though the pedagogical structure of the circumstances of learning has moved away from the principle of legitimate peripheral participation with respect to the target practice, legitimate peripheral participation is still the core of the learning that takes place. This leads us to distinguish between a *learning curriculum* and a *teaching curriculum*. A learning curriculum consists of situated opportunities (thus including exemplars of various sorts often thought of as 'goals') for the improvisational development of new practice (Lave, 1989). A learning curriculum is a field of learning resources in everyday practice *viewed from the perspective of learners*. A teaching curriculum, by contrast, is constructed for the instruction of newcomers. When a teaching curriculum supplies – and thereby limits – structuring resources for learning, the meaning of what is learned (and control of access to it, both in its peripheral forms and its subsequently more complex and intensified, though possibly more fragmented, forms) is mediated through an instructor's participation, by an external view of what knowing is about. The learning curriculum in didactic situations, then, evolves out of participation in a specific community of practice engendered by pedagogical relations and by a prescriptive view of the target practice as a subject matter, as well as out of the many and various relations that tie participants to their own and to other institutions.

A learning curriculum is essentially situated. It is not something that can be considered in isolation, manipulated in arbitrary didactic terms, or analysed apart from the social relations that shape legitimate peripheral participation. A learning curriculum is thus characteristic of a community. In using the term community, we do not imply some primordial culture-sharing entity. We assume that members have different interests, make diverse contributions to activity and hold varied viewpoints. In our view, participation at multiple levels is entailed in membership in a *community of practice*. Nor does the term community imply necessarily co-presence, a well-defined, identifiable group, or socially visible boundaries. It does imply participation in an activity system about which participants share understandings concerning what they are doing and what that means in their lives and for their communities.

The concept of community underlying the notion of legitimate peripheral participation, and hence of 'knowledge' and its 'location' in the lived-in world, is both crucial and subtle. The community of practice of midwifery or tailoring involves much more than the technical knowledge-able skill involved in delivering babies or producing clothes. A community of practice is a set of relations among persons, activity, and world, over time and in relation with other tangential and overlapping communities of practice. A community of practice is an intrinsic condition for the existence of knowledge, not least because it provides the interpretive support necessary for making sense of its heritage. Thus, participation in the cultural practice in which any knowledge exists is an epistemological principle of learning. The social structure of this practice, its power relations, and its conditions for legitimacy define possibilities for learning (i.e., for legitimate peripheral participation).

It is possible to delineate the community that is the site of a learning process by analysing the reproduction cycles of the communities that seem to be involved and their relations. For the quartermasters, the cycle of navigational practice is quite short; a complete reproduction of the practice of quartermastering may take place every five or six years (as a novice enters, gradually becomes a full participant, begins to work with newcomer quartermasters who in their own turn become full participants and reach the point at which they are ready to work with newcomers). The reproduction cycle of the midwives', the tailors', or the butchers' communities is much longer. In A. A., its length is rather variable as individuals go through successive steps at their own pace. Observing the span of developmental cycles is only a beginning to such an analysis (and a rough approximation that sets aside consideration of the transformation and change inherent in ongoing practice – see below), for each such cycle has its own trajectory, benchmarks, blueprints, and careers (Stack, 1989).

In addition to the useful analytic questions suggested by a temporal focus on communities of practice, there is a further reason to address the delineation of communities of practice in processual, historical terms. Claims *about* the definition of a community of practice and the community of practice actually in process of reproduction in that location may not coincide – a point worth careful consideration.

For example, in most high schools there is a group of students engaged over a substantial period of time in learning physics. What community of practice is in the process of reproduction? Possibly the students participate only in the reproduction of the high school itself. But assuming that the practice of physics is also being reproduced in some form, there are vast differences between the ways high school physics students participate in and give meaning to their activity and the way professional physicists do. The actual reproducing community of practice, within which schoolchildren learn about physics, is not the community of physicists but the community of schooled adults. Children are introduced into the latter community (and its humble relation with the former community) during their school years. The reproduction cycles of the physicists' community start much later, possibly only in graduate school (Traweek, 1988).

In this view, problems of schooling are not, at their most fundamental level, pedagogical. Above all, they have to do with the ways in which the community of adults reproduces itself, with the places that newcomers can or cannot find in such communities, and with relations that can or cannot be established between these newcomers and the cultural and political life of the community.

In summary, rather than learning by replicating the performances of others or by acquiring knowledge transmitted in instruction, we suggest that learning occurs through centripetal participation in the learning curriculum of the ambient community. Because the place of knowledge is within a community of practice, questions of learning must be addressed within the developmental cycles of that community, a recommendation which creates a diagnostic tool for distinguishing among communities of practice.

The Problem of Access: Transparency and Sequestration

The key to legitimate peripherality is access by newcomers to the community of practice and all that membership entails. But though this is essential to the reproduction of any community, it is always problematic at the same time. To become a full member of a community of practice requires access to a wide range of ongoing activity, old-timers, and other members of the community; and to information, resources, and opportunities for participation. The issue is so central to membership in communities of practice that, in a sense, all that we have said so far is about access. Here we discuss the problem more specifically in connection with issues of understanding and control, which along with involvement in productive activity are related aspects of the legitimate peripherality of participants in a practice.

The artifacts employed in ongoing practice, the technology of practice, provide a good arena in which to discuss the problem of access to understanding. In general, social scientists who concern themselves with learning treat technology as a given and are not analytic about its interrelations with other aspects of a community of practice. Becoming a full participant certainly includes engaging with the technologies of everyday practice, as well as participating in the social relations production processes, and other activities of communities of practice. But the understanding to be gained from engagement with technology can be extremely varied depending on the form of participation enabled by its use. Participation involving technology is especially significant because the artifacts used within a cultural practice carry a substantial portion of that practice's heritage. For example, the alidade used by the quartermasters for taking bearings has developed as a navigational instrument over hundreds of years, and embodies calculations invented long ago (Hutchins, 1996). Thus, understanding the technology of practice is more than learning to use tools; it is a way to connect with the history of the practice and to participate more directly in its cultural life.

The significance of artifacts in the full complexity of their relations with the practice can he more or less *transparent* to learners. Transparency in its simplest form may just imply that the inner workings of an artifact are available for the learner's inspection: The black box can be opened, it can become a 'glass box.' But there is more to understanding the use and significance of an artifact: knowledge within a community of practice and ways of perceiving and manipulating objects characteristic of community practices are encoded in artifacts in ways that can be more or less revealing. Moreover, the activity system and the social world of which an artifact is part are reflected in multiple ways in its design and use and can become further 'fields of transparency,' just as they can remain opaque. Obviously, the transparency of any technology always exists with respect to some purpose and is intricately tied to the cultural practice and social organization within which the technology is meant to function: it cannot he viewed as a feature of an artifact in itself but as a process that involves specific forms of participation, in which the technology fulfils a mediating function. Apprentice quartermasters not only have access to the physical activities going on around them and to the tools of the trade; they participate in information flows and conversations, in a context in which they can make sense of what they observe and hear. In focusing on the epistemological role of artifacts in the context of the social organization of knowledge, this notion of transparency constitutes, as it were, the cultural organization of access. As such, it does not apply to technology only, but to all forms of access to practice.

Productive activity and understanding are not separate, or even separable, but dialectically related. Thus, the term *transparency* when used here in connection with technology refers to the way in which using artifacts and understanding their significance interact to become one learning process. Mirroring the intricate relation between using and understanding artifacts, there is an interesting duality inherent in the concept of transparency. It combines the two characteristics of *invisibility* and *visibility*: invisibility in the form of unproblematic interpretation and integration into activity, and visibility in the form of extended access to information. This is not a simple dichotomous distinction, since these two crucial characteristics are in a complex interplay, their relation being one of both conflict and synergy.

It might be useful to give a sense of this interplay by analogy to a window. A window's invisibility is what makes it a window, that is, an object through which the world outside becomes visible. The very fact, however, that so many things can be seen through it makes the window itself highly visible, that is, very salient in a room, when compared to, say, a solid wall. Invisibility of mediating technologies is necessary for allowing focus on, and thus supporting visibility of, the subject matter. Conversely, visibility of the significance of the technology is necessary for allowing its unproblematic – invisible – use. This interplay of conflict and synergy is central to all aspects of learning in practice: It makes the design of supportive artifacts a matter of providing a good balance between these two interacting requirements. (An extended analysis of the concept of transparency can be found in Wenger, 1990.)

Control and selection, as well as the need for access, are inherent in communities of practice. Thus access is liable to manipulation, giving legitimate peripherality an ambivalent status: depending on the organization of access, legitimate peripherality can either promote or prevent legitimate participation. In the study of the butchers' apprentices, Marshall (1972) provides examples of how access can be denied. The trade school and its shop exercises did not simulate the central practices of meat cutting in supermarkets, much less make them accessible to apprentices; on-the-job training was not much of an improvement. Worse, the master butchers confined their apprentices to jobs that were removed from activities rather than peripheral to them. To the extent that the community of practice routinely sequesters newcomers, either very directly as in the example of apprenticeship for the butchers, or in more subtle and pervasive ways as in schools, these newcomers are prevented from peripheral participation. In either case legitimacy is not in question. Schoolchildren are legitimately peripheral, but kept from participation in the social world more generally. The butchers' apprentices participate legitimately, but not peripherally, in that they are not given productive access to activity in the community of practitioners.

An important point about such sequestering when it is institutionalized is that it encourages a folk epistemology of dichotomies, for instance, between 'abstract' and 'concrete' knowledge. These categories do not reside in the world as distinct forms of *knowledge,* nor do they reflect some putative hierarchy of forms of knowledge among practitioners. Rather, they derive from the nature of the new practice generated by sequestration. *Abstraction* in this sense stems from the disconnectedness of a particular cultural practice. Participation in that practice is neither more nor less abstract or concrete, experiential or cerebral, than in any other. Thus, legitimate peripheral participation as the core concept of relations of learning places the explanatory burden for issues such as 'understanding' and 'levels' of abstraction or conceptualization not on one type of learning as opposed to another, but on the cultural practice in which the learning is taking place, on issues of access, and on the transparency of the cultural environment with respect to the meaning of what is being learned. Insofar as the notion of transparency, taken very broadly, is a way of organizing activities that makes their meaning visible, it opens an alternative approach to the traditional dichotomy between learning experientially and learning at a distance, between learning by doing and learning by abstraction.

Discourse and Practice

The characterization of language in learning has, in discussions of conventional contrasts between formal and informal learning, been treated as highly significant in classifying ways of transmitting knowledge. Verbal instruction has been assumed to have special, and especially effective properties with respect to the generality and scope of the understanding that learners come away with, while instruction by demonstration – learning by 'observation and imitation' – is supposed to produce the opposite, a literal and narrow effect.

Close analysis of both instructional discourse and cases of apprenticeship raise a different point: issues about language, like those about the role of masters, may well have more to do with legitimacy of participation and with access to peripherality than they do with knowledge transmission. Indeed, as Jordan (1989) argues, learning to become a legitimate participant in a community involves learning how to talk (and be silent) in the manner of full participants. In A. A. telling the story of the life of the nondrinking alcoholic is clearly a major vehicle for the display of membership. Models for constructing A. A. life stories are widely available in published accounts of alcoholics' lives and in the storytelling performances of old-timers. Early on, newcomers learn to preface their contributions to A. A. meetings with the simple identifying statement 'I'm a recovering alcoholic', and, shortly, to introduce themselves and sketch the problems that brought them to A. A. They begin by describing these events in non-A. A. terms. Their accounts meet with counterexemplary stories by more-experienced members who do not criticize or correct newcomers accounts directly. They gradually generate a view that matches more closely the A. A. model, eventually producing skilled testimony in public meetings and gaining validation from others as they demonstrate the appropriate understanding.

The process of learning to speak as a full member of a community of practice is vividly illustrated in an analysis of the changing performances of newcomer spirit mediums in a spiritist congregation in Mexico (Kearney, 1977). This example is interesting partly because the notion of 'proper speech' is so clearly crystallized in the collective expectations of the community, while at the same time, if the community were forced to acknowledge the idea that mediums must *learn* their craft, this would negate the legitimacy of spirit possession. That learning through legitimate peripheral participation nonetheless occurs makes this example especially striking.

Spiritist cult communities center around women who are adept at going into trance. They act as mediums, transmitting the messages of a variety of spirits. The spirits are arranged in a complex hierarchy of more- and less-important forms of deity. It takes a great deal of practice to speak coherently while in trance, especially while taking on a variety of personae.

> It is quite apparent from biographical data I have on mediums that they typically begin 'working' with various [unimportant] exotic spirits who have idiosyncratic speech patterns, and then eventually switch to working with the [highly revered] Divinities who typically speak in a much more stereotypic manner . . . . Recently several novice mediums have been 'entered' by 'beings from outer space'. These beings appeared quite intent on speaking to those present via the mediums, but of course their language was incomprehensible to the audience. During the course of repeated visits, however, and with help from nonpossessed spiritualists, they slowly 'began to learn to speak the Spanish language', and to articulate their messages . . . A . . . characteristic of advanced mediums as compared with novices is the large repertoire and wider range of identities displayed by the former.
>
> Kearney 1977.

In the *Psychology of Literacy*, Scribner and Cole (1981) speculate that asking questions – learning how to 'do' school appropriately may be a major part of what school teaches. This is also Jordan's conclusion about Yucatec midwives' participation in biomedical, state-sponsored training courses. She argues that the verbal instruction provided by health officials has the effect of teaching midwives how to talk in biomedical terms when required. Such talk only serves to give them 'face validity' in the eyes of others who believe in the authoritative character of biomedicine. But Jordan argues that it has no effect on their existing practice.

This point about language use is consonant with the earlier argument that didactic instruction creates unintended practices. The conflict stems from the fact that there is a difference between talking *about* a practice from outside and talking *within* it. Thus the didactic use of language, not itself the discourse of practice, creates a new linguistic practice, which has an existence of its own. Legitimate peripheral participation in such linguistic practice is a form of learning, but does not imply that newcomers learn the actual practice the language is supposed to be about.

In a community or practice, there are no special forms of discourse aimed at apprentices or crucial to their centripetal movement toward full participation that correspond to the marked genres of the question-answer-evaluation format of classroom teaching, or the lecturing of college professors or midwife-training course instructors. But Jordan makes a further, acute, observation about language, this time about the role of *stories* in apprenticeship: she points out that stories play a major role in decision making (1989). This has implications for what and how newcomers learn. For apprenticeship learning is supported by conversations and stories about problematic and especially difficult cases.

> What happens is that as difficulties of one kind or another develop, stories of similar cases are offered up by the attendants [at a birth], all of whom, it should be remembered, are experts, having themselves given birth. In the ways in which these stories are treated, elaborated, ignored, taken up, characterized as typical and so on, the collaborative work of deciding on the present case is done . . . . These stories, then, are packages of situated knowledge . . . . To acquire a store of appropriate stories and, even more importantly, to know what are appropriate occasions for telling them, is then part of what it means to become a midwife
>
> Jordan 1989: 935.

Orr (1990) describes comparable patterns of story telling in his research on the learning of machine-repair work: technicians who repair copier machines tell each other 'war stories' about their past experiences in making repairs. Such stories constitute a vital part of diagnosing and carrying out new repairs. In the process, newcomers learn how to make (sometimes difficult) repairs, they learn the skills of war-story telling, and they become legitimate participants in the community of practice. In A. A. also, discussions have a dual purpose. Participants engage in the work of staying sober and they do so through gradual construction of an identity. Telling the personal story is a tool of diagnosis and reinterpretation. Its communal use is essential to the fashioning of an identity as a recovered alcoholic, and thus to remaining sober. It becomes a display of membership by virtue of fulfilling a crucial function in the shared practice.

It is thus necessary to refine our distinction between *talking about* and *talking within* a practice. Talking within itself includes both talking within (e.g., exchanging information necessary to the progress of ongoing activities) and talking about (e.g., stories, community lore). Inside the shared practice, both forms of talk fulfill specific functions: engaging, focusing, and shifting attention, bringing about coordination, etc., on the one hand; and supporting communal forms of memory and reflection, as well as signalling membership, on the other. (And, similarly, talking about includes both forms of talk once it becomes part of a practice of its own, usually sequestered in some respects.) For newcomers then the purpose is not to learn *from* talk as a substitute for legitimate peripheral participation; it is to learn *to* talk as a key to legitimate peripheral participation.

Motivation and Identity: Effects of Participation

It is important to emphasize that, during the extended period of legitimate participation typical of the cases of apprenticeship described here, newcomers participate in a community of practitioners as well as in productive activity. Legitimate peripheral participation is an initial form of membership characteristic of such a community. Acceptance by and interaction with acknowledged adept practitioners make learning legitimate and of value from the point of view of the apprentice. More generally, learning in practice, apprentice learners know that there is a field for the mature practice of what they are learning to do – midwifing, tailoring, quartermastering, butchering, or being sober. The community of midwives, tailors, quartermasters, butchers, or nondrinking alcoholics and their productive relations with the world provide apprentices with these continuity-based 'futures'.

To be able to participate in a legitimately peripheral way entails that newcomers have broad access to arenas of mature practice. At the same time, productive peripherality requires less demands on time, effort, and responsibility for work than for full participants. A newcomer's tasks are short and simple, the costs of errors are small, the apprentice has little responsibility for the activity as a whole. A newcomer's tasks tend to be positioned at the ends of branches of work processes, rather than in the middle of linked work segments. A midwife's apprentice runs errands. Tailors' apprentices do maintenance on the sewing machine before the master begins work, and finishing details when the master has completed a pair of trousers; a lot of time in between is spent sitting beside the master on his two-person bench. For the quartermasters, the earliest jobs are physically at the periphery of the work space. In many cases, distinctions between play and work, or between peripheral activity and other work, are little marked. In all five cases of apprenticeship, however, it is also true that the initial, partial contributions of apprentices are useful. Even the A. A. newcomer, while reinterpreting his or her life, produces new material that contributes to the communal construction of an understanding of alcoholism. An apprentice's contributions to ongoing activity gain value in practice – a value which increases as the apprentice becomes more adept. As opportunities for understanding how well or poorly one's efforts contribute are evident in practice, legitimate participation of a peripheral kind provides an immediate ground for self-evaluation. The sparsity of tests, praise, or blame typical of apprenticeship follows from the apprentice's legitimacy as a participant.

Notions like those of 'intrinsic rewards' in empirical studies of apprenticeship focus quite narrowly on task knowledge and skill as the activities to be learned. Such knowledge is of course important; but a deeper sense of the value of participation to the community and the learner lies in *becoming* part of the community. Thus, making a hat reasonably well is seen as evidence that an apprentice tailor is becoming 'a masterful practitioner', though it may also be perceived in a more utilitarian vein in terms of reward or even value. Similarly, telling one's life story or making a Twelfth Step confers a sense of belonging. Moving toward full participation in practice involves not just a greater commitment of time, intensified effort, more and broader responsibilities within the community, and more difficult and risky tasks, but, more significantly, an increasing sense of identity as a master practitioner.

When the process of increasing participation is not the primary motivation for learning, it is often because 'didactic caretakers' assume responsibility for motivating newcomers. In such circumstances, the focus of attention shifts from co-participating in practice to acting upon the person-to-be-changed. Such a shift is typical of situations, such as schooling, in which pedagogically structured content organizes learning activities. Overlooking the importance of legitimate participation by newcomers in the target practice has two related consequences. First, the identity of learners becomes an explicit object of change. When central participation is the subjective intention motivating learning, changes in cultural identity and social relations are inevitably part of the process, but learning does not have to be mediated – and distorted – through a learner's view of 'self' as *object.* Second, where there is no cultural identity encompassing the activity in which newcomers participate and no field of mature practice for what is being learned, exchange value replaces the use value of increasing participation. The commoditization of learning engenders a fundamental contradiction between the use and exchange values of the outcome of learning, which manifests itself in conflicts between learning to know and learning to display knowledge for evaluation. Testing in schools and trade schools (unnecessary in situations of apprenticeship learning) is perhaps the most pervasive and salient example of a way of establishing the exchange value of knowledge. Test taking then becomes a new parasitic practice, the goal of which is to increase the exchange value of learning independently of its use value.

Contradictions and Change: Continuity and Displacement

To account for the complexity of participation in social practice, it is essential to give learning and teaching independent status as analytic concepts. Primary reliance on the concept of pedagogical structuring in learning research may well prevent speculation about what teaching consists of, how it is perceived, and how – as perceived – it affects learning. Most analyses of schooling assume, whether intentionally or not, the uniform motivation of teacher and pupils, because they assume, sometimes quite explicitly, that teacher and pupils share the goal of the main activity (e.g., Davydov and Markova, 1983). In our view, this assumption has several consequences. First, it ignores the conflicting viewpoints associated with teaching and learning, respectively, and obscures the distortions that ensue (Fajans and Turner, 1988). Furthermore, it reflects too narrowly rationalistic perspective on the person and motivation. The multiple viewpoints that are characteristic of participation in a community of practice, and thus of legitimate peripheral participation, are to be found in more complex theories of the person-in-society, such as those proposed by critical psychologists. Finally, assumptions of uniformity make it difficult to explore the mechanisms by which processes of change and transformation in communities' practice and processes of learning are intricately implicated in each other.

In considering learning as part of social practice, we have focused our attention on the structure of social practice rather than privileging the structure of pedagogy as the source of learning. Learning understood as legitimate peripheral participation is not necessarily or directly dependent on pedagogical goals or official agenda, even in situations in which these goals appear to be a central factor (e.g., classroom instruction, tutoring). We have insisted that exposure to resources for learning is not restricted to a teaching curriculum and that instructional assistance is not construed as a purely interpersonal phenomenon; rather we have argued that learning must be understood with respect to a practice as a whole, with its multiplicity of relations – both within the community and with the world at large. Dissociating learning from pedagogical intentions opens the possibility of mismatch or conflict among practitioners' viewpoints in situations where learning is going on. These differences often must become constitutive of the content of learning.

We mentioned earlier that a major contradiction lies between legitimate peripheral participation as the means of achieving continuity over generations for the community of practice, and the displacement inherent in that same process as full participants are replaced (directly or indirectly) by newcomers-become-old-timers. Both Fortes (1938) and Goody (1989) have commented on this conflict between continuity and displacement, which is surely part of all learning. This tension is in fact fundamental – a basic contradiction of social reproduction, transformation, and change. In recent accounts of learning by activity theorists (e.g., Engeström, 1987), the major contradiction underlying the historical development of learning is that of the commodity. Certainly this is fundamental to the historical shaping of social reproduction as well as production. But we believe that a second contradiction – that between continuity and displacement – is also funda-mental to the social relations of production and to the social reproduction of labor. Studies of learning might benefit from examining the field of relations generated by these interrelated contradictions. For if production and the social reproduction of persons are mutually entailed in the repro-duction of the social order, the contradictions inherent in reproducing persons within the domestic group and other communities of practice do not go away when the form of production changes, but go through transfor-mations of their own. How to characterize these contradictions in changing forms of production is surely the central question underlying a historical understanding of forms of learning, family, and of course, schooling.

The continuity–displacement contradiction is present during apprentice-ship, whether apprentice and master jointly have a stake in the increasingly knowledgeable skill of the apprentice, as among the tailors and midwives, or whether there is a conflict between the master's desire for labor and the apprentice's desire to learn (see Goody, 1982), as among the meat cutters. The different ways in which old-timers and newcomers establish and main-tain identities conflict and generate competing viewpoints on the practice and its development. Newcomers are caught in a dilemma. On the one hand, they need to engage in the existing practice, which has developed over time: to understand it, to participate in it, and to become full members of the community in which it exists. On the other hand, they have a stake in its development as they begin to establish their own identity in its future.

We have claimed that the development of identity is central to the careers of newcomers in communities of practice, and thus fundamental to the concept of legitimate peripheral participation. This is illustrated most vividly by the experience of newcomers to A. A., but we think that it is true of all learning. In fact, we have argued that, from the perspective we have developed here, learning and a sense of identity are inseparable: they are aspects of the same phenomenon.

Insofar as the conflicts in which the continuity–displacement contradic-tion is manifested involve power – as they do to a large extent – the way the contradiction is played out changes as power relations change. Conflicts between masters and apprentices (or, less individualistically, between generations) take place in the course of everyday participation. Shared participation is the stage on which the old and the new, the known and the unknown, the established and the hopeful, act out their differences and discover their commonalties, manifest their fear of one another, and come to terms with their need for one another. Each threatens the fulfillment of the other's destiny, just as it is essential to it. Conflict is experienced and worked out through a shared everyday practice in which differing viewpoints and common stakes are in interplay. Learners can be overwhelmed, overawed, and overworked. Yet even when submissive imitation is the result, learning is never simply a matter of the 'transmission' of knowledge or the 'acquisition' of skill; identity in relation with practice, and hence knowledge and skill and their significance to the subject and the community, are never unproblematic. This helps to account for the common observation that knowers come in a range of types, from clones to heretics.

Granting legitimate participation to newcomers with their own viewpoints introduces into any community of practice all the tensions of the continuity–displacement contradiction. These may be muted, though not extinguished, by the differences of power between old-timers and newcomers. As a way in which the related conflicts are played out in practice, legitimate peripheral participation is far more than just a process of learning on the part of newcomers. It is a reciprocal relation between persons and practice. This means that the move of learners toward full participation in a community of practice does not take place in a static context. The practice itself is in motion.

Since activity and the participation of individuals involved in it, their knowledge, and their perspectives are mutually constitutive, change is a fundamental property of communities of practice and their activities. Goody (1989) argues that the introduction of strangers into what was previously strictly domestic production (a change that occurred within an expanding market in West Africa in the recent past) led masters to think more comprehensively about the organization of their production activities. She points out that the resulting division of work processes into segments to be learned has been mirrored in subsequent generations in new, increasingly specialized occupations. Legitimate peripherality is important for developing 'constructively naive' perspectives or questions. From this point of view, inexperience is an asset to be exploited. It is of use, however, only in the context of participation, when supported by experienced practitioners who both understand its limitations and value its role. Legitimacy of participation is crucial both for this naive involvement to invite reflection on ongoing activity and for the newcomer's occasional contributions to be taken into account. Insofar as this continual interaction of new perspectives is sanctioned, everyone's participation is legitimately peripheral in some respect. In other words, everyone can to some degree be considered a 'newcomer' to the future of a changing community.

References

Bourdieu, P. (1977) *Outline of a theory of practice*, Cambridge: Cambridge University Press.

Davydov, V. and Markova, A. (1983) A concept of educational activity for school children, *Soviet Psychology*, 11 (2), pp. 50–76.

Engeström, Y. (1987) *Learning by expanding*, Helsinki: Orienta-Konsultit Oy.

Fajans, J. and Turner, T. (1988) Where the action is: An anthropological perspective on activity theory, with ethnographic applications. Paper presented at the annual meeting of the American Anthropological Association.

Fortes, M. (1938) Social and psychological aspects of education in Taleland, Supplement to *Africa*, 11 (4).

Goody, E. (ed.) (1982) *From craft to industry*, Cambridge: Cambridge University Press.

Goody, E. (1989) Learning and the division of labor, in M. Coy (ed.) *Anthropological perspectives on apprenticeship*, New York: SUNY Press.

Hutchins, E. (1996) Learning to navigate, in S. Chaiklin and J. Lave (eds.) *Understanding practice*, New York: Cambridge University Press, pp. 35–64.

Jordan, B. (1989) Cosmopolitical obstetrics: Some insights from the training of traditional midwives, *Social Science and Medicine* 28 (9), pp. 925–44.

Kearney, M. (1977) Oral performance by Mexican spiritualists in possession trance, *Journal of Latin American Lore,* 3 (2), pp. 309–28.

Lave, J. (1989) The acquisition of culture and the practice of understanding, in J. Stigler, R. Shweder, and G. Herdt (eds.) *The Chicago symposia on human development*, Cambridge, Cambridge University Press.

Marshall, H. (1972) Structural constraints on learning, in B. Geer (ed.) *Learning to Work*, Beverly Hills, CA: Sage Publications.

Orr, J. (1990) Sharing knowledge, celebrating identity: War stories and community memory among service technicians, in D. S. Middleton and D. Edwards (eds.) *Collective remembering: Memory in society* (pp. 169–189), Beverley Hills, CA: Sage Publications.

Scribner, S. and Cole, M. (1981) *The psychology of literacy*, Cambridge, MA: Harvard University Press.

Stack, C. (1989) Life trajectories and ethnography. Proposal to the Group on Lifespan Research, University of California, Berkeley.

Traweek, S. (1988) Discovering machines: Nature in the age of its mechanical reproduction, in F. Dubinskas (ed.) *Making time: Ethnographies of high technology organisations*, Philadelphia: Temple University Press.

Wenger, E. (1990) Toward a theory of cultural transparency: elements of a social discourse of the visible and the invisible, Palo Alto, CA: Institute for Research on Learning.

4

Perspectives on the Nature of Science

R. Driver, J. Leach, R. Millar and P. Scott

Can We Talk of 'Understanding the Nature of Science'?

The Absence of Consensus

Researching into, or even thinking and talking about, students' understanding of the nature of science immediately raises one important issue: to talk of someone's 'understanding' of something seems to imply that the thing in question is well understood, that there is an agreed 'expert' understanding against which their ideas can be set. This is the case when we are considering students' ideas and understandings of science content. If we take, for example, a science domain such as electric circuits, then at the level to which this is studied at school, there is consensus among scientists about the phenomena and about how these should be explained. We might want to treat students' ideas with a certain respect, as prior conceptions or even 'alternative' conceptions rather than misconceptions; but we can use a consensually accepted understanding as a template against which to set students' understandings. The accepted view provides us with a 'map' of the domain.

In contrast, there is less consensus among scholars about the 'nature of science'. Philosophers of science have adopted – and continue to adopt – a range of positions on the major questions and issues about science and scientific knowledge. And it is problematic, at best, to suggest that such views 'progress' or 'approach the truth'. It may reasonably be claimed that scientific knowledge progresses, that we know more now than we used to know about the natural world, but this cannot be so easily claimed of our understanding of *science*. The ideas of today's philosophers of science do not overturn, or subsume, those of earlier writers. Indeed, more recent studies of scientific practice have tended to emphasize the variety, and local contingence, of scientific practices rather than painting a picture of a general 'method' or 'approach'. So far from clarifying our understanding of the nature of science, or leading towards consensus, their effect has been to broaden the range of views and positions on offer.

Natural Sciences

It is important to make clear that we are imposing some limits on this diversity. First, we have chosen to focus on understanding of the nature of science, and not the nature of technology, or of science-and-technology. We would draw the distinction between science and technology largely in terms of purpose, with science seeking to provide explanations of natural events and phenomena, while technology is concerned with the solution of practical problems, drawing on a range of knowledge sources, including science, in reaching acceptable solutions, and sometimes leading to the development of new knowledge (including scientific knowledge) in the process.

Second, 'science' refers to the natural sciences. The boundary between natural and social sciences is not, however, a firm or clearly defined one. There is a longstanding debate about the extent to which there are, or should be, similarities and differences between the methods of the natural and social sciences (see, for example, Bernstein, 1976). In broad terms, however, a distinction can be drawn between studies in which the research subjects are conscious beings, whose consciousness could influence (in various ways) the empirical data collected, and studies of inanimate objects (Harré 1972, pp. 188–9). This, however, still leaves a considerable 'gray area' of studies of living creatures (including humans) in situations where it is a matter of debate whether (and if so, to what extent) their consciousness has an effect on the data.

Even within the natural sciences, there is considerable methodological diversity, some of which may have epistemological implications. In many sciences, for instance, experimentation is a key aspect of the process of gaining knowledge. By experiment, we mean a planned intervention, in which a part of the natural world is manipulated in order to obtain data. Some sciences, however, such as astronomy and geology, study objects which cannot be brought into the laboratory and processes which cannot be replicated. Here planned and structured observation often has to take the place of experiment, as a means of testing explanations and predictions (though much experiment may, of course, have been involved in developing the instruments used in these sciences). Also, some sciences seek historical explanations rather than experimental/predictive ones. Gould (1991) argues that palaeontology and evolutionary biology must base their interpretations on the available historical record. The events they study may have happened for contingent reasons, which by their very nature cannot be replicated. The key methodological challenge for such sciences is to legitimate their interpretations of the historical records, since experiment is not an option. Gould's conclusion is that the crucial work in the 'historical' sciences is the detailed *description* of the available evidence.

If differences in subject matter lead to differences in practices, which in turn rest on epistemological differences, perhaps it is more plausible to think of multiple 'natures of sciences'? The very fact, however, that we can recognize and talk about a group of disciplines as natural sciences implies a measure of similarity and family resemblance. Further, since the sciences have quite distinctive (though admittedly in places overlapping) areas of content, some of this similarity resides in shared epistemological and methodological commitments and institutional practices. It is to this common core of ideas about commitments, methods and practices that we refer when talking of 'the nature of science'.

Perspectives on the Nature of Science: an Historical Overview

Science is *a body of knowledge* about the natural world; and a *set of practices,* both material and social, which have been used to obtain, and continue to be used to extend, that knowledge. Our grounds for confidence in this body of knowledge and in the efficacy of these practices have exercised philosophers over the centuries. Here we provide only a brief overview of some of the major strands in this ongoing discussion. Fuller accounts may be found in the books by Chalmers (1982), Losee (1972), Newton-Smith (1981) and Gillies (1992).

Explanation in Science

The central aim of science is to provide *explanations* for natural phenomena. But what do we mean by an 'explanation'? In one sense, an explanation is simply what is accepted by the person who has given it, and by the person who has received it, as an explanation. We learn from experience what counts as an explanation. One factor crucial to the emergence of science was a shift in the nature of acceptable explanation of events, away from accounts in terms of reasons ('final causes' in Aristotle's terms) to accounts in terms of an observed regularity or an underlying causal model. So, for example, Galileo's understanding of motion depended critically on his decision to ask *how* falling objects fall, rather than *why* they fall. In general, science seeks to exclude teleological explanations, in which a future state of affairs is used to account for events leading up to it.

Various attempts have been made to describe the structure of acceptable explanation in the sciences. One approach is to appeal to the logical structure of an explanation:

> an explanation as to *why* things happen, or *why* they are as they are, consists of a statement of an accepted law (or laws) and some other statement(s) relating the particular circumstances to it (or to them) so that from all these the *emplicandum* (the thing to be explained) can be deduced.
>
> (Trusted, 1987, p. 52, emphasis in original)

For example, imagine we have a syringe containing 100 ml of air at atmospheric pressure. The end of the syringe is sealed. We now push the piston inwards, until the volume of the air is 50 ml, and measure the air pressure. We find it is 2 atmospheres. We can explain this by stating the general law that, for a fixed mass of gas, the pressure is inversely proportional to the volume (Boyle's Law). In this particular case, we have halved the volume. So we can deduce that the pressure should be doubled. The outcome is explained because it is a logical deduction from the general law and the specific starting conditions. This type of explanation is referred to as a Deductive-Nomological (or DN) explanation.

Hemple (1965) provides the classical statement of this view of scientific explanation; an accessible introductory discussion is provided by Trusted (1987). As an account of scientific explanation, the DN model is, however, open to several objections. First, it has difficulty in distinguishing cause and effect clearly: an argument of the same logical structure can explain a storm by a falling barometer and vice versa. Second, as Cartwright (1983, pp. 44–53) points out, science does not, in fact propose universal generalizations. All generalizations are accompanied by an explicit or implicit *ceteris paribus* clause; that is, they have the qualification 'all other things being equal'. The law is followed under certain special conditions. This means, as Cartwright notes, that they cannot, logically, explain anything, since any departure from the predicted behaviour can always be attributed to the prevailing conditions.

An alternative approach is to emphasize theories, rather than generalizations or laws, as fundamental to explanation in science. A theoretical model describes an imagined world. Events in the real world are then seen as a natural outcome of the behaviour and properties of objects in this imagined world – and hence are 'explained'. Ogborn (1994) proposes a model of explanation as a *history* in a *possible world*. The content of an explanation is 'a set of events in a possible world which lead to what is to be explained, in which that set of events is a possible world' (p. 4). He goes on to show the power of this model in providing a structure for considering a wide range of phenomena associated with explanation. This has close similarities to Johnson-Laird's (1983) account of the role of mental models in constructing explanations – allowing ideas to be 'played through' in the imagination to provide a possible account of an observed event.

Theoretical models clearly differ from empirical generalizations (or laws) (though both, as we shall see later, share one important feature: they make claims which go beyond the data on which they are based). Many laws, however, are underpinned by theoretical models. So, for example, in the example above of compressing a gas, Boyle's Law is supported by a theoretical model (the kinetic theory of gases) in which pressure is interpreted in terms of collisions between molecules of the gas and the walls of the container. The presence of such a model in the background is, however, irrelevant to the logical form of a DN explanation. And many quite acceptable explanations remain at the level of the empirical law, even when there is an underlying theoretical model. For example, if someone asks 'why is the handle of a saucepan made of plastic and not of metal, like the rest of the pan?', then the answer 'because plastics are poor conductors of heat' would normally be taken as an explanation. There would not normally be a perceived need to go on to explain free electron models of thermal conduction in metals, and the different atomic/molecular structure of insulators in order to explain satisfactorily the choice of plastic as the handle material.

There are also quite striking differences in kind among theoretical models (for a fuller discussion, see Harré, 1972). Some, like the kinetic theory of matter, introduce unobservable objects such as atoms and molecules, with distinctive properties like constant motion with an average speed related to the temperature. Other theoretical models, such as the germ theory of disease, give a key role to objects which are not observable with the naked eye, but which can be observed using instruments, in this case microscopes. Some theories, like the heliocentric model of the solar system or the plate tectonic model of the evolution of the Earth's surface, introduce no new unobservable objects, but seem much more like a description of the system, from a particular viewpoint, or over a longer time-span than human lives. Yet others propose formal entities such as force or energy, which are not, in principle, observable, but provide one means (though not necessarily the only means) of structuring phenomena and events. The unifying characteristic of theories is that they provide a mental model; by 'running' the model in the mind, predictions can be made and explanations given. Some models can be expressed mathematically, allowing the behaviour of more complex situations and systems to be simulated and predicated.

Observations First: the Inductive View

If science aims to provide explanations for phenomena and events, then perhaps the central question to be asked about science as a knowledge form is: why should we have confidence in the scientific account? What is it about the scientific approach which enables it to provide 'reliable knowledge' (Ziman, 1978)? For Chalmers (1982, p. 1), the 'widely held common-sense view of science' is that:

> Scientific knowledge is proven knowledge. Scientific theories are derived in some rigorous way from the facts of experience acquired by observation and experiment. Science is based on what we can see and hear and touch, etc.

This is both an *empiricist* and an *inductive* view. *Empiricism* is the view that secure knowledge is that which comes directly from experience. *Induction* is the process of inferring generalizations from a series of specific (or *singular*) observations. Examples might include the statement that 'the sun rises every morning in the east', based upon the repeated observation that, every morning so far, it has done so; or proposing that 'all non-metals are electrical insulators' on the basis of tests carried out on a collection of metallic and non-metallic specimens. Although the idea of induction dates back at least to Aristotle (Losee, 1972, p 8), the claim that induction is distinctively the 'method' of science is most closely associated with Francis Bacon (1561–1626). Philosophers, however, have long been aware (Losee, 1972, pp. 31ff.) of a fundamental problem about induction: unlike deductive reasoning, where we start from a set of initial propositions and use logical rules of argument to reach a conclusion (so that, if the premises are sound, then the conclusion *must* be valid), we can never be completely sure that an inductive generalization is true. The next singular observation we make may show that it is false. The second example above is a case in point.

If we now add graphite to our collection of materials, we discover a non-metal which is not an electrical insulator. The generalization 'all non-metals are electrical insulators' is seen to be false. A first response to this objection might be to argue that, provided sufficient observations have been made, covering a sufficiently wide range of situations and cases, then we can be confident that a generalization is valid. But that begs the question of how many is 'sufficient', or what a 'sufficiently wide range' might be. We have to accept that, if scientific generalizations are arrived at through inductive reasoning, then it cannot be logically demonstrated that they are true. By the same reasoning, theoretical models, if they are derived inductively from experience, can never be shown to be true.

Philosophers have responded to this in a variety of ways. In the eighteenth century, David Hume's analysis of induction led him to conclude that generalizations can have no logical basis in singular pieces of evidence (Ayer, 1981). Hume conceded, however, that humans do indeed think in these ways; he acknowledged that he, himself, did so when 'out of his study'. This he regarded as a 'habit of the mind' – a psychological propensity rather than a logical step. Hume was prepared to accept that induction was, indeed, the method of the sciences; but he argued that it was grounded in human psychology rather than in logic.

For many philosophers, however, this is an uncomfortable conclusion. J. S. Mill (1803–1873) developed a logic of experimentation based on four 'methods', of which the most important were the Method of Agreement and the Method of Difference (Mill, 1843, in Brown *et al.*, 1981, pp 76–82). The former involves listing instances in which a particular phenomenon occurs, and then searching for common factors associated with each of these instances. If one can be found, then this suggests, according to Mill, that it is probable that this is the cause of the phenomenon. The Method of Difference involves listing instances and non-instances of a phenomenon and then looking for a factor which is present when the phenomenon occurs, but absent when it does not. Mill's arguments did not, however, allay concerns about the inductive method; these methods may underlie much practical reasoning, but they do not lead to results which must, logically, follow. They do not, therefore, provide any assurance that the inductive method leads to true generalizations or laws.

The American philosopher, C. S. Pierce, a contemporary of Mill, introduced the term 'abduction' for the process of working back from observation to an account of an underlying model or principle which could account for what was observed. He acknowledged that there was no 'method' for doing so, but that the process involved creativity and imagination. Most empiricists would now share this view, that there is no automatic, or algorithmic, method of deriving a generalization or theoretical model from a set of singular observations; modern empiricists would argue that, however the generalization or theory comes to be proposed, our grounds for confidence in it lie in the set of singular observations which underpin it (van Fraassen, 1980).

In the twentieth century, inductive reasoning has been taken up and developed by the philosophical movement known as 'logical positivism' (Ayer, 1946). Logical positivists argue that the aim of philosophy is not to establish which propositions are true or false, but to clarify the meaning of statements. Some are *analytic*: they follow logically from previous assumptions but, since they are logically entailed by those assumptions, do not tell us anything new about the world. Others, including all scientific statements, are *synthetic*: they propose a link between two or more things which are not necessarily (i.e. logically and inevitably) related in this way. Such statements must be verifiable by observation, at least in principle. All other statements, according to the logical positivists, are non-sensical and meaningless – that is, literally 'without meaning'. The logical positivist view of synthetic statements, and hence of scientific knowledge, is an inductive one, with a particular emphasis on verifiability and observation.

While accepting the logical problem of induction, logical positivists (Carnap, 1950) have claimed, using arguments based on formal logic and the mathematics of probability, that induction can lead, logically, to generalizations which are *probably* true, and that additional observations can increase this probability. Against such claims, it is usually argued that, however many singular observations are made, the ratio:

$$\frac{\text{Number of actual observations made}}{\text{Number of situations to which the generalization applies}}$$

is always zero for universal generalizations, as these claim to apply to *all* possible cases. So the probability that the generalization is true remains zero.

The Problem of Induction Solved? Popper and Falsification

Against the background of logical positivism, Karl Popper (1934) produced his now classic critique of induction. Popper argues that induction cannot be shown to lead logically to true generalizations, or even to ones which are 'probably true'. Unlike Hume, however, he does not resolve the problem this creates for philosophy of science by appealing to 'habits of the mind'. Instead, he argues that induction is *not* the method of science. Science, Popper claims, is the method of conjectures and refutations – a 'hypothetico-deductive' approach. Science progresses by proposing testable hypotheses; these are then subjected to rigorous tests in which predictions deduced from the hypothesis are compared with observation *with a view to falsifying the hypothesis*.[1] Unlike verification, which is impossible (as no finite number of observations can *prove* that a generalization is true), a single observation which conflicts with a generalization can, logically, falsify it. Popper's example is the statement 'All swans are white', which cannot be proved by any number of observations of white swans, but can be falsified by one observation of a non-white swan.

Popper argues that science makes progress through the replacement of hypotheses by newer ones with greater empirical content; that is, they account for a larger number of observations. The stimulus to such progress is the realization that current hypotheses are deficient and this can only come through their falsification. So the aim of experimental tests is the falsification of hypotheses. The key criterion that a hypothesis must meet to be called 'scientific' is that it has testable consequences which could lead, in principle, to its falsification. If it is stated in such terms that no conceivable observation could ever falsify it, then it is not, for Popper, scientific.

Another important consequence of Popper's approach is to separate the process of conceiving of a scientific idea from that of justifying it. The former involves the proposing of bold conjectures which account for known data and lead to testable consequences. According to Popper, there is little that we can say about this process; a novel theory or hypothesis is a creative product of an individual mind and there is no pattern in the way these arise. The latter involves severe testing with a view to falsification. The 'method of science' does not lie in the way new ideas are conceived but, rather, in the rigorous and systematic way such ideas are tested.

There are, however, a number of problems with this falsificationist view. First, the view that all experimentation is carried out within a hypothetico-deductive context seems somewhat narrow, and to make too many assumptions about the branch of science one is thinking about and its stage of development. It seems clear, for example, that when scientists undertake an initial exploration of a new area, their primary concern is often simply to collect data and information about the area. They have no theory in mind as they probe, and their data-gathering cannot convincingly be portrayed as theory-testing (see, Hacking, 1983, especially chapter 10). [. . .] Second, the strong emphasis on falsification as an aim does not ring true of actual scientific practice. As Lakatos is once said to have remarked: 'You know a scientist who wants to falsify his theory?' (Newton-Smith, 1981, p. 52). If a scientist undertakes experimental work in order to test a hypothesis, the intention (and the hope) is invariably to corroborate it rather than to falsify it. This is not simply a reflection of the natural human desire to be right rather than wrong; many of the episodes in science which are celebrated as 'crucial' experiments are verifications rather than falsifications. Eddington's measurements of the deflection of light from stars during a solar eclipse, which corroborated the predictions of Einstein's general theory of relativity, and Fresnel's observation of the bright spot at the centre of the shadow of a disc, are just two examples. In general, few scientific investigations appear to be undertaken in the hope of falsifying a hypothesis.

A second line of criticism centres on the absence of any obvious place for the notion of 'truth' in the hypothetico-deductive approach. If induction is logically invalid, and hypotheses are bold conjectures, then we can never have grounds for believing any conjecture to be 'true'. It is, at best, 'not yet falsified'. So what is the purpose of science, if we cannot attain the truth (or, more precisely, we cannot ever be sure if we have attained it)? Popper's answer is that theories can have differing degrees of *verisimilitude* or 'nearness to the truth'. We can compare the relative verisimilitude of theories and so can claim that science makes progress. His argument, however, has been subjected to significant criticism, along lines similar to those used against probabilistic interpretations of induction (for a fuller discussion, see Newton-Smith, 1981, Chapter 3).

Observation is Theory-laden

A serious challenge both to the falsificationist approach and to induction is the argument that all observation is theory-laden. Hanson (1958) uses a series of examples to show how the reports people give of what they see presuppose theories of different sorts, and concludes:

> There is a sense, then, in which seeing is a 'theory-laden' undertaking. Observation of *x* is shaped by prior knowledge of *x*. Another influence on observation rests in the language or notation used to express what we know, and without which there would be little we could recognise as knowledge.
>
> (Hanson, 1958, p. 146)

In the context of science teaching, we might see this 'theory-ladenness' of observation in pupils' drawings of what they observe when using a microscope to look at cells; those who have seen textbook diagrams of cells produce very different drawings from those who have not (Hainsworth, 1956). Similarly, if pupils are asked to map a magnetic field using iron filings and sketch what they observe, their drawings differ according to the prior knowledge of magnetic field patterns which they bring to the task (Gott and Welford, 1987).

If the theory-ladenness of all observation is accepted, then the basic empiricist idea that we can have secure knowledge based upon sense experience is overturned. Even observation statements depend on, and are infected by, the theoretical commitments of the observer. There is no 'pure' bedrock of observable 'fact'. The inductive view, which begins with observation, is seriously compromised. Recognizing this, logical positivists have tried to argue that there is a clear observational-theoretical distinction (Carnap, 1966). Falsificationism is equally challenged, since it depends on the idea that hypotheses can be tested by comparing predictions based upon them with observation. But these observations themselves incorporate theoretical ideas. So a conflict between a prediction and an observation statement may be attributed to a problem with the theory (or theories) which are implicit in the observation statement itself, and not with the hypothesis being tested. As a result, falsification can never be clear-cut.

Popper himself accepted this argument and proposed that all statements, even 'basic statements' reporting an observation, should be seen as conjectural. They may be consensually accepted as a basis for theory-testing, but his is ultimately a *decision* made by the scientific community (see Newton-Smith, 1981, pp. 59–64). Feyerabend talks of 'quickly decidable sentences' (quoted in Maxwell, 1962, p. 13) – statements which can readily be agreed by all concerned. Newton-Smith (1981, p. 28) argues that:

> while we cannot have absolute faith in any particular report . . . we are entitled to have general faith in the low-level O-reports (observational reports) we are inclined to make. Our success in coping with the world gives us grounds for this general confidence. If such judgments were not by and large reliable, we should not be still here to make judgments.

Others (Maxwell, 1962; Putnam, 1962; Shapere, 1982) have similarly argued that there is a continuum from the less to the more theoretical, and that any line drawn to divide this into two categories is necessarily arbitrary. While a rigid distinction cannot be made between statements which are 'purely observational' and others which contain theoretical terms and ideas, statements can differ in the amount of theoretical 'baggage' they carry. Finally, it is important to note that, while an observation statement may be theory-laden, it is not necessarily laden with the theory which it is being used to test.

For all these reasons, the distinction between observation and theory remains a useful one, despite the acknowledged difficulties in drawing any clear line between observation statements and theoretical ones.

From Theories to Research Programmes

The criticisms of the naïve falsificationist position outlined above led some philosophers to develop more sophisticated forms of falsificationism. The best known of these is in the work of Imre Lakatos (1970, 1978), who argues that it is misleading to represent the scientific process as involving 'a two-cornered fight between theory and experiment'. Instead, 'history of science suggests that (1) tests are – at least – three-cornered fights between rival theories and experiments and (2) some of the most interesting experiments result, *prima facie*, in confirmation rather than falsification' (Lakatos, 1978, p. 31). Lakatos acknowledges that scientists do not reject a theory just because an observation has been reported which apparently falsifies it. Even if the observation is accepted as valid, they will hold on to the theory, often hoping that some modification or new piece of information will turn up which will reconcile the theory and the apparently anomalous observation. In short, theories are never rejected unless a plausible alternative theory is available. For Lakatos the issue then becomes the process by which rival theories are compared.

He develops his arguments around the central notion of a 'research programme'. This has a 'hard core' of basic assumptions, which must not be modified or rejected. Around this, there is a 'protective belt' of auxiliary hypotheses and theories relating to such matters as initial conditions, how instruments work, and so on. The stipulation that the hard core cannot be changed, even in the light of apparent anomalies, Lakatos calls the 'negative heuristic' of a research programme. The 'positive heuristic' is a set of loose guidelines on how the research programme might develop in the face of anomalies. Lakatos then argues that research programmes can be either 'progressive' or 'degenerating', depending on whether they predict new and interesting phenomena which are subsequently observed, or simply provide *ad hoc* (and *post hoc*) accounts of observations. Popper was similarly critical of *ad hoc* adjustments to theories to account for anomalous observations, but Lakatos sets this in the context of research programmes rather than single theories.

Using this framework of ideas, Lakatos attempts to show how certain theory choices in the history of science can be portrayed as rational – based on the weight of evidence and on reason, rather than whim. His approach, however, has been criticized as providing only a rationalization of theory choice after the event, but providing no guidance to scientists facing such theory choices in the present. Lakatos's criteria for theory choice are so general that they cannot be applied in actual situations of theory choice. Hence Feyerabend (1970, p. 215) refers to Lakatos's method as 'a verbal ornament'. Feyerabend's own solution is to argue that there is no 'method of science' or rule for deciding between rival theories:

> The idea that science can, and should, be run according to fixed and universal rules is both unrealistic and pernicious . . . All methodologies have their limitations and the only 'rule' that survives is 'anything goes'.
>
> (Feyerabend, 1975, pp. 295–6)

Another influential view which agrees with Lakatos in rejecting the notion that a theory can ever be tested in isolation is the so-called Duhem-Quine thesis. Duhem's original argument was that an experiment in physics can never test an isolated hypothesis but only a group of hypotheses:

> The physicist can never subject an isolated hypothesis to experimental test; when the experiment is in disagreement with the predictions, what he learns is that at least one of the hypotheses constituting this group is unacceptable and ought to be modified; but the experiment does not designate which one should be changed.
>
> (Duhem, 1904/5, cited in Gillies, 1992, pp. 98–9)

Hence, any anomaly can be dealt with in a large number of ways. It will certainly not necessarily lead to rejection of a core theory. While Duham explicitly limited the scope of this idea to physics, and considered that it did not apply to several of the other sciences, Quine proposed that it can apply quite generally, to all statements. He argues that 'any statement can be held true come what may, if we make drastic enough adjustments elsewhere in the system'(Quine, 1951, p. 43).

Letting History Speak: Kuhn's Revolution

The publication of Thomas Kuhn's *The Structure of Scientific Revolutions* (1962) itself caused a revolution in thinking about science. Kuhn's basic thesis appears innocuous enough: that we should pay more dispassionate attention to the details of the history of science in theorizing about the nature of science and the progress of scientific ideas. On the basis of historical studies, Kuhn proposes two distinct types of scientific activity. One he calls 'normal science'. This is the kind of science practised by most scientists most of the time. It involves working within existing frameworks of theory and practice, articulating the implications and working out further applications of the accepted theoretical ideas in the branch of science. Kuhn refers to this activity, somewhat provocatively, as 'puzzle-solving'. From time to time, however, anomalous results may begin to accumulate in a branch of scientific activity. If it is impossible to accommodate these within the current theoretical framework, they will precipitate a crisis in the field. This is eventually resolved when an alternative theory emerges and is accepted by the community of practitioners in the field. This change, which can occur over a relatively short period, Kuhn calls a 'scientific revolution'. Following the revolution a new normal scientific tradition takes over.

In the account above, we have deliberately avoided using the term 'paradigm' which plays a key role in Kuhn's book. The reason is that Kuhn has been criticized for having used the term in a wide variety of different senses (Masterman, 1970), to the extent that its meaning is unclear. Kuhn acknowledges the force of this criticism and attempts in a later book (Kuhn, 1977) to clarify his intentions. He argues that the key sense of 'paradigm' is its original one: a concrete examplar of a practice, or problem solution. Individuals learn how to practise science in any given field, he argues, by learning the paradigms which guide practice in that field. For the network of facts, laws, theories and practices shared by the scientists who work in a given field, Kuhn suggests the term 'disciplinary matrix'. (Some social scientists, however, have continued to use 'paradigm' for this wider set of commitments.) In Kuhn's (1977) terminology, a scientific revolution is the period between the dominance of an old disciplinary matrix and a new one.

The aspect of Kuhn's ideas which caused controversy was his account of scientific revolutions. Kuhn likens the change to a 'gestalt switch' – a new disciplinary matrix represents a new way of looking at the world. He argues that the old and the new views cannot be compared directly. They may even be incommensurable; that is, the same terms can have quite different meanings within the two systems of thinking. A crisis in a field of science is resolved, in the final analysis, by a decision of the scientific community of workers in that field: 'What better criterion [for theory choice] than the decision of the scientific group could there be?' Kuhn asks (1970, p. 170). As critics were quick to point out, this makes theory choice seem ' a matter of mob psychology' (Lakatos, 1970, p. 178). Another consequence of Kuhn's position is that a change of disciplinary matrix does not necessarily represent 'progress' and certainly not progress *towards* anything.

In response to these criticisms, Kuhn (1977, pp. 321–2) identifies five 'characteristics of a good scientific theory':

1. A theory should be accurate within its domain, that is, consequences deducible from a theory should be in demonstrated agreement with the results of existing experiments and observations.

2. A theory should be consistent, not only internally or with itself, but also with other currently accepted theories applicable to related aspects of nature.
3. It should have broad scope: in particular, a theory's consequences should extend far beyond the particular observations, laws or sub-theories it was initially designed to explain.
4. It should be simple, bringing order to phenomena that in its absence would be individually isolated and, as a set, confused.
5. A theory should be fruitful of new research findings: that is, it should disclose new phenomena or previously unnoted relationships among those already known.

These 'standard criteria . . . together with others of much the same sort, . . . provide *the* shared basis for theory choice' (Kuhn, 1977, p. 322, emphasis in original). This seems scarcely radical. All Kuhn appears to be arguing is the unexceptional position that there is no algorithm for applying these (and similar) criteria to any given case, or for determining the relative weight to be given to each if they point towards different conclusions. Those who argue that theory choice is based on rational criteria, such as Popper, Lakatos and Laudan (1977), would agree. Kuhn chooses, however, to maintain a non-rationalist stance, by arguing that these criteria cannot be rationally justified but are simply the generally accepted ones. In practical terms, however, there seems little difference between these positions, with terms like 'rational' and 'irrational' used primarily as a rhetoric of approbation or denigration.

The 'Sociological Turn'

Kuhn's emphasis on the scientific community as the arbiter of change was quickly seized upon by sociologists, who saw it as opening up the possibility of a sociology of scientific knowledge (SSK). The idea of a 'sociology of knowledge' was first developed in a systematic way by Karl Mannheim (see, for example, Mulkay, 1979, pp. 10–17). Mannheim, however, saw scientific knowledge as lying outside the scope of sociological explanation. While a sociological account of scientific error might be produced, accepted (or true) scientific knowledge was not, in Mannheim's view, open to a sociological account. In the 1970s, several groups of sociologists began to challenge this position. The so-called 'strong programme' in the sociology of scientific knowledge (Bloor, 1976) is based on the premise that a symmetrical approach should be adopted in accounting for both the successes and failures of science. It is, in Bloor's view, unacceptable to apply one set of criteria and arguments in accounting for scientific ideas which later come to be seen as erroneous, and a different set for those which have come to be accepted. According to Bloor (1976, pp. 4–5):

The sociology of scientific knowledge should adhere to the following four tenets . . .:

1. It would be causal, that is, concerned with the conditions which bring about belief or states of knowledge. Naturally there will be other types of causes apart from social ones which will co-operate in bringing about belief.
2. It would be impartial with respect to truth or falsity, rationality or irrationality, success or failure. Both sides of these dichotomies will require explanation.
3. It would be symmetrical in its style of explanation. The same types of cause would explain, say, true and false beliefs.
4. It would be reflexive. In principle, its patterns of explanation would have to be applicable to sociology itself.

Note the emphasis, in Bloor's first tenet, on causes. Sociology, as science, is interested in the *causes* of beliefs – with, as Bloor puts it, 'the conditions which bring about belief or states of knowledge'. This contrasts with the philosopher's focus on the *rationality* of beliefs or knowledge, which is an essentially different project.

In line with Bloor's second and third tenets, SSK has embraced a *relativist* methodology. Relativism denies that things are true or false in virtue of an independent reality. Things can only be true or false for a particular group at a certain time – that is all the terms 'true' and 'false' can mean. So studies have presented evidence to support their argument that specific pieces of scientific knowledge (including currently accepted ideas, on an equal footing with ideas now seen as erroneous) are socially constructed and negotiated, and can be attributed to the interests, of the location within social groupings, of the scientists involved (Barnes and Shapin, 1979, Collins 1981a). One important influence on the development of SSK was anthropological studies which provided examples of viable and coherent belief systems based upon alternative accounts of the natural order, yet able to operate successfully at the practical level (see Giere, 1988, pp. 50–61; Gjertsen, 1989, pp. 234–257). Acknowledging limits to the possible extent of variation in viable accounts of the world, one leading practitioner of SSK has argued that 'sociologists as a whole would acknowledge that the world in some way constrains what is believed to be' (Barnes, 1974, p. vii). Collins (1981b, p. 54) counters this with a methodological principle which he sees as central to SSK; 'the appropriate attitude for conducting this kind of enquiry is to assume that 'the natural world in no way constrains what is believed to be'. This, it should be noted, is proposed as a *methodological principle* to guide sociological work, and not (necessarily) as an epistemological position.

Critics have questioned the success of studies carried out within SSK in showing exactly how specific scientific ideas have been caused by specific social factors (see, for example, Chalmers, 1990, pp. 80–114). Collins and Cox (1976) respond by challenging the critics of SSK to show in detail, in specific cases, precisely how the natural world causes specific pieces of scientific knowledge to be held as such. The variety of views about the natural world which have been held by different societies undermines, they

suggest, the claim that the natural world 'compels' any particular interpretation of it.

Later developments of the sociological programme have included richly
detailed accounts of everyday life in scientific research laboratories, with a
focus on the social interaction involved and the processes by which outputs
(mainly in the form of texts) are produced and transformed as they pass
into wider circulation (Latour and Woolgar, 1979; Lynch, 1985). Others
have focused on scientists' discourse and on the ways in which different
types of account are used in different social situations (Gilbert and Mulkay,
1984; Mulkay, 1985).

As a result of the work of sociologists, the idea that scientific knowledge is,
in some sense, 'socially constructed', is one which has passed into widespread
use. (The term has resonances with the title of Berger and Luckmann's
(1967) influential book, *The Social Construction of Reality*. Berger and Luckmann, however, were writing quite explicitly of 'social reality', which they
contrast with natural reality.) It is sometimes difficult to be sure exactly what
is meant by the claim that scientific knowledge is socially constructed. One
version is unproblematical and can be readily conceded. This is the argument
that decisions about which areas of scientific enquiry should be pursued (and
supported with funds) are based on factors external to science. Clearly, the
interests of agencies external to science, notably the military and industry,
have ensured that certain branches of science are more developed than
others. As a result, the corpus of knowledge we recognize as science is, it can
reasonably be argued, a consequence of social pressures. Under different
conditions we would have some pieces of knowledge we do not now possess,
and some which we do have would be unknown.

A stronger argument, and one which raises much more fundamental
issues, is that the *contents* of accepted science are socially constructed. This
is the core argument of SSK. In one sense this, too, can be readily accepted.
The process by which a knowledge claim from an individual scientist or
research group is transmuted into 'specific knowledge' involves a peer
review process within which the controls on publication of findings are
central. A knowledge claim can only become 'knowledge' through an institutionalized, and hence social, process. But rather more than this is
usually intended by the claim that the content of accepted science is socially constructed. The key issue, which is still strongly disputed, is whether
it is the social processes affecting the relevant scientific community, or
features of the natural world, which are the principal determinant of scientific knowledge. As Giere (1988, pp. 55–6) puts it: 'The real issue is the
extent to which, and by what means, nature constrains scientific theorizing'.

In reflecting on this issue, it may be important to recognize that the
physical sciences are the 'hard case' for SSK. If we are thinking instead of a
science such as ethology, or social biology, then it is much easier to concede
that researchers' interests and social locations may influence their observations and interpretations. Thus, for instance, it has been claimed that
scientific work on the social behaviour of chimpanzees is influenced by the

gender of the researchers. Longino (1990) provides an interesting discussion on scientific knowledge but stopping short of a complete relativism.

Realism and Instrumentalism

The ways in which philosophers and sociologists talk about science is so different from the way the enterprise is experienced by working scientists that some have been led to question whether they are referring to the same thing. While insiders' accounts cannot be taken as specially privileged – indeed Lakatos is said to have remarked that a practising scientist has as much need of philosophy as a fish of hydrodynamics – it is a matter of some concern if philosophical accounts of science differ radically from those of thoughtful practitioners (Polanyi, 1958; Ziman, 1967, 1978).

Scientists' view of science are usually characterized by an unproblematic, commonsense realism; science is taken to be an attempt to obtain knowledge of a real, physical, external world, which behaves as it does quite independently of our views about it. This does not, of course, imply the possibility of certain knowledge; we can have, at best, fallible knowledge of this real world. Ogborn (1994) argues that the success of science in producing consensually agreed knowledge of aspects of the natural world is a contingent historical fact, which could not have been guaranteed at the outset, and is the result of sustained *work*. In major part, it is a consequence of the 'decision' of scientists to limit their areas of interest to questions about which such consensus is obtainable.

The alternative to realism is instrumentalism, the view that theories are simply tools for thinking. They are useful if they lead to predictions which are borne out by observation and experience. But there is no claim that the entities and processes they talk about correspond to anything in the world.

Realists argue that, while we can entertain any ideas we want about the natural world, only certain ideas enable us to *act* successfully. Our ideas about the world are sustained not through thinking about it, but by acting in it. Bhaskar (1978) distinguishes the transitive nature of thought, in which any idea can be sustained, from the intransitive nature of the world, which, by behaving simply as it does, and not in accordance with our wishes, sustains some ideas but not others. Hacking (1983) tells how he became persuaded that electrons are real through his conversations with scientists who talked of 'spraying electrons' at targets. It was their ability to do things with electrons which made them real.

Newton-Smith (1981, p. 21) proposes that the fundamental claim of realism is that theoretical statements in science are either true or false, and which they are depends on how the world is, independently of us. Harré (1986), however, argues that we can never tell whether any theoretical statement is true or false, so a defence of this version of realism is hopeless. He proposes instead a 'referential realism', based on the argument that we have good reason to believe that 'many of the referring expressions that occur in theoretical discourses have referents in the world that exists independently of human cognitive and practical activity' (p. 191). That is, there are good grounds for believing that many of the things of which theories speak correspond to things which exist in the world independently of our theorizing about them.

Hacking makes a distinction between *realism about entities* and *realism about theories*. An example might help to clarify this distinction. A theory of the structure of the atom might propose various things about the smaller objects out of which an atom is 'made' and how these interact. It is possible to be realist about the atom as an entity (to accept that there really are atoms) without necessarily accepting as true the theoretical account of the atom's structure. This could be regarded, quite consistently, as largely instrumental – simply leading to good predications. Hacking (1983, pp. 28–9) argues for a realism about both entities and theories, though on slightly different grounds for each. Cartwright (1983), on the other hand, argues for a realism about entities but not about theories.

As we have noted, at the core of several recent realist arguments is an emphasis on action, as opposed to mere talk. Ogborn (1994) links this argument to Piaget's claim that the child's conception of objects, of space and time is constructed through action on the world, and the internalization of these actions. Hence scientific thinking, and the kind of provisional 'certainty' about things to which it can lead, are seen as a natural development of commonsense thinking.

Post-modernist Developments

A current strand of thought about the nature of science calls into question the status of the knowledge of scientific experts in comparison to that of other members of the public. Studies of scientific knowledge used for specific social purposes (e.g. Layton *et al.*, 1993) are challenging the image of scientific knowledge as a universal and privileged 'given'. Instead, they portray local knowledge developed to address specific needs and interests in specific social contexts and raise the question of whose knowledge has the right to be labelled as 'science'. Commenting on the views of participants in their case studies, Layton *et al.* (1993, pp. 138–9) remark:

> Those in the case studies who sought to use scientific knowledge to ground the actions they wished to take found themselves, like many post-modernists, questioning much of what was presented as 'given' and discovering that, in some cases, e.g. estimates of risk, scientific 'facts' involve a large element of social construction/ subjectivity and/or were related to circumstances far removed from those in which they conducted their daily lives (e.g. the management of an energy budget).

Rather than seeing science as an endeavour to establish claims about a world which exists independently of the knower, such a post-modernist perspective adopts a view of local knowledges being established within particular situations or standpoints. The perspective can perhaps be seen to embrace a view of knowledge in action but from an instrumentalist rather than a realist position. It is not proposing total relativism in relation to the truth of scientific knowledge claims, but rather that scientific knowledge claims are limited in scope by the physical and social settings to which the knowledge is related. [. . .]

References

Ayer, A. J. (1946) *Language, Truth and Logic*, London: Gollancz.

Ayer, A.J. (1981) *Hume*, Oxford: Oxford University Press.

Barnes, B. (1974) *Scientific Knowledge and Sociological Theory*, London: Routledge and Kegan Paul.

Barnes, N. and Shapin, S. (eds.) (1979) *Natural Order: Historical Studies of Scientific Culture*, London: Sage.

Berger, P. and Luckmann, T. (1967) *The Social Construction of Reality*, Harmondsworth: Penguin.

Bernstein, R. J. (1976) *The Restructuring of Social and Political Theory*, London: Methuen.

Bhaskar, R. (1978) *A Realist Theory of Science*, London: Harvester Wheatsheaf.

Bloor, D. (1976) *Knowledge and Social Imagery*, London: Routledge and Kegan Paul.

Brown, S., Fauvel, J. and Finnegan, R. (1981) *Conceptions of Inquiry*, London: Methuen.

Carnap, R. (1950) *Logical Foundations of Probability*, Chicago, IL: University of Chicago Press.

Carnap, R. (1966) *Philosophical Foundations of Physics: An Introduction to the Philosophy of Science*, New York: Basic Books.

Cartwright, N. (1983) *How the Laws of Physics Lie*, Oxford: Oxford University Press.

Chalmers, A. F. (1982) *What is This Thing Called Science?*, 2nd edn., Milton Keynes: Open University Press.

Chalmers, A. F. (1990) *Science and its Fabrication*, Milton Keynes: Open University Press.

Collins, H. M. (ed.) (1981a) Knowledge and controversy: Studies of modern natural science, *Social Studies of Science* (spec. issue), 11 (1).

Collins, H. M. (1981b) Son of seven sexes: The social destruction of a physical phenomenon, *Social Studies of Science*, 11 (1), 33–62.

Collins, H. M. and Cox, G. (1976) Recovering relativity: Did prophesy fail? *Social Studies of Science*, 6, 423–44.

Feyerabend, P. (1970) Consolations of the specialist, in I. Lakatos and A. Musgrave (eds.), *Criticism and the Growth of Knowledge*, pp. 197–230, Cambridge: Cambridge University Press.

Feyerabend, P. (1975) *Against Method,* London: Verso.

Giere, R. N. (1988) *Explaining Science: A Cognitive Approach*, Chicago, IL: University of Chicago Press.

Gilbert, G. N. and Mulkay, M. (1984) *Opening Pandora's Box: A Sociological Analysis of Scientists' Discourse*, Cambridge: Cambridge University Press.

Gillies, D. (1992) *Philosophy of Science in the Twentieth Century*, Oxford: Blackwell.

Gjertsen, D. (1989) *Science and Philosophy: Past and Present*, Harmondsworth: Penguin.

Gott, R. and Welford, G. (1987) The assessment of observation in science, *School Science Review*, 69 (247), 217–27.

Gould, S. J. (1991) *Wonderful Life*, Harmondsworth: Penguin.

Hacking, I. (1983) *Representing and Intervening*, Cambridge: Cambridge University Press.

Hainsworth, M. D. (1956) The effect of previous knowledge on observation, *School Science Review*, 37, 234–42.

Hanson, N. R. (1958) *Patterns of Discovery*, Cambridge: Cambridge University Press.
Harré, R. (1972) *The Philosophies of Science*, Oxford: Oxford University Press.
Harré, R. (1986) *Varieties of Realism*, Oxford: Blackwell.
Hempel, C. (1965) The logic of explanation, in *Aspects of Scientific Explanation*, pp. 135–75, Baltimore, MD: Williams and Wilkins.
Johnson-Laird, P. N. (1983) *Mental Models*, Cambridge: Cambridge University Press.
Kuhn, T. S. (1962) *The Structure of Scientific Revolutions*, Chicago, IL: University of Chicago Press.
Kuhn, T. S. (1970) *The Structure of Scientific Revolutions*, 2nd edn, enlarged, Chicago, IL: University of Chicago Press.
Kuhn, T. S. (1977) *The Essential Tension*, Chicago, IL: University of Chicago Press.
Lakatos, I. (1970) Falsification and the methodology of scientific research programmes, in I. Lakatos and A. Musgrave (eds.), *Criticism and the Growth of Knowledge*, pp. 91–196, Cambridge: Cambridge University Press.
Lakatos, I. (1978) *The Methodology of Scientific Research Programmes*, Cambridge: Cambridge University Press.
Latour, B. and Woolgar, S. (1979) *Laboratory Life: The Construction of Scientific Facts*, Princeton, NJ: Princeton University Press.
Laudan, L. (1977) *Progress and its Problems: Towards a Theory of Scientific Growth*, London: Routledge and Kegan Paul.
Layton, D., Jenkins, E., Macgill, S. and Davey, A. (1993) *Inarticulate Science? Perspectives on the Public Understanding of Science and Some Implications for Science Education*, Nafferton: Studies in Education Ltd.
Longino, H. E. (1990) *Science as Social Knowledge*, Princeton, NJ: Princeton University Press.
Losee, J. (1972) *A Historical Introduction to the Philosophy of Science*, Oxford: Oxford University Press.
Lynch, M. (1985) *Art and Artifact in Laboratory Science: A Study of Shop Work and Shop Talk in a Research Laboratory*, London: Routledge and Kegan Paul.
Masterman, M. (1970) The nature of a paradigm, in I. Lakatos and A.Musgrave (eds.), *Criticism and the Growth of Knowledge*, pp. 59–90, Cambridge: Cambridge University Press.
Maxwell, G. (1962) The ontological status of theoretical entities, *Minnesota Studies in the Philosophy of Science*, 3, 3–14.
Mulkay, M. (1979) *Science and the Sociology of Knowledge*, London: George Allen and Unwin.
Mulkay, M. (1985) *The Word and the World*, London: George Allen and Unwin.
Newton-Smith, W. H. (1981) *The Rationality of Science*, London: Routledge and Kegan Paul.
Ogborn, J. (1992) *Explanation: A Theoretical Framework*, Hatts Working Paper. London: University of London, Institute of Education.
Polanyi, M. (1958) *Personal Knowledge*, London: Routledge and Kegan Paul.
Popper, K. R. (1934) *Logik der Forschung*. Published in English (1959) as *The Logic of Scientific Discovery*, London: Hutchinson.
Putnam, H. (1962) What theories are not, in E. Nagel, P. Suppes and A. Tarsk (eds.), *Logic, Methodology and Philosophy of Science*, pp. 240–44, Stanford, CA: Stanford University Press.
Quine, W. V. O. (1951) Two dogmas of empiricism. Reprinted in *From a Logical Point of View*, 2nd edn, 1961, London: Harper Torchbooks.
Shapere, D. (1982) The concept of observation in science and philosophy, *Philosophy of Science*, 49, 231–67.
Trusted, J. (1987) *Inquiry and Understanding*, London: Macmillan.
Van Fraassen, B. C. (1980) *The Scientific Image*, Oxford: Oxford University Press.
Ziman, J. (1967) *Public Knowledge*, Cambridge: Cambridge University Press.
Ziman, J. (1978) *Reliable Knowledge*, Cambridge: Cambridge University Press.

Notes

1 In this discussion of Popper's ideas, we use the term 'hypothesis' to cover both 'generalization' and 'theory'. Popper's example of the black swan involves a universal generalization. Popper (1959, p. 59) writes that 'scientific theories are universal statements', and couches most of his discussion in terms of 'singular statements' and 'universal statements'. Earlier in this chapter, we drew a distinction between laws (generalizations) and theories (models). It seems clear, however, that Popper does not see his argument as depending upon any distinction between the two but as applying equally to both.

5

The Curriculum as Socially Organised Knowledge

Michael Young

Introduction

The history, social divisions and the many competing interests and value systems found in a modern society are expressed in the school curriculum as much as they are in its system of government or its occupational structure. Likewise, curriculum debates, implicitly or explicitly, are always debates about alternative views of society and its future. These links between the curriculum and society provide both the topic and the rationale for the sociological approach to the curriculum set out in this chapter.

The chapter is based on a paper first published in 1971 (Young, 1971) and the analysis which it presents inevitably reflects the time and context. The specific examples, which are taken largely from the secondary curriculum in England and Wales, will be of primary interest to the educational historian. However, the intractable character of academic/vocational divisions (Finegold *et al.*, 1990) and the international concern with the issue of parity of esteem between academic and vocational learning (Lasonen, 1996: Lasonen and Young, 1998) suggest that the idea of exploring the links between the stratification of knowledge in the curriculum and wider social divisions is as relevant now as it was nearly thirty years ago. In order to enable the reader to separate those elements of the analysis specific to the earlier context from those of current relevance, the first two parts of this chapter are concerned with that earlier context. Part 1 considers a number of educational policy issues in the period 1950–1970 and Part 2 considers the intellectual context through an analysis of developments in the sociology of education in the UK up to 1971. Part 3 develops the theoretical framework which links social change and the curriculum through the concept of the stratification of knowledge.

The Secondary Curriculum in Context: Educational Policy Themes 1950–1970

It is possible to trace three stages in the public debates on education in England and Wales between 1950 and 1970 through three interrelated themes:

(i) equality of opportunity;
(ii) the organisation and selection of pupils for secondary education, and
(iii) the curriculum.

In the first stage, the facts of educational 'wastage' were documented by the Early Leaving Report (HMSO, 1953) and the Crowther Report (Crowther, 1959) and the social class basis of differences in educational opportunities was demonstrated by sociologists such as Glass (1954) and Floud *et al.* (1957). The research complemented the public reports and both were used by successive governments as a justification for expanding secondary and higher education. However, the research also threw up a set of questions concerning the basis of selection at 11+ and the fact that it was as much a social as an educational process. This exposure of 'wastage of talent', especially of able working class children, led to the second phase of public debate which began in the mid 1960s and focused on critiques of the 11+ test for grammar school, leading to demands for the comprehensive reorganisation of what was then a tripartite system of secondary education. Public debate in the second phase became increasingly political, an indication that the policies involved, such as the abolition of selective schools, threatened significant and powerful interests in society that are no less with us today. However, the manifest inefficiency and less well-publicised injustice of the 11+ test made its abolition a realistic political commitment for reformist politicians of the time.

It was only towards the end of the 1960s that the focus of the debate moved again from questions of the organisation of secondary schooling to the content of education and therefore to the curriculum itself. The likely reasons for this shift are worth referring to briefly as they set the context for what was later to become a more explicit focus on the curriculum from the 1970s onwards by both policy makers and researchers. Three reasons can be distinguished as follows:

Government Pressure for More and Better Technologists and Scientists

The origins and implications of the concern to increase the numbers of pupils studying science were widely discussed at the time, although some cast doubts on whether pupils in secondary schools were 'swinging from science' (Mcpherson, 1969; Blaug and Gannicott, 1969; Gorbutt, 1970). However, the 'swing' became an 'official' problem with the publication of the Dainton Report (Dainton, 1968) and the various solutions that it proposed. In retrospect, the most interesting recommendation of the Dainton Report that was little noticed at the time was that the 'swing from science' was unlikely to be reversed without some change in the narrow form of subject specialisation that was forced on pupils by A Levels [. . .].

The Commitment to Raising the School Leaving Age

Throughout the 1960s there were proposals, not in fact implemented until 1973, that the school leaving age should be raised to 16. The reasoning behind the proposals arose from the obvious if neglected fact that the length of a student's school career is probably the single most important determinant of the level of attainment he or she is likely to reach. However, a compulsory additional year for all pupils posed quite new curriculum problems since a significant section of the cohort already wanted to leave school at 14 or 15. Various alternatives for 'more meaningful curricula' were introduced including a new teacher assessed national examination, the Certificate of Secondary Education, which gave teachers a new flexibility in planning a curriculum that still would lead to a public examination. Curriculum alternatives for those making up the new Vth and VIth Forms were to become a major preoccupation of the Schools Council[1] after it was launched in 1964 and were to provide the policy context for more fundamental questions to be raised about relations between curriculum and social priorities (Young, 1972).

Comprehensive Reorganisation of Secondary Education

Following the government circular on secondary reorganisation 10/65, many local education authorities merged grammar schools and secondary modern schools to create comprehensive schools. This meant that many grammar school teachers were obliged, for the first time, to receive a non-selective pupil intake. Thus, teachers who for years had successfully produced good A Level results from highly selective groups of pupils were faced with pupils who appeared neither to know how to learn academic subjects nor to want to. This inevitably generated new curriculum problems that had not arisen when pupils were separated into secondary modern, technical and grammar schools.

Educational and Political Debates about the Curriculum in the 1960s

In the UK, the public debate about the curriculum in the 1960s and afterwards took place on two levels, the 'political' and the 'educational'. At the political level, the main protagonists were the Marxist 'Left' (Anderson, 1969) and the conservative or Black Paper 'Right' (Cox and Dyson, 1969a, 1969b). The 'Left' criticised contemporary curricula for 'mystifying the students' and 'fragmenting knowledge into compartments'. They also claimed that typical higher education curricula denied students the opportunity to understand society as a 'totality' and therefore acted as little more than a mechanism of social control. The conservative 'Right' criticised progressive teaching methods, mixed-ability teaching and the various curricular innovations designed to broaden the teaching of English and history, as well as the expansion of what they saw as the 'soft' social sciences. However, the 'politics of the curriculum' at the time remained firmly outside party politics. Furthermore, apart from the requirement for compulsory religious instruction, the formal autonomy of the headteacher over the school curriculum was not questioned. This autonomy was in practice limited, especially in the upper forms of secondary schools, by the control of curricula by the universities, both through their entrance requirements and their domination of all but one of the school examination boards.

Three features of the educational debates about the curriculum at the time should also be mentioned. They are the emphasis on secondary curricula, the important role of philosophers of education and the marginal role of sociologists. Virtually all the curriculum debates in the 1960s focused on the area which had in practice undergone least change, the secondary school curriculum. The absence of debate over changes in the primary curriculum appeared to point to the much greater autonomy of that part of the educational system with the lowest status. However, as has since become apparent, this relative autonomy of the primary curriculum at the time depended not only on the low status of primary school teachers but also on a 'hands off' view of the curriculum on the part of politicians which was taken for granted at the time but which was to change dramatically two decades later.

By the end of the 1960s an approach to the philosophy of education associated with Peters and Hirst had established a dominant role in educational studies and in the curriculum of teacher education. It was to have a profound influence on debates about the curriculum. Starting from a view of knowledge which they traced back to Kant (Hirst, 1969), they criticised the new topic-based and integrated syllabi which they saw as neglecting the fundamental 'forms of knowledge' which everyone needed to make sense of the world. It was not subjects, which Hirst recognised were the socially constructed ways that teachers organise knowledge, but forms of understanding, which he claimed were not open to debate or change. However, in the debates that followed, the distinction between school subjects and forms of understanding easily got lost and the philosophy of education became associated with opposition to a socio-historical view of the curriculum (Pring, 1972; White and Young, 1975 and 1976) and at the time served to limit debates about the curriculum.

Despite their significant role in debates about educational inequality and secondary reorganisation, sociologists played little role in the curriculum debates of the 1960s. In order to understand why, and to provide the basis for the sociological approach to the curriculum developed later in this chapter, it is necessary to look in more detail at the sociology of education of the time.

Sociology of Education and the Curriculum 1950–1970

Education is always, as Williams (1961) so evocatively pointed out, a set of cultural choices, some conscious and some unconscious. It follows that the curriculum is always a selection and organisation of the knowledge available at a particular time. However, at least until the 1970s, sociologists of education did not see their task as trying to relate the principles of selection and organisation of knowledge in curricula to the wider social structure. I want to suggest that this may be explained by examining the ideological and methodological assumptions of sociology of education at the time and the institutional context within which it developed.

British sociology in the late 1950s drew its political priorities from Fabian socialism and its methodology from the political arithmetic tradition of research associated with Booth and Rowntree. Sociologists such as Halsey and Floud broadened the definition of poverty from lack of income to lack of education and identified lack of educational opportunities as a significant way in which working class life chances were limited. However, in their concern to promote greater equality of opportunity, these early studies pointed not only to the need to expand educational opportunities but also to identifying the characteristics of those who failed, the early leavers and the drop-outs. Partly because they wanted evidence to justify educational expansion, their explanations of school failure focused on the educability of those who failed rather than on features of the education system that failed them. A curriculum example of that system might have been how grammar schools obliged pupils from about 14 to take up to 10 different subjects which had very little relation either to each other or to the rest of their lives and then at 16 to drop all but three, usually selected from a narrowly specialised group.

The sociological studies of the time set out to show how the distribution of life chances through education could be seen as an aspect of the class structure. Inevitably, this led to an over-mechanistic conception of 'social class' which isolated the 'social class' characteristics of individuals from the 'social class' content of their educational experience. It may clarify this point to represent the model of explanation of school failure of such studies diagramatically (Table 5.1).

Though presenting a somewhat over-simplified picture, Table 4.1 does show that, in terms of the model, the curriculum and content of education

Table 5.1

Assumptions	Independent variables	Dependent variables
Criteria of educational success – curricula, methods and evaluation. What counts as 'knowledge and knowing' in school.	Social characteristics of the groups who succeed and fail.	Distribution of success and failure at various stages in terms of participation and attainment.

is taken as a 'given' and not as a possible variable to be investigated; furthermore, the model inevitably represents successes as normal and educational failures as a form of 'deviance' from the norm. What such a model cannot consider is how differential rates of educational success and failure may be explained in terms of the criteria and definitions of success that are used (Keddie, 1971). To ask such questions is to consider how definitions of success arise and are legitimised as methods of assessment, selection and organisation of knowledge. However, to treat such definitions as objects of study raises not just theoretical and methodological questions; it also raises political questions about the distribution of power and the ability of some to define what counts as educational success. Furthermore, bearing in mind the reformist mission of the sociologists of education of the time, it is difficult to see to what policies a refocusing of the model of educational failure might have pointed.

Turning to the institutional context, teaching and research in the sociology of education expanded in the 1960s in teacher training colleges and university departments of education, where previously it had hardly existed. The new specialists had to legitimise their contribution to the education of teachers and justify their particular field of expertise – particularly when the philosophers had defined the curriculum and knowledge as 'their area'. They mapped out areas previously unexplored in educational studies. They started from the social context of education with an emphasis on social class, relationships to the economy, the occupational structure and the family and moved to the consideration of schools as organisations and pupil subcultures. It is perhaps not surprising that a consensus emerged, at least for a time, among sociologists and non-sociologists alike, that the curriculum was not a field for sociological research.

Although this discussion has focused on British sociology, the general points are more widely applicable. Structural-functionalism, which was the perspective of the majority of sociologists in the USA, presupposes an agreed set of societal values or goals which define, among other things, the selection and organisation of knowledge in curricula. Thus, sociology of education in the USA was primarily concerned with socialisation, seen as the 'organisation' and 'processing' of people, and with notable exceptions, for example the pioneering early work of Apple (1979) and Wexler (1983) continued to take the organisation of knowledge for granted.

Towards a Framework for Analysing the Curriculum as Socially Organised Knowledge

The previous section has suggested that it was the taken for granted assumptions of the sociology of education of the 1960s that accounted for its neglect of the curriculum. The next section of this chapter turns this critique into a positive programme for raising sociological question about the curriculum. It does so by starting from the assumption that those in positions of power will attempt to define what is to be taken as knowledge in society, how accessible to different groups any knowledge is and what are the accepted relationships between different knowledge areas and between those who have access to them and make them available. It is the exploration of these issues that is the basis of an approach to the curriculum as socially organised knowledge. Drawing on Bernstein (1968), the approach gives rise to three interrelated questions about curricula concerning the stratification of knowledge, the extension of the scope of knowledge (or degree of specialisation) and the relations between knowledge areas.

The power of some to define what is 'valued' knowledge leads to the question of accounting for how knowledge is stratified and by what criteria. The idea of knowledge being stratified has two aspects – what might be referred to as its 'prestige' and 'property' components. Differences in prestige refer to the different ways that different kinds of knowledge are valued – for example, pure and applied, academic and vocational, and general and specialist. The property aspect of the stratification of knowledge refers to how access to knowledge are controlled, in modern societies, largely by professionals and other experts. Thus the 'property' aspect of stratification points to the distribution of knowledge in use and its associated reward structure. It suggests that in different societies the dominant conception of knowledge is likely to be associated with dominant ideas about property in general – whether this is private, state or communal.

The restriction of the access of some knowledge areas to specific groups is also a question of power. In relation to curricula it poses the questions what is the scope of curricula provided for different groups and what factors may influence what is seen as the degree and kind of specialisation appropriate to different groups of learners at different ages.

The third question points to relations between knowledge areas between those with access to them. Relations between knowledge areas are also expressions of power; in this case the power of some to maintain or break down knowledge boundaries. Relations between knowledge areas can be seen on a continuum between being insulated and being connective.

We can therefore conceptualise options for organising the curriculum in terms of three dimensions which can, for simplicity, be seen as continua between (i) high and low stratification, (ii) broad and narrow degrees of specialisation and (iii) insulated and connective relations between knowledge areas.

There is a more fundamental question, only hinted at in this chapter, as to whether, as knowledge expands, it necessarily becomes more stratified. The growth of knowledge and the access to it have undoubtedly been paralleled by an increasing differentiation and specialisation. It is also likely that increasing differentiation is a condition which allows for some groups to legitimise 'their knowledge' as superior – in other words, the growth of knowledge is a condition for its greater stratification. The high value of some knowledge is institutionalised by the creation of schools, colleges and universities to transmit it as the curriculum.

Although the differential social evaluation of knowledge often follows from increasing differentiation, there is no necessary relationship between the two processes. It is possible that greater differentiation could be associated with reduced stratification in a society where the fragmenting tendencies of differentiation are balanced by the integrative trend of less stratification. My argument is that patterns of social evaluation must be explained, independently of the process of differentiation, in terms of the power that certain groups have to restrict access to certain kinds of knowledge and the opportunity for those who have access to knowledge to legitimise its status.

The general hypothesis underlying the analysis is of a shift from 'curricula of the past', which were insulated, narrowly specialised and highly stratified to 'curricula of the future', which I predict will need to be connective, broad and with low degrees of stratification. However, as will be indicated, this does not imply any straightforward or smooth process of evolutionary change.

The framework presented focuses on the principles of the organisation and selection of knowledge and only implicitly suggests how these might be related to changes in the social structure. The assumption here is that the most explicit relation between the organisation of knowledge and the wider society will be on the dimension of stratification. Moves to 'destratify' or give equal value to different kinds of knowledge, or 'restratify' (or legitimise other criteria of evaluation), by posing a threat to the existing power structure, are likely to be resisted. However, a qualification needs to be made to these general propositions. Power is not distributed in a monolithic way in most modern societies; there is unlikely to be a consensus about definitions of knowledge among the different economic, political, bureaucratic, cultural and educational interest groups, except at a very general level. One would imagine, for example, that business and academic elites would not, except if faced with a common threat, share assumptions in their definitions of knowledge. Another aspect of the relations between knowledge and power will be apparent in any attempt to reduce the degree of specialisation in the curriculum and to make the relations between knowledge areas more connective. These are also likely to pose threats to the patterns of social relations implicit in the more specialised and insulated forms and likewise will be resisted. A good example is in the long history of attempts to broaden the A Level curriculum.

The Academic Curriculum and the Stratification of Knowledge

In the remaining part of this chapter, I want to focus primarily on the academic curriculum associated with the upper forms of secondary schools, both private and state, as a test case of the theoretical framework I have outlined. It is undoubtedly an area of the curriculum which has been highly resistant to change and should therefore provide evidence of relations between patterns of dominant values, the distribution of rewards and power and the organisation of knowledge as well as the explanatory poten-tial of the concept of the stratification of knowledge.

All curricula involve assumptions that some kinds and areas of know-ledge are more 'worthwhile' than others. In England and Wales, the aca-demic curriculum is based on the assumption that learning should become highly specialised as early as possible and give minimum emphasis to rela-tions between the different subjects. Changes in the academic curriculum can be conceptualised as involving changing valuations of a less stratified, less specialised and more connective organisation of knowledge. Further, as we assume some pattern of social relations is associated with any curric-ulum, these changes will be resisted in so far as they are perceived to undermine the values, relative power and privileges of the dominant groups involved.

Before looking in more detail at the stratification of knowledge, I should like to make brief reference to other dimensions of specialisation and connectedness earlier referred to in Table 5.1. By referring to the degree of specialisation, we are by implication concerned with the distribution of resources (pupil and teacher time, resources and materials).[2] This suggests why, in spite of many rhetorical statements about the importance of curric-ulum breadth that have been made by politicians and others since Crowther in 1959 and which have culminated in the manifesto commit-ments of the New Labour government (DfEE, 1997), existing patterns of specialisation remain firmly entrenched.

The question of the connectedness of knowledge areas raises basic ques-tions about how knowledge areas are defined and about the interests in-volved in keeping knowledge areas separate. The question also raises more fundamental issues about the categories a society uses to make sense of itself and the physical world. Subjects or even broad fields like 'arts' and 'sciences' cannot be treated as if they continued independently of any social changes (Gibbons *et al.*, 1994)

The key question to which I now return in this chapter is the idea of the stratification of knowledge in the academic curriculum. It is through this idea, I suggest, that we are led to consider the social basis of different kinds of knowledge and that we can begin to raise questions about relations between the power structure of society and curricula, the access to know-ledge and the opportunities to legitimise it as 'superior' and the relation between knowledge and its functions in different kinds of society.

If knowledge is highly stratified, there will be a clear distinction between what is taken to count as knowledge which will provide the criteria for deciding what knowledge to include and exclude in curricula. It would follow that highly stratified curricular models presuppose and legitimate a rigid hierarchy between teacher and taught. This issue has recently been explored in relation to the academic curriculum of higher education by

Gibbons *et al.* (1994). They argue that external pressures on the university to produce more useful knowledge more quickly is undermining the traditional forms of academic hierarchy and in particular relations between the producers and consumers of knowledge.

So taken for granted by most people, in education and outside, is the idea that knowledge is stratified that it is difficult to conceive of the possibility of a curriculum based on knowledge which is differentiated but not stratified. That it poses a revolutionary alternative is apparent when one considers whether the terms 'teacher', 'pupil' and 'examination' in the sense normally used would have any meaning at all within such a curriculum. This argument suggests that the stratification of knowledge is not only deeply implicit in our ideas of what education 'is' and what teachers 'are' but that some stratification of knowledge is in principle a feature of any curriculum and any teaching. However, acceptance of such a principle does not deny the possibility that the degree of stratification of knowledge is a social and historical product that can change.

As previously suggested, the contemporary British educational system remains dominated by an academic curriculum with a rigid stratification of knowledge. It is not surprising, therefore, that high status and rewards are associated with areas of the curriculum that involve:

- formal assessment
- the 'ablest' children
- homogeneous ability groups of pupils.

Two contradictory implications follow from this argument. If curricula are developed on the basis of criteria other than those associated with high status knowledge, this will only occur if they are designed for 'low status' pupils. An example, referred to earlier in this chapter, was the early work of the Schools Council on a curriculum for the 'young school learner'. The Council accepted the existing stratification of knowledge but produced most of its early recommendations for reform in low-status knowledge areas (Young, 1972). However, proposals such as Mathematics for the Majority, which were designed for less-able pupils only and therefore did not challenge any criteria of high status knowledge nor threaten the interests of those in positions of power, came up against another aspect of the stratification of knowledge. Despite the fact that they had achieved little in the conventional mathematics curriculum, low-ability pupils accepted the academic definitions of what counted as mathematics and rejected the curricular and pedagogic innovations which involved alternative definitions of knowledge; they wanted 'real mathematics' like fractions (Spradberry, 1976).

The idea of knowledge being stratified in the curriculum can be extended by asking two further questions. First, by what criteria are different areas of, kinds of, and approaches to knowledge associated with high status? No criteria will be universal to all academic curricula; they will inevitably have developed in particular social and historical contexts. However, if identified, they may be related to social, political and economic factors and suggest reasons for changes and resistance to change in the academic curriculum. Second, can we relate the extent to which knowledge is stratified in society and the kinds of criteria on which such stratification may be based,[3] to features of social structures?

The first question requires an attempt to identify some of the social characteristics of academic curricula and to show how over time they have become legitimised as high status by those in positions of power. A number of sources suggest what these might be. First, there are comparative perspectives on pre- and post-literate societies. In discussing the way in which the emphasis of formal education has moved from 'learning' to 'teaching', Mead (1938) links the idea of groups holding some kinds of knowledge as superior to the notion of a 'hierarchical arrangement of cultural views of experience' and the increasing emphasis on the importance of changing the beliefs, habits, knowledge, ideas and allegiances that children bring with them to school. Second, in studies of the consequences of literacy for contemporary culture, Goody and Watt (1962) argue that so great is the discontinuity between the private, oral traditions of family and home and the public literate tradition of the school that 'literate skills form one of the major axes of differentiation in industrial societies'. They go on to suggest that reading and writing (which are the activities that occupy most of the time of young people when they are at school) are inevitably solitary activities and so a literate culture brings with it an increasing individualisation. This curricular individualisation is brought out most clearly in the dominance of written modes of assessment in school. In comparing literate and non-literate cultures, Goody and Watt suggest that the peculiar characteristic of the former is the priority that they give to

> an abstraction which disregards an individual's social experience . . . and a compartmentalisation of knowledge which restricts the kind of connections which the individual can establish and ratify with the natural and social world
>
> Goody and Watt (1962)

The third source of criteria for high-status knowledge is the evidence of the link in modern education systems between formal education, examinations and specialist knowledge (Weber, 1952). Weber discussed the process of what he called the 'bureaucratic domination of the nature of education'. He suggested that the major constraint on what counts as knowledge in modern societies and therefore in curricula was whether something could be objectively, and in practice quantitatively, assessed. As the Scottish physicist, Lord Kelvin, said of science 'when you cannot express it in numbers, your knowledge is of a meagre and unsatisfactory kind'. This is not so far from the assumption that appears to underlie much modern educational policy that if you cannot examine or test for it, it's not worth knowing.

We can draw together the main ideas of the previous paragraphs to suggest the dominant characteristics of high-status knowledge and how they represent the organising principles underlying academic curricula. These are literacy – an emphasis on writing as opposed to oral communication; individualism – an avoidance of group work or co-operativeness and a focus on how academic learning is assessed; abstractness of knowledge and its structuring and compartmentalising independently of the knowledge of the learner.[4] Finally, and linked to abstractness, is what I refer to as the unrelatedness of academic curricula; this refers to the extent to which academic curricula can be 'at odds' with daily life and common experience.

If high status is accorded to knowledge in terms of these criteria, we would expect academic curricula to be organised on such principles. In other words academic curricula will tend to be abstract, literate, individualistic and unrelated to non-school knowledge. Curricula can therefore be ranked on these characteristics which then become four dimensions in terms of which knowledge is stratified. Low-status curricula will be identified according to the extent to which they are organised in terms of oral presentation, group activities and assessment, concreteness of the knowledge involved and its relatedness to non-school knowledge. These criteria are typical, in varying degrees, of many secondary vocational curricula. The academic/vocational divide, therefore, can be seen as an example of the stratification of knowledge having the effect of maintaining wider divisions and inequalities in society generally.

One way of viewing these characteristics of the academic curriculum is to see them as the historical outcome of how mass education was established on a model of bookish learning for priests which was extended first to lawyers and doctors but which, increasingly, has come to dominate the curricula of all older age groups in industrial societies (Goodman, 1969). If such curricular characteristics persist, it may not be because they are the most pedagogically effective but because they are the conscious or unconscious cultural choices which accord with the values, beliefs and interests of dominant groups at a particular time. It is in terms of these choices that educational success and failure are defined. Why, then, do such characteristics of curricula persist? The conventional explanation of the persistence of an academic curriculum with such characteristics is that it transmits the specialist knowledge needed by key occupations in a modern society. An alternative view that arises from the approach to the curriculum developed in this chapter is that any very different cultural choices, or the granting of equal status to sets of cultural choices that reflected variations in terms of the suggested characteristics, would involve an unacceptable redistribution of rewards in terms of wealth, prestige and power and the labels of educational success and failure.

Three important limitations of this approach must be mentioned. First, there is a danger in contrasting conventional and sociological explanations of the curriculum which equate the former uncritically with common sense and therefore by definition as inferior. In reality academic criteria are not just social or just an expression of ruling views of the world; they are also ways of making explanations available that do work in the real world as well as in the classroom. It is this epistemological reality, together with what may be possible politically at a particular time, that will limit the extent to which curricula reorganisation is possible. Second, the categories are formal and do not relate directly to issues of curriculum content. In any analysis of texts, syllabi, school reports, examination questions or 'marking' criteria that make up the curriculum, it is not the 'abstractness' of the student's work that is judged but the particular subject forms of abstractness, whether a scientific law or a historical explanation. Third, by its primary emphasis of the social organisation of knowledge and not its social functions, this approach does not make explicit that access to certain kinds of knowledge is also potential access to the means of changing the criteria of the social evaluation of knowledge itself and therefore to the possibility of creating new knowledge. However, changing knowledge criteria is a practical activity and inevitably concrete, collective and related, as well as likely to involve oral and written communication. It may therefore be that it is through the devaluing of practical activity and in elevating the value of 'knowledge for its own sake' through the separation of knowledge from practical action that the academic curriculum serves its most significant social function. 'Really useful knowledge', as the Chartists referred to it (Johnson, 1980), involves combining theory and practice, something rarely experienced through the academic curriculum.

Finally let us return to how we might account for the criteria implicit in the different ways educational knowledge is stratified in curricula. At least in the case of Europe, it is possible to trace schematically a set of stages from non-literate societies where there are no separate educational institutions to feudal societies where formal education in separate institutions is largely restricted to a priestly caste and where schools remained largely independent of the economic and political forces of the time. Gradually, as schools and colleges became differentiated and increasingly dependent on the economies of their societies, the new economic and political classes began to play a major role in determining the stratification of knowledge, in how knowledge areas are kept separate and in defining degrees of specialisation for different groups. Comparative studies might shed light on these relationships and why, for example, they shaped such a narrow form of curricular specialisation and such a high degree of insulation of knowledge areas in the secondary schools of England and Wales.

To sum up, this chapter has presented a framework for a sociological approach to the organisation of knowledge in curricula. It is inevitably schematic and reflects the concerns and context of its time. However, though the social and economic context has changed out of all recognition since 1971, when the paper on which this chapter is based was published, many of the features of academic curricula which it identifies are still with us and still taken for granted. Part of the difficulty of conceiving real curriculum alternatives is that many curricular assumptions are so much part of our taken-for-granted world. Approaching the curriculum as socially organised knowledge is both a tool for analysis and for conceptualising alternatives. What the chapter has tried to do is to show that academic curricula are as much the products of people's actions in history as any other form of social organisation. They are not given, nor in today's language do they represent, a gold standard. They can therefore be changed. The issue is one of purposes and the extent to which the existing curriculum represents a future society we can endorse or a past society we want to change.

Notes

1   This was a government funded agency that supported curriculum development projects, producing materials and approaches to various areas of the curriculum.
2   It is a paradox of the English educational system worth exploring, that while those most in need of education get least of it, those with the longest educational careers have curricula of the most limited scope.
3   Ben-David (1963) in comparing university curricula in the USA, USSR and UK, among other countries, shows wide variations in the criteria on which the stratification of knowledge is based in different countries.
4   There are problems in the use of the term 'abstract' because it presupposes some kind of absolute notion of what is 'abstract', and neglects the way in which one can have different 'kinds of abstraction', some of which may be 'labelled' concrete by others using different 'abstraction' criteria. While 'abstractness' seems to be a satisfactory category for describing academic curricula, the problems raised by Horton (1968) mean that as an analytic category it presupposes just those assumptions that one would want to treat as problematic. It may be possible to reconceptualise the problem by treating 'abstractness' as an 'educators' category' to be explained.

References

Anderson, P. (1969) Patterns of National Culture, in Cockburn, A. and Anderson, P. (eds) *Student Power*, Penguin, Harmondsworth.
Apple, M. (1979) *Ideology and Curriculum*, Routledge and Kegan Paul, London.
Ben-David, J. (1963) The Professions and the Class Structure, *Current Sociology*, V(12).
Bernstein, B. (1968) On the Curriculum (unpublished).
Blaug, M. and Gannicott, K. (1969) Manpower Forecasting since Robbins; a Science Lobby, in *Action Higher Education Review*, Autumn.
Cox, C. B. and Dyson, A. E. (1969a) The Fight for Education, Black Paper 1, *Critical Quarterly*.
Cox, C. B. and Dyson, A. E. (1969b) The Crisis in Education, Black Paper 2, *Critical Quarterly*.
Crowther, G. (1959) 15th-18th Report of the Central Advisory Council for Education, HMSO, London.
Dainton, F. S. (1968) *Enquiry into the Flow of Candidates in Science and Technology into Higher Education*, HMSO, London.
Department for Education and Employment (1997) *Qualifying for Success*, HMSO, London.
Early Leaving Report (1953) HMSO, London.
Finegold, D., Keep, E., Miliband, D., Raffe, D., Spours, K. and Young, M. (1990) *A British Baccalaureate: Overcoming Divisions Between Education and Training*, Institute for Public Policy Research, London.
Floud, J., Halsey, A. H. and Martin, F. (1957) *Social Class and Educational Opportunity*, Heineman, London.

Gibbons, M., Limoges, C., Nowotny, H., Schwartzman, S., Scott, P. and Trow, M. (1994) *The New Production of Knowledge*, Sage, London.

Glass, D. (1954) *Social Mobility in Britain*, Routledge and Kegan Paul, London.

Goodman, P. (1969) The Present Moment in Education, *New York Review of Books*, April.

Goody, J. and Watt, I. (1962) The Consequences of Literacy, *Comparative Studies in History and Society*, V(3).

Gorbutt, D. (1970) Subject Choice and the 'Swing from Science': a Sociological Critique, MA Thesis, University of London.

Hirst, P. (1969) The Logic of the Curriculum, *Journal of Curriculum Studies*, I(2), May.

Horton, R. (1968) Neo-Tylerianism: Sound Sense or Sinister Prejudice?, *Man*, 3 (8).

Johnson, R. (1980) Really Useful Knowledge, in Clarke, J. *et al.* (ed) *Working Class Culture*, Hutchison, London.

Keddie, N. (1971) Classroom Knowledge, in Young, M. (ed) *Knowledge and Control*, Collier-Macmillan.

Lasonen, J. (ed) (1996) Surveys of Strategies for Post-16 Education to Improve Parity of Esteem for Initial Vocational Education, in Eight European Countries, University of Jyväskylä, Finland.

Lasonen, J. and Young, M. (1998) Strategies for Achieving Parity of Esteem in European Secondary Education Institute for Educational Research, University of Jyväskylä, Finland.

Mcpherson, A. (1969) Swing from Science Retreat from Reason? *Universities Quarterly*, Winter.

Mead, M. (1938) Our Educational Emphases in Primitive Perspective, *American Journal of Sociology*, 43.

Pring, R. (1972) Knowledge out of Control, *Education for Teaching*, Autumn No 89.

Spradberry, J. (1976) Pupil Resistance to Curriculum Change: the case of the Mathematics for Majority Project, in Whitty, G. and Young, M. (1976) *Explorations in the Politics of School Knowledge*, Nafferton Books.

Weber, M. (1952) Essays in Sociology, translated and edited by H. Gerth and C. W. Mills, Routledge, London.

Wexler, P. (1983) *Beyond Equality*, Bobbs Merril, New York.

White, J. and Young, M. (1975) The Sociology of Knowledge (Part 1) Education for Teaching No. 98.

White, J. and Young, M. (1976) The Sociology of Knowledge (Part 2) Education for Teaching No. 99.

Williams, R. (1961) *The Long Revolution*, Chatto and Windus, London.

Young, M. (1971) (ed) *Knowledge and Control: New Directions for the Sociology of Education*, Collier Macmillan.

Young, M. (1972) On the Politics of Educational Knowledge, *Economy and Society*, 1.

6

Music, Music Education and the Bourgeois Aesthetic: Developing a Music Curriculum for the New Millennium

Gary Spruce

Introduction

Over the course of a generation, the character and quality of music education in British schools has undergone a radical transformation. Lessons based upon 'musical appreciation' and 'theory' are no longer the norm. Instead, children are given opportunities to experience music from a wide range of styles and cultures as composers, performers and active, critical listeners.

The transition from a didactic information-about-music curriculum to an experiential one has received official endorsement at various stages of its development through, for example, HMI's *Music from 5–16* (1985) the GCSE examination and music's inclusion as a foundation subject in the National Curriculum. By the late nineteen-eighties, the creative, experiential approach to music in Britain's schools was sufficiently well-established for it to be able to resist an attempt by right-wing politicians and university academics to hi-jack the report of the national curriculum music working party and return British music education to propositional knowledge about classical music and study of its supporting theoretical systems.

It can be safely argued, therefore, that British music education is in better shape than it has ever been. The music classroom where children are actively involved in gaining knowledge *of* music, rather than *about* it, is the rule rather than the exception. However, the question must now be: where does music education go from here? All in the garden is not green. Indeed it would be a remarkably sanguine music educator who would suggest that it is. OFSTED reports that 25 per cent of Key Stage 3 music lessons are unsatisfactory (OFSTED, 1996, p. 20) (higher than any other subject); in a recent study carried out by The National Foundation for Educational Research (NFER) an equivalent percentage of children expressed dissatisfaction with the arts education they received in schools – with music being particularly singled out for criticism (Harland, Kinder and Hartley, 1995); the recruitment and retention of music teachers is becoming increasingly problematic. Consequently, the status of music *as a curriculum subject* and,

71

by association, music teachers *as educators*, remains relatively low. Why then, despite changes in pedagogical methodology and subject content possibly greater than in any other subject, does music education still find itself in a relatively vulnerable position?

This chapter will argue that at least part of the reason lies in society's perception of what 'good' music actually is – its nature and purpose. It will suggest that despite a radical readjustment of pedagogical style and surface curriculum content, further progress is inhibited by a relationship to music which remains rooted in the nineteenth century. In order for music education to build upon the successes of recent years, and not only to reflect but to influence society's conception of what music and music education is about, we need to abandon some commonly-held and long-standing beliefs about music. Beliefs which are predominantly culturally-rooted and, in the way they impact upon music education, are unaffected by the radical developments in classroom practice. It is our *relationship* to, and our *perception* of, music that now needs to be questioned if we are to move forward to create a curriculum that is relevant and appropriate for the next millennium. Otherwise, we are in danger of grounding a music curriculum for the twenty-first century in a nineteenth-century aesthetic.

Music as Escapism

> Lose Yourself In The World's Greatest Music Festival (Slogan of the 1997 *Henry Wood Promenade Concerts*)

> Get Lost in Britten (Advertisement for the *Benjamin Britten Weekend Festival*, part of the 1997 Proms)

> Why . . . suggest that listeners wish to learn about the music from a presenter? Better by far to listen to the music untainted by subjective theories. A composer communicates the ineffable through sound – any more is irrelevant . . . Schopenauer got it right. Music . . . is the most powerful of all the arts, and therefore attains its ends entirely from its own resources. (Letter to the *Radio Times*, 23rd-29th August 1997.)

These three contemporary quotes demonstrate clearly the prevailing music establishment's view of the nature and purpose of 'good' music. One listens to music in order to escape from the mundanities and predictableness of everyday life to a higher plane of existence. Music which does not achieve this transcendent quality, or which is not dedicated to this aim, is assumed, unquestioningly, to be inherently inferior.

However, despite the hegemony of this particular view of music, which causes it to operate '. . . upon the presumption of [its] universality and timelessness' (Donogho, 1987, p. 330), this is a relatively recent way of experiencing and relating to music. Its roots lie in the late eighteenth century Enlightenment forming the foundation of nineteenth century romanticism and the emergent, bourgeois aesthetic. Moritz, writing between

1785 and 1788, expresses well the aesthetic's central tenets; the similarities to the above contemporary quotes being, I think, quite evident:

> As long as the beautiful draws our attention completely to itself, it shifts it away from ourselves for a while, and makes us seem to lose ourselves in the beautiful object; just as this losing, this forgetting of the self, is the highest degree of the pure and unselfish pleasure that beauty grants us. At that moment we give up our individual, limited existence in favour of a kind of higher existence.
>
> (Moritz quoted in Dalhaus, 1989, p. 5)

The unquestioning acceptance of the appropriateness of this aesthetic for evaluating all music, rather than existing simply 'to breathe life into an otherwise musically lifeless framework' (Walker, 1996, p. 6) has ensured its continuing hegemony over the cultural life of contemporary western society. Music education has, then, reflected this view by perpetuating the notion of a hierarchy of musical styles with western art music at the pinnacle.

The Roots of the Romantic Aesthetic

Until the mid-eighteenth century, music performed an essentially social, utilitarian function. Its purpose was to support the rites and rituals of powerful social institutions. Music was composed and performed for specific occasions and thereafter discarded or reworked for future use. The notion of the 'masterpiece' to be preserved for posterity was alien to such an understanding of music's role. Similarly, the composer was a functioning member of society whose task was to compose and prepare performances to support the ceremonies of ruling and powerful elites – typically the church and court. There was little distinction between composer and performer.

By the nineteenth century, however, the focus had changed to a more romanticised vision. A vision of composers as free to articulate their own emotions and, by association, those of their audiences: 'what all have felt but none so well express'd' (Pope quoted in Wolterstorff, 1987, p. 107).

There was as Hauser puts it '. . . the discovery of the concept of genius, and the idea that the work of art is the creation of an autocratic personality, that this personality transcends tradition, theory and rules, even the work itself' (Arnold Hauser quoted in Wolff, 1987, p. 3).

The artist was seen as articulating those parts of the human psyche that the conventions of nineteenth century society insisted must ordinarily remain repressed. Thus was born the Romantic paradigm of the creative artist as being difficult and deeply individualistic, 'a misunderstood genius who struggles heroically against tradition and its agent, society' (James, 1993, p. 196). Musically, this was exemplified by composers and performers such as Berlioz, Liszt and Paganini. A contemporary description of Paganini perfectly illustrates the kind of Byronic presence demanded by audiences:

I can see with the eye of memory, the whole man before me now; his gaunt, angular form; his black elf-locks falling in weird confusion over his neck and shoulders; his cadaverous face and shaggy brows; his long hairy hands with the veins standing out like cordage.

(James, 1993, p. 197).

However, the notion of the artist as an autonomous individual somehow detached from society and immune from its expectations and demands was essentially illusory. They were very much a product of the society in which they existed. For, as Shepherd says:

a particular medium or set of media, may only have an active influence on the structuring of consciousness and realities within a society if they are permitted or encouraged to by groups with sufficient political power.

(Shepherd, 1991, p. 17).

Arguably similarly illusory, but equally central to the bourgeois aesthetic, was the notion of 'musical autonomy'. The musical work (for the terms 'music' and 'musical work' are here considered as synonymous) was considered to exist of itself and for itself. Music was perceived as possessing an autonomous existence, its 'meaning' being situated entirely in the formal relationship and interplay of the musical materials – the rhythm, harmony, melody etc. Music was perceived as '[shaping] itself in accordance with self-contained abstract principles unrelated to the outside social world' (Leppert and McClary, 1987, p. xii).

In addition, the understanding of music's expressive quality changed from the baroque concept of *Afektenlehre* – music as *representing* emotions – to the romantic ideal of music actually *expressing* these emotions – a kind of musical transubstantiation. Music that expressed such passions could, so the received wisdom went, only be appreciated by those with developed sensibilities. Thus, by the middle years of the nineteenth century Berlioz writes, without fear of reproach, 'music is not for everyone, nor everyone for music' (Strunk quoted in James, 1993, pp. 210–11). Thus music and musical consumption became an object or tool of social delineation.

The transformation of music from a socially situated phenomenon to one which is objectified and taken over by an emerging bourgeoisie for its own purposes, begins in the latter half of the eighteenth century. The rowdy factionalism which contributed to the decline in the fortunes of Italian opera, and which caused Handel to withdraw from it in favour of composing oratorio, also resulted in:

rich patrons finding opera no longer novel, bored with Lenten oratorios and tired of rubbing shoulders with the hoi polloi in theatres and pleasure gardens they turned to a new musical experience.

(Brewer, 1997, p. 396)

This 'new experience' was the arguably more complex instrumental music of foreigners: in particular Haydn, Mozart and J. C. Bach. To begin with, these concerts took place in fashionable London houses. However, as demand grew, buildings were built for the specific purpose of performing this music: the first London concert halls. Charges for these concerts and regu-

lations governing admission ensured that only those from the higher eche-
lons of society were able to attend.

> The directors granted subscriptions only on personal application and subscribers
> were not allowed to transfer tickets to anyone outside their immediate family.
> Between a third and half of the concert public were families of peers, knights and
> baronets. In the 1780s, after the success of the Handel centenary, the king and
> the court became prominent supporters of these concerts.
>
> (Brewer, 1997, p. 401)

Consequently attendance at these concerts became an indicator of one's
superior social standing. The concerts:

> served to mark off the nobility from the crowd and to affiliate them culturally to
> the court. Having lost the status attendant upon their military role, they received
> compensation in aesthetic coin. Becoming cultured rather than learning how to
> use a rapier became the prime duty of the gentleman . . . where the élite had used
> to participate in popular culture (festivals, carnivals and the like) they now began
> to withdraw and establish a sense of 'high' culture excluding the 'low'.
>
> (Donogho, 1987, p. 342)

Finally, in the late nineteenth century, as Hirschkop points out, 'popular
music undergoes a similar process of confinement and pricing through the
establishment of cafe concerts and cabarets' (Hirschkop, 1989, p. 296). The
inevitable result of this was that by the middle of the twentieth century,
musical divisions were firmly delineated and the function of music in
society marginalised. As John Shepherd puts it, music was relegated 'to the
status of 'cultural capital', in the case of serious music, or that of "mere
leisure and entertainment", in the case of popular music' (Shepherd, 1991,
p. 138). Thus was achieved the separation of high and low culture music
and with it, social and cultural delineation.

The objectification of music, which had originally possessed an aesthetic
and cultural rationale, now took on a market imperative, the consumers of
which were not only the aristocracy but the emerging professional middle
classes:

> A middle class audience evolved to support such institutions as concert hall,
> music society, chamber music recitals, along with a class of professionals gearing
> performances and compositions to public taste. Haydn's journey from Esterhazy
> to London was not merely geographical, it was historical too; from a life of
> patronage to that of the entrepreneur in a free market.
>
> (Donogho, 1987, p. 339)

The idea of ownership of the musical object emerged and, with it the
concept of copyright and the music publisher or composer as controller of
musical dissemination. Notation becomes more prescriptive as composers
seek to emphasise the autonomous existence of the musical object by attempting to use notation to codify exactly the musical sound they imagined.
Notation becomes part of the compositional process by defining the parameters of the medium to an extent that it never had in Renaissance and
Baroque music. The musical manuscript now no longer acted solely as an
aid to performance, but became the saleable commodity, the object of

attention. Its meaning is perceived as being encapsulated entirely within the codification. The consequence of this objectification of music into discrete musical works, is the idea of a repertoire and with it the creation of a 'canon' of great works central to the bourgeois aesthetic.

> In this new order music is no longer a continuum of melodies, ornaments and instrumental techniques which can be drawn upon by an improvisatory practice, but a collection of discrete, individual performable works. And this in turn implies the notion of a repertory which can extend in space (as it does when Liszt starts to perform the works of others in 1830) and through history (as it does when Mendelssohn revives Bach in 1829). So many works and performances implies a market.
>
> (Hirschkop, 1989, p. 296)

Musical Notation, Music Education and the Romantic Aesthetic

Earlier in this chapter I referred to the assumption that 'music' and 'musical work' are synonymous. However, as Dalhaus points out, 'the idea that music is exemplified in works, no matter how firmly it has been rooted in the past century and a half, is far from self evident' (Elliot, 1994, p. 12). Objectification of music is part and parcel of art music's assumed autonomy and completeness. Only through autonomy, completeness and objectification could musical works 'be stripped of their social and historical connotations . . . [and] . . . prized as examples of the aesthetic which would now partially fill the gap left by the demise of other forms of social authority' (Hirschkop, 1989, p. 288). Notation is a critical part of the process of objectification. It places a distance between the music, the creator and the performer. Thus:

> music appears as pure form, self contained and devoid of social meaning, because it becomes an object of consumption, capable of being used without reference to a supporting or cultural ritual. This endows music with an autonomous *value* . . . asserted and measured in the act of exchange.
>
> (Hirschkop, 1989, pp. 295–6)

It is not surprising therefore that western music education has traditionally elevated the ability to read music over purely musical skills. Even today, it sometimes acts as a precursor to, or substitute for, active engagement with musical sound. Along with 'music appreciation', musical literacy was, for many years, the mainstay of the music curriculum. Both emphasised the autonomous nature of music and the superior status of a bourgeois-defined western canon.

The hegemony of musical theory not only articulates bourgeois objectification of music but also the status traditionally accorded to intellectual abstraction over subject application; a tradition which is rooted in the mediaeval *quadrivium* (music, arithmetic, geometry and astronomy). In ancient and mediaeval times this was reflected in a musical distinction between the *cantores* (those who practised music) and the *musici* (those who engaged in theoretical discussion of it). Far greater status was accorded to the latter, with the *cantores*, in Jamie James's words, being considered little more than 'performing monkeys' (James, 1993). For the classics-based tradition of English education, this form of the music curriculum must have seemed right and proper. Furthermore, it had the advantage of being facts-based, easily assessable, and therefore academically legitimate. 'O' level music perpetuated such a model of music learning well into the nineteen-eighties.

The inherent status accorded to objectified (notated) music by implication devalues music that has little or no mediation with notation (much non-western music), or music whose relationship to notation is ambivalent; for example, jazz and folk music. Moreover, the social functionalism and lack of 'transcendence' of much of 'non-art' music further removes it from the bourgeois romantic aesthetic and therefore serious consideration as music. In non-western music, jazz and folk, it is typically the *act* of making music that communicates, rather than any product of it. The distinction between composer and performer and rehearsal and performance is constantly blurred. 'Composition' is frequently a collective exercise proceeding from open and public rehearsals. Thus the music is constantly developing. The notion of preserving music in one definitive form by means of notation is wholly alien to such cultural perceptions of its nature and function. In these traditions, music is:

> a living organism; any performance of it shows it not in a final form but only at a particular stage in its development. To such non-literate composers the final written form of a western classical composition is dead, the score a sarcophagus, while the non-literate composition remains as full of possibilities as does any other living creature.
>
> (Small, 1987, pp. 230–1)

However, the consequence of its lack of objectification means that it cannot be 'possessed' by a particular section of society in order to act as a symbol of power and authority; in fact it is quite often the agent for social change.

Finally, mastery of notation requires cognitive skills which are not specifically musical but arguably more closely related to high status linguistic and mathematical intelligences (Gardner, 1982). Thus children who achieve success in these high status areas are also likely to do well in this theoretically-based paradigm of music education. Children who do not possess high linguistic and logico-mathematical skills, but who may nevertheless possess pure musical skills, are unlikely to be successful in such a music curriculum model and therefore be, once more, labelled as failures. Thus the musical potential of many children remains unexploited and, as there is social/class correlation with achievement in linguistic/ mathematical subjects, this model of music education functions as a tool of social delineation.

Popular Music, Music Education and Social Delineation

Brian Simon has pointed out how, since its inception, English state education has served to perpetuate social hierarchies:

> educational restructuring was not spearheaded by those representing economic or industrial interests. . . . Rather this role was played at a crucial stage by those representing the aristocracy and gentry, who were concerned to preserve social stability and reinforce emerging social hierarchies.
>
> (Simon, 1987, p. 106)

Wolff argues that music has the propensity to articulate these divisions with 'different social groups [using] culture as a kind of capital, confirming their social position, excluding other social groups, and guaranteeing the reproduction of these social divisions from one generation to another' (Wolff, 1987, p. 7).

Hirschkop takes the argument a stage further showing how textual objects (literature and music) are used to reflect and reinforce social hierarchies:

> ruling institutions produce an official discourse, a body of texts which takes account of these different languages but arranges them in an hierarchy, so that the subordinate popular languages appear as deviant, uneducated, hysterical or savage in relation to a valued high or correct language.
>
> (Hirschkop, 1989, p. 286)

The role of art music as 'cultural capital', situated at the apex of a musical hierarchy, has particular significance in terms of its relationship with other music (rock and non-western) within the music curriculum of British schools. Shepherd and Vulliamy (1994) describe how the struggle for the soul of the music national curriculum between the musical world and right-wing politicians and academics was symbolic as a struggle for the role of Englishness: 'the very public nature of the debates concerning what should count as school music exemplify an ideological struggle concerning the nature of Englishness and what should lie at the heart of English culture' (Shepherd and Vulliamy, 1994, p. 27).

In education, the bourgeois-defined inherent superiority of western art music is articulated either through outright rejection of pop and non-western music as, to use the words of Shepherd and Vulliamy, appropriate 'knowledge within schools' or as 'what counts or should count as music in schools' (Shepherd and Vulliamy, 1994, p. 27). The notion of western music autonomously encapsulating beauty and moral order (an essentially Platonic view) is frequently contrasted with pop music's 'association with drug abuse and youthful revolt' (Rainbow, 1996, p. 16) to support such a view.

Even for those who do not subscribe to the rather extreme notion of pop music as a threat to moral and social order, the fact is it operates functionally by overtly articulating particular life-styles: 'to like rock, to like a certain kind of rock rather than another, is also a way of life, a manner of reacting: it is a whole set of tastes and attitudes' (Foucault and Boulez, quoted in Norris, 1989, p. 301) is in itself sufficient reason for unfavourable comparison with the autonomous and socially detached art music.

> Underlying all the other distinctions critics draw between 'serious' and 'popular' music is an assumption about the source of musical value. Serious music matters because it transcends social forces; popular music is aesthetically worthless because it is determined by them (because it is 'useful' or 'utilitarian'). . . . If we venture to suggest that the value of, say, Beethoven's music can be determined by the social conditions determining its production and consumption we are dismissed as philistines . . .
>
> (Frith, 1987, p. 133)

The hegemony of western classical music is then rationalised by evaluating non-art music on art music's terms: as an autonomous object, detached from its social and cultural context, valued only in terms of the relationships between its musical materials. An exercise in which non-art music can only come off worse. Thus the bourgeois aesthetic is confirmed as intrinsically superior and, by association, so are its consumers and creators and indeed all who are in any way associated with it.

Thus, despite the increasing acceptance in schools of rock groups and non-western ensembles, it is arguable that music of the western classical tradition still enjoys much greater status by virtue of its ability to articulate, as Lucy Green puts it, 'Western Culture and Western values' (Green, 1988, p. 67). Indeed, despite the fact that music teachers entering the profession since the seventies have been raised in 'a cultural milieu . . . in which the strict discursive divides between the "classical" the "popular" and the "folk" would have seemed far less pertinent to prospective music teachers than in previous years' (Shepherd and Vulliamy, 1994, p. 36), this diversity was rarely reflected in the curriculum of the universities and conservatories (Dunbar-Hall, 1996):

> both the study of popular music styles and methods for teaching them are missing from many tertiary courses; the mainly art music backgrounds of many music teachers act against an understanding of popular music; there is a shortage of critical material in this area to which music teachers can refer; and an accepted model for teaching popular music has not been developed.
>
> (Dunbar-Hall, 1996, p. 216)

Thus for many teachers their higher education is an affirmation of the inherent superiority of western classical music. Music teachers may then carry into the classroom notions of the intrinsic inferiority of pop music and unwittingly use it in such a way that it perpetuates social and educational divisions. In a case study carried out into the use of pop music in schools Graham Vulliamy described how:

> teachers, although aware of a split between pop and classical music, acted on the grounds of unspoken assumptions that involved treating 'working-class' pupils as less musical and pop as less valuable. The teachers gave high-stream, mainly 'middle-class' pupils the opportunity of instrumental lessons in preference to low stream, mainly 'working-class' pupils, on the unspoken assumption that the former make better musicians. They played more pop with low streams and tended to use it mainly to keep the children quiet or as a treat at the end of a lesson,

revealing an assumption that pop does not really count as music and is concomitantly more suitable for low than high-stream pupils

(Green, 1988, p. 58).

The result of such practice is that both the children who are being taught, and the music itself, is stigmatised.

Music Notation and Popular Music: Implications for Practice

Teaching Musical Literacy

Encouraged by initiatives such as the Schools Council Music Project (1977), many teachers developed a vision of music education's purpose as identifying and fulfilling the musical potential of all children. They believed that this vision could only be realised if the criteria for success were related specifically to musical skills, experiences and understanding. The teaching of notation was consequently rejected by many teachers on the grounds that it is not vital to musical skill or experience. Also, that it excluded many children who were already educationally disenfranchised by a curriculum that concentrates almost exclusively on what Gardner describes as 'linguistic and logical-mathematical intelligences' (Gardner, 1982). They argued that, as the vast majority of the world's music is not notated, and that only certain types of music are transcribable through staff notation, notation is restrictive to musical creativity and discourages the serious consideration of music from non-literate societies.

Paul Terry (1994) supports such a point of view when he writes that:

> The learning of staff notation will only be of value to specialist performers who intend to spend the greater part of their professional lives performing or studying an existing musical literature. If the National Curriculum is genuinely intended to encourage all pupils at Key Stages 1 to 4 to engage with sound, then there is no practical reason why they need to be burdened with an anachronistic notational system: technology allows students to compose directly onto a retrievable system. Many universities and institutions of further education may insist on the 'traditional value' of musical literature, but traditions belong to the past: our students are creating sound structures for the present and future.

(Terry, 1994, p. 110)

Lucy Green (1988) believes, however, that many of the arguments put forward for not teaching music notation are misguided and based upon a confusion about how music and musical experience relate to the individual. She draws parallels between developing musical literacy skills and those required for using music technology arguing that 'notational elites are no greater a threat than technological elites' (Green, 1988, p. 131). She suggests that basing a rejection of the teaching of notation upon a paradigm of a non-literate society is essentially illogical. We must start from where we are at, and not attempt to recreate the conditions of an unrealisable 'pre-industrial state of grace' (Green, 1988, p. 131). She goes on to suggest that the immediacy of musical experience, which many associate with non-

literacy, is spurious: 'all experience of music, pre-literate or literate, requires familiarity with style and is therefore never "immediate" but mediated through conventional meaning, and learnt' (Green, 1988, p. 131).
Music is essentially socially-based. She criticises both the 'romantic aesthetic' – the notion of music as something which 'is an immediate reflection
of our "innermost feelings"' – and those who argue that music can lack an
objectified existence and that notation is '. . . a betrayal of music's
authentic state'.

> In fact, objectified musical meaning in notation merely allows a distance between
> the musical object and the subject which creates the possibility for thought away
> from the real material processes in time.
>
> (Green, 1988, p. 133)

In finding a middle ground she draws parallels between the improviser and
the person who relies upon notated music:

> It is not possible to be a musician, to play, improvise or even listen to music in
> any other way than by mediating with the processes and materials of music as
> they pass in time . . . the improviser mediates with external musical materials just
> as does the performer of notated music: each has to retain and project in every
> moment, posit themselves as the listening other. . . . Improvisation is . . . no more
> free than any musical mediation: otherwise the result would not count as music.
> That is why improvisers who nonetheless imagines themselves to be free from
> rules, find it necessary to impose rules all the time.
>
> (Green, 1988, p. 133).

The critical point she is making is that notation is not inherently aligned to
a bourgeois aesthetic. However, in order to function meaningfully as part
of an authentic musical experience, notation needs to be liberated from its
bourgeois functions, traditions and associations; particularly the idea of
notation as a valid abstract concept which confers upon it spurious autonomous value. Notation has no autonomous value. Its value is only in terms
of how it supports, informs and encourages people's engagement with
musical sound as listeners, performers and composers. Notation should
never be the musical *raison d'être*.

From a music education perspective, the teaching of musical notation
should seek to reconstitute an umbilical link between notation and musical
sound by being rooted in an authentic musical experience which is *recog-
nisable as such* by the child. In order to do this, the teaching of notation will
be based upon differentiation by need and appropriateness. When deciding
how (or indeed whether) to teach notation, the teacher will consider the
needs and aspirations of the musical learner and the type of notation and
the conceptual level which are appropriate to fulfil these aspirations. Thus,
the kit drummer, singer, rhythm or bass guitarist, classical pianist and steel
pan player and composer, may require competence in realising notation of
different types or at different conceptual levels. Some will require skills in
the kind of notation which purports to codify all of the musical elements:
pitch, rhythm, timbre etc. (essentially, staff notation). Others may need
skills in the type of notation which concentrates upon one particular musi-

cal element: for example, rhythm. For others, competence in the use of a particular music software package will best address their needs.

Concentration upon one kind of notation need not, however, restrict their development as musicians or the range of musical styles with which they can engage. For, having developed competence in the particular aspect of music literacy most suited to their initial needs, children can 'cross over' to other musical styles using the literacy skills developed in their own sphere in tandem with a developed aural ability. This almost inevitably results in those musicians who are not entirely dependent upon notation for the realisation of musical sound.

Teaching Popular Music

Popular music (by which I mean typically the music that children listen to outside of school) is a tremendous resource for the music teacher. It can be a stimulus for children's compositions and performances and provide exemplar musical material with which the children are familiar. Inasmuch as such music is usually experienced and learnt aurally, it can assist in the development of children's aural facility, whilst the ability to read musical notation is not necessary for an effective engagement with it. Furthermore, the strong delineated meanings of pop music mean that for many children 'their music' is central to their perception of life and the way in which they relate to the world.

However, as I have suggested earlier in this chapter, pop music can have a negative impact upon the curriculum if its low status, in terms of the bourgeois aesthetic, is implicitly reinforced by using pop music only with working class children or those who are perceived as academically 'less able'. Popular music needs to be underpinned by a strong supporting philosophy if it is to take a positive place in the music curriculum. (Otherwise it can be looked upon as a kind of panacea with which difficult classes can be 'bought off'.)

Such a philosophy requires, as first step, a questioning of the basic premise that lies behind the division of art and non-art music: that the former is autonomous and transcendent and the latter entirely socially situated. The notion that this distinction is inherent in the two types of music, and that art music can be understood *only* musicologically and pop music *only* sociologically, is a myth which serves to perpetuate the notion of the inherent superiority of western music.

Simon Frith argues that all music can be understood equally in terms of its relationship to society and its potential for transcendence: 'Abba's value is no more (and no less) bound up with experience of transcendence than Mozart's; the meaning of Mozart is no less (and no more) explicable in terms of social forces' (Frith, 1987, p. 134).

Dunbar-Hall (1996) articulates a model for the teaching of popular music based upon the notion of music as possessing two sets of properties: the 'etic' (the musical elements and their relationship to each other) and the 'emic' (the product of cultural knowledge). He argues that:

> based upon the combination of music's two-sided character as the combination of analysable facts and interpreted meanings, a teaching model based on the etic and emic characteristics of popular music includes consideration of the range of qualities that make up any piece of music.   (Dunbar-Hall, 1996, p. 225)

However, this only gets us so far. For, whereas we may recognise the two-sides of the musical coin, there still remains the *perceived* autonomous nature of art music and the utilitarian, socially-based, pop music, with the greater status accorded to the former. We can attempt to redress the balance by arguing, as Elliot does, that all music is socially based:

> In the case of the *Eroica*, a human being named Ludwig van Beethoven did something. And what he did was to compose something in the context of a specific time and place and a specific tradition of music making. In the case of *Cotton Tail*, a person named Duke Ellington did something. And what he did was to compose, arrange, perform, improvise and record something in the context of another time, and place and another tradition of music making.
> (Elliot, 1994, p. 15)

However, this is not the way we experience this music. One (the *Eroica*) is experienced as an autonomous musical object whilst the other (*Cotton Tail*) is experienced primarily, though not exclusively, in terms of its social and cultural context. What is needed, perhaps, is a recognition that, whereas both popular and art music have transcendent capabilities and are to an extent socially rooted, they are different in the way in which each relates to the social and transcendent.

In an article which applies the sociolinguistic theories of Bakhtin (1895–1975) to a consideration of the distinction between art and popular musical forms, Hirschkop appropriates the terms 'poetic' to describe autonomous, art music and 'novelistic' to describe socially-based popular music. Hirschkop recognises that there is probably no escape from the perception of art music as transcendent and popular music as socially-based. He argues that in the case of art music, for example, no amount of intellectual justification for a socially situated context will distract from a transcendent, aesthetic experience. For, one 'is not able to oppose [one's] own poetic consciousness' (Hirschkop, 1989, p. 292).

However, that is not to deny that art music does have a social dimension. It is simply different to the way in which popular music relates to, and reacts with, its social context. He argues that popular music embraces its social context *consciously*, producing artefacts which are specific to its time and place. Classical music, on the other hand, although being affected by its social situation and frequently reflecting the virtues of the culture in which it is created, is rarely consciously social in the way that popular music almost invariably is. It is this that distinguishes classical music from popular music, 'the "novelised" forms of musical practice usually, though not exclusively, found in the open spaces of public squares and streets' (Hirschkop, 1989, pp. 298–9).

Hirschkop articulates here an inherent and important distinction between art and popular music based upon how each relates to its social context. However, this distinction is a positive one, not founded upon bourgeois mythology, but recognising the distinction in function between the two forms. It is a distinction that recognises the validity of popular music and which can form the basis of its place in the music curriculum.

Similarly, Frith (1987) argues for an aesthetic of popular music which is neither purely social or purely transcendent but that mediates between the social and individual worlds. He argues this can function in four ways, all of which in some way mediate between the individual and society. First, as a form of self-definition within a sub-group of society; second as a means of 'managing the relationship between public and private emotional lives' – '. . . popular music gives shape and voice to emotions that otherwise cannot be expressed without embarrassment or incoherence'; third, '. . . to shape popular memory, to organise our sense of time' (Frith, 1987, pp. 140–3). Frith points out that this function is particularly important for young people:

> Youth is experienced as an intense presence, through an impatience for time to pass and a regret that it is doing so, in a series of speeding, physically insistent moments that have nostalgia coded into them.
>
> (Frith, 1987, p. 143)

Finally, pop music is something possessed both individually and as part of a social group. It 'occupies the space between the individual and society' (Swanwick, 1996).

Frith goes on to make the point that transcendency is not an experience unique to art music, but can also be possessed by popular music and that moreover, music transcendent effect relies upon its social context:

> people do hear the music they like as something special: . . . it seems to provide an experience that transcends the mundane, that takes us 'out of ourselves'. It is special, that is, not necessarily with reference to other music, but to the rest of life. This kind of specialness, the way in which music seems to make possible a new kind of self-recognition, frees us from the everyday routines and expectations that encumber our social identities, is a key part of the way in which people experience and thus value music: if we believe we possess our music, we also often feel we are possessed by it. Transcendence is, then, as much a part of the popular music aesthetic as it is of the serious music aesthetic; but . . . in pop, transcendence marks not music's freedom from social forces but its patterning by them. (Of course, in the end, the same is true of serious music, too.)
>
> (Frith, 1987, p. 144)

So, in order to break down the status distinctions between art and popular music, and to begin the emancipation of popular music into the music curriculum, it is imperative that we recognise that all music possesses both a social and an aesthetic existence. Having recognised that, the perception of art music as possessing an inherent status, which raises it above all popular music, can begin to be challenged. For at that point, all examples of music can be valued in terms of how they relate to a specific and appropriate set of criteria. We can then, both socially and educationally, move towards creating a culture in which, in the words of Shepherd and Vulliamy:

> The value of music [is] not judged across cultures according to a scheme of absolutes taken to be objective, but only in relation to a criteria developed as an integral aspect of the socially constructed reality of the group or society creating the music to be evaluated. Popular music as introduced into the secondary school curriculum [cannot] therefore be judged according to an 'objective' set of criteria – which without exception [turns] out to be abstracted from the technical and aesthetic criteria of music of the western canon – but only according to criteria which were . . . associated with those who created and appreciated the music.
>
> (Shepherd and Vulliamy, 1994, p. 29)

Developing a New Music Curriculum

I have tried to demonstrate in the preceding pages how the nineteenth century bourgeois aesthetic continues to exert a significant influence on present day thinking about music and music education through the promotion of a hierarchy of musical styles.

In arguing for music education to break free from the hegemony of this understanding of western art music, I am not espousing cultural or social relativism that then becomes dependent, if it is to have any educational value, upon an understanding of social context. Indeed, I fully agree with Swanwick when he writes that:

> Having fairly recently escaped from the clutches of propositional knowledge associated with the history of western classical music we must be careful not to replicate this state of affairs with the history and social context of music from India, the Caribbean, Africa, China and the Pacific.
>
> (Swanwick, 1996, p. 20)

Rather, I am suggesting that one of the purposes of music education should be to explore the variety of ways in which music occurs. Thus music education becomes, not just about music as 'object' or music as 'sound materials', but also about ways in which music is experienced and thought about. I am not therefore arguing for the elimination of the 'romantic aesthetic' from music education, but rather that it be taught as just one way among many of experiencing the phenomenon of music. This implies, then, music philosophy as *part* of the music curriculum rather than something which simply mediates between teacher, pupil and curriculum. It is not the aim of this chapter to explore in any detail how this might be achieved, only to make the point that integrating music philosophy into the music curriculum does not imply substituting talking about music for actively engaging with it. Individual, social and musical experience all occur at the human-musical interface. It is this interface that we now might wish to consider as an area for development in a music curriculum for the new millennium. Above all, however, music must be liberated from the divisions wrought by the continuing hegemony of the romantic aesthetic. This is where we must start. For, as Williams writes:

> Our specialisms will be finer if they have grown from a common culture, rather than being a distinction from it. And we must at all costs avoid the polarization of our culture. . . . We must emphasise not the ladder but the common highway for every man's ignorance diminishes me, and every man's skill is a common gain of breath.
>
> (Benn, 1984, p. 115)

References

Brewer, J. (1997) *The Pleasures of the Imagination*. London: Harper/Collins.

Dalhaus, C. (1989) *The Idea of Absolute Music*. Translated by R. Lustig. Chicago: The University of Chicago Press.

Donogho, M. (1987) Music and History. In P. Alperson *What is Music? An Introduction to the Philosophy of Music*, pp. 327–349. Pennsylvania: Haven Publications.

Dunbar-Hall, P. (1996) Designing a Teaching Model for Popular Music. In G. Spruce (ed) *Teaching Music,* pp. 216–227. London: Routledge.

Elliot, D. (1994) Rethinking Music: First Steps to a New Philosophy of Music Education, *International Journal of Music Education,* **24**, pp. 9–20.

Frith, S. (1987) Towards an Aesthetic of Popular Music. In R. Leppert and S. McClary (eds) *Music and Society. The Politics of Composition, Performance and Reception*, pp. 133–151. Cambridge: Cambridge University Press.

Gardner, G. (1982) *Frames of Mind*. London: Heinemann.

Green, L. (1988) *Music On Deaf Ears*. Manchester: Manchester University Press.

Harland, J., Kinder, K. and Hartley, K. (1995) *Arts In Their View. A study of youth participation in the arts*. Slough: National Foundation for Educational Research.

Hirschkop, K. (1989) The Classical and the Popular: Musical form and social context. In C. Norris, (ed), pp. 283–302.

HMI. (1985) *Music from 5–16. Curriculum Matters 4*. London: HMSO.

James, J. (1993) *The Music of the Spheres*. London: Little, Brown and Company.

Leppert, R. and McClary, S. (1987) Introduction. *Music and Society. The Politics of Composition, Performance and Reception*, pp. xi-xx. Cambridge: Cambridge University Press.

Norris, C. (ed) (1989) *Music and the Politics of Culture*. London: Lawrence and Wishart.

OFSTED (1996) *Subjects and Standards. Key stages 3&4 and Post-16*. London: HMSO.

Rainbow, B (1996) Onwards From Butler: School Music 1945–1985. In G. Spruce (ed) *Teaching Music,* pp. 9–21. London: Routledge.

Schools Council (1977) Music in the secondary schools curriculum. Working Paper 2, London Schools Council.

Simon, B. (1987) Systemisation and Segmentation in Education: the case in England. In D. Muller, R. Ringer, and B. Simon, (eds) *The Rise of the Modern Educational System*, pp. 88–111. Cambridge: Cambridge University Press.

Shepherd, J. (1991) *Music As Social Text*. Cambridge: Polity Press.

Shepherd, S. and Vulliamy, G. (1994) The Struggle for Culture: a sociology case study of the development of the national music curriculum, *British Journal of the Sociology of Education,* **15** (1), pp. 27–40.

Small, C. (1987) *Music of the Common Tongue*. London: Calder Publications.

Swanwick, K. (1996) Music education liberated from new praxis, *International Journal of Music Education,* **28**, pp. 16–24.

Terry, P. (1994) Music notation in secondary education: some aspects of theory and practice, *British Journal of Music Education*, **11**, pp. 99–111.

Walker, R. (1996) Music education freed from praxis, *International Journal of Music Education*, **27**, pp. 2–15.

Williams, R. (1958) Conviction. In T. Benn (ed) *Writings on the Wall: A radical and socialist anthology 1215–1984*, p. 115. London: Faber and Faber.

Wolff, J. (1987) The Ideology Of Autonomous Art. In R. Leppert and S. McClary *Music and Society. The Politics of Composition, Performance and Reception*, pp. 1–13. Cambridge: Cambridge University Press.

Wolterstorff, N. (1987) The Work of Making a Work of Music. In P. Alperson *What is Music? An Introduction to the Philosophy of Music*, pp. 103–131. Pennsylvania: Haven Publications.

SECTION 2:
LEARNING AND ASSESSMENT

7

Expert Knowledge and Processes of Thinking

Robert Glaser

Highly competent performance is intrinsically fascinating, regardless of whether we witness it in memory experts, quiz kids, Olympic players, medical diagnosticians, chess masters, or mathematicians and biophysicists. In the past 15 years or so, describing competence and the processes that underlie it has become a significant endeavor in the study of human cognition. The tactic in these studies has been to explore the well-established performances that proficient people display, which have developed over time, and the components and properties of knowledge and skill that characterize highly competent performance. The results of this work define objectives for human attainment – goals for learning that can inform teaching practices at all levels. Expertise is proficiency taken to its highest level, and understanding of the experts' hard-won knowledge and skill can be used to foster the novices' progress and, perhaps, to expand the proficiencies of experts themselves.

The seeds for work on expertise were sown in the widely cited Newell and Simon (1972) book, *Human Problem Solving.* Newell and Simon described the observations of Adrian de Groot, a famous Dutch chess master who compared chess masters' and novice chess players' accounts of their thinking as they confronted various chess problems (de Groot, 1965, 1966). de Groot's findings anticipated key ideas in our current understanding of the nature of expertise. Although de Groot was unsuccessful in attempting to distinguish stronger from weaker players' performances using various assessments of memory or facility with the general problem-solving heuristics, he succeeded in identifying a critical difference by asking them, after 5 second's viewing, to recall and reproduce the positions of chess pieces that would occur in a game. Experts reproduced the board layouts perfectly, but this ability was less apparent in weaker players. Pure memory capacity was not involved, for strong and weak players alike had trouble remembering randomly arranged layouts of chess pieces; rather, perceptual abilities and knowledge organization clearly were characteristic of highly competent players. Strong players automatically viewed particular configurations of pieces as laden with meaning: a given configuration suggested possible moves and helped the player anticipate the consequences of those moves.

The perceptual aspects of problem solving in chess seem to be crucial. Research that has followed up on de Groot's work has shown that chess masters recognize clusters of related pieces as familiar constellations and they store each cluster in memory as a single symbol or pattern. Less-skilled players have to describe the board as a larger number of simpler patterns – hence, they cannot hold in memory all of the information required to reproduce a layout. When the same number of pieces is arranged in a scrambled pattern on the board, few of the resulting configurations are familiar even to grandmasters. They then need more symbols to describe the position than they can hold simultaneously in short-term memory – hence, their recall is as poor as weaker players'. Chess masters, thus, do not show greater memory capacity for chess pieces in general, but only for the board's instantiations of chess principles as they crop up in a game. The quantities of patterns demanded by their expertise are of a high order of magnitude. In the many years required to attain chess mastery, a player might be expected to acquire a 'vocabulary' of subpatterns comparable in extent to the verbal knowledge required to read English (Chase and Simon, 1973).

The study of expert/novice differences in other domains has deepened our appreciation of the significance of the experts' perceptions of patterns. This perceptiveness, we can now suggest, is one of the critical manifestations of experts' highly organized, integrated structures of knowledge. In electronics, for example, skilled technicians reconstructing symbolic drawings of circuit diagrams do so according to the functional nature of the elements in the circuit, such as amplifiers, rectifiers, and filters. Novice technicians, however, reconstruct the diagrams on the basis of the spatial proximity of the elements (Egan and Schwartz, 1979).

Expert radiologists' readings of x-rays show that the expert first builds a mental representation of possible abnormalities and that this representation guides the diagnosis and must satisfy tests of applicability before it is allowed to control viewing and interpretation. The expert works efficiently to reach a stage where an appropriate general model or schema guides the diagnosis. Less-expert interns do not confirm the applicability of the patterns they invoke, and an incomplete model may be triggered and control their efforts (Lesgold *et al.*, 1988)

Like the chess results, such evidence shows that the expert in a domain takes in and uses information in *chunks* – in organizations and integrations of knowledge, or meaningful patterns – extremely rapidly. Whether the domain is chess configurations, functional interpretations of circuit diagrams, or representations of anatomical abnormalities in x-rays, the central underlying properties or meaningful deep structure of the situation is key to experts' perceptions, whereas the surface features and structural properties (such as proximity and literal descriptive aspects) organize the less-than-expert individuals' perceptions.

This aspect of expertise has been investigated in studies of scientific problem solving. In experiments where novices and experts were asked to classify a set of elementary physics mechanics problems in terms of the requirements for solutions, the two groups tackled the task on entirely different bases. The novices used surface features to group rotation problems, inclined plane problems, or spring problems in their classifications. In contrast, the experts grouped problems that had little surface resemblance; they saw as similar problems that involved the principle of conservation of energy or Newton's second law. The experts were able to tie the surface features of problems to deeper principles, and inducing these principles was predictive of fast, efficient, and accurate methods of solution (Chi *et al.*, 1982).

Another observable difference between expert and novice problem solvers' performances is their pause-times for retrieving successive equations. Experts appear to invoke sets of equations; eliciting one equation activates rapid retrieval of related equations. Novices do not exhibit such chunking in setting up equations. It appears that, for experts, physics equations are stored in functional configurations, so that accessing one procedure leads to another (Larkin, 1979).

The results of research to date has made it clear that experts' knowledge structures play a critical role in their performances. Experts, as the studies mentioned indicate, have a great deal of domain-specific information, and this information is highly organized and conceptually integrated. This organized knowledge appears to account for the experts' capacities for rapid pattern recognition and categorization.

Coordinate with these abilities, experts in science and maths often make use of qualitative reasoning to approach a problem that will require quantitative solution. Expert physicists, for example, appear to exercise a form of *physical intuition* (Simon and Simon, 1978) prior to their retrieval of equations – that is, before they even consider calculations or specific solution procedures. In contrast, novices rush into quantitative manipulations and plug in formulas (Larkin *et al.*, 1980; McDermott and Larkin, 1978). This initial qualitative phase of problem solving is key in the investigation of expert performance.

One aspect of such qualitative analysis is the representation of a problem in terms of a *runnable mental model.* This model specifies the main causal connections of the components of a situation and, like other aspects of problem representation, has a formative influence on performance. For example, in a statics problem involving a ladder leaning against a wall, the mental model would probably include the ladder, the floor, the wall, and the points of contact, as well as gravity and the forces operating at points of contact. Once this kind of representation has been constructed in memory and the expert has a feel for the situation, the equations of equilibrium can be constructed readily (Simon and Simon, 1978).

Research on algebra students' initial representations of problems is revealing here. In confronting pseudo word-problems (i.e., problems about physically unrealizable situations), a few highly proficient students immediately perceived the incongruity in the problems (Paige and Simon, 1966). The rest proceeded to invoke equations before realizing that the solutions would be meaningless (e.g., a negative quantity would be obtained for the length of an object). The good solvers apparently constructed a representation that provided a basis for inferences about problem features and their relations that were not available from the problem statement. This model gave them a basis for questioning the problem content and monitoring applicability of solution procedures.

Six Generalizations

In general, then, experts' highly integrated structures of knowledge lie behind many salient features of their performances. Current understanding of expertise now allows a set of generalizations about its nature. The implications and impact of experts' knowledge are far reaching in shaping their thinking, as these generalizations indicate.

1. *Experts' proficiency is very specific.* The precision of experts' performances derives from the specialized knowledge that drives their reasoning. Specificity of performance is evidenced by the disruption of proficiency in instances where random or meaningless patterns or poorly structured problems are presented. Under these conditions, experts lose their rapid perceptual and representational ability and resort to general problem solving strategies. It may be, however, that certain task domains are more generalizable than others, so that adults who are experts in applied mathematics or aesthetic design, or younger students who have learned measurement and quantitative concepts, have transferable forms of expertise. Nevertheless, competence in one domain is no guarantee of effectiveness in others.

2. *Experts perceive large, meaningful patterns.* These patterns guide experts' thinking in everyday working activities. Pattern recognition occurs so rapidly that it appears to take on the character of intuition. In contrast, the patterns that novices recognize are smaller, less articulated, more literal and surface-oriented, and far less related to abstracted principles. Like other aspects of experts' performance, this extraordinary representational ability depends on the organization of knowledge existing in memory.

3. *Experts' problem solving entails selective search of memory or use of general problem-solving tactics.* Whereas novices display a good deal of search and processing of a general nature, experts' fast-access pattern recognition and representational capability facilitate approaches to problems that reduce the roles of these processes. Even where it can be assumed that experts and novices have similar cognitive capacities, the experts' performances have an efficiency that derives primarily from

their knowledge being structured for retrieval, pattern recognition, and inferencing.

4. *Experts' knowledge is highly procedural and goal-oriented.* In experts' highly structured knowledge base, concepts are bound to procedures and the rules and conditions for their application. This functional knowledge is closely tied to knowledge of the goal structure of a problem. Experts and novices may be equally competent at recalling small specific (multiple-choice type) items of domain-related information, but high-knowledge individuals far more readily relate these items of information in cause-and-effect sequences that link the goals and subgoals needed for problem solution.

5. *Experts' knowledge enables them to use self-regulatory processes with great skill.* Experts proficiently monitor their own problem-solving activities; they have the ability to step back, so to speak, at appropriate points, and observe their solution processes and the outcomes of their performances. Their self-awareness is also shown in their allocation of attention and their sensitivity to information feedback as they work. Use of self-regulatory processes sometimes slows experts as they initially encode a difficult problem, although they are faster problem solvers overall. Here, novices' reliance on surface features allows them speed initially.

6. *Experts' proficiency can be routinized or adaptive.* Competence is influenced by the task demands and by the conditions for work; thus, experts' attained proficiencies can be context-bound. Under some conditions, maybe most, their performances become routinized as well as efficient and accurate. Under others, experts develop the capability for *opportunistic planning*, which is manifested by their revising problem representations readily and accessing multiple possible interpretations of a situation. The conditions and demands of education and of work can foster combinations of highly competent routine and adaptive expertise.

A Note on Expert Performances in Unfamiliar Territory

The picture of expertise presented thus far does not take into account the competence (or perhaps the lack of competence) that experts demonstrate when they work at the frontiers of knowledge – when the problems they confront are from unfamiliar domains or are not well structured, so that patterns and solution procedures cannot readily be perceived.

Working such problems – which can be called *ill-structured problems or problems of discovery* – requires: (a) the resolution of open constraints; (b) decisions about imposing parameter values that are entailed in the problem presentation or conceptualization; (c) a search for analogies; and (d) most importantly, pursuit of equivalents to the powerful principles that underlie solutions for well-structured or familiar problems. In these novel situations, the definition of subproblems for which patterns can be seen that enable particular approaches is a key step. The solver must invent an organization that synthesizes potential understandings – that is, the solver must come up with some representation or model as a basis for proceeding (Simon, 1973; Voss and Post, 1988).

What is of interest here is that, somewhat like novices, experts bring *general* problem-solving processes to bear. They do decompose an ill-structured problem into a better structured set of subproblems, but with greater facility than a novice would. They also are able to select parameter values for open constraints that lead to a possible meaningful solution by supplying testable candidate problem representations. In general, where problems do not yield to straightforward approaches, experts can usefully resort to analogies with systems they understand well and search for matches and mismatches. They may attempt to impose some model of the workings of another phenomenon on the problem at hand to try to understand how the model would behave in the new context. They may pose extreme-case arguments or construct simpler problems of a similar sort and bring those solutions to the original problem.

This use of general heuristics does not take on significance as a substitute for domain knowledge. On the contrary, general heuristics serve mostly in the attempt to gain access to domain knowledge that can be used for problem solution. In a sense, the use of general heuristics reflects the attempt to move ill-structured problems of discovery into the familiar domain where extant knowledge can be brought into play. Rather than using general heuristics in a decontextualized way – as free-floating interrogators of a situation – the expert uses them to make contact with available knowledge and the solution processes it might afford. The abstract use of general heuristics in courses on thinking skills or reasoning may not be successful for this reason.

Expertise and Writing Skill

As an illustration of how the properties of expertise interact, the domain of writing competence is interesting. An increasing amount of analysis is being undertaken on the nature of novice and expert writing. Writing is a skill that we must rely on in much of our schooling and working lives. It is a basic skill of educated people, yet involves, it seems, a neverending process of acquiring competence. Writing can be viewed as a form of domain-specific problem solving; through structuring and expressing our ideas in written texts, we think and learn to think in our fields. For these reasons, it is an apt arena in which to examine the interdependence of the various aspects of expert performance. Consider then the specificity, integrated knowledge, problem representation, task monitoring, and goal orientation of experts' performances in writing.

Specificity

Writing, in a fundamental way, requires linguistic knowledge, that is, a strong vocabulary; a good grasp of grammar and syntax; and an awareness of rhythm, voice, and figures of speech. The student, the poet, the playwright, and the novelist all develop this knowledge, more or less, as does the academician or scientist writing about research. The domain specificity of writing expertise is now widely acknowledged by teachers and educators. In an illuminating analysis of the import of this for education, David Bartholomae observed that:

> Every time a student sits down to write for us, he has to invent the university for the occasion – invent the university or a branch of it, that is, like history or anthropology, or economics, or biology. He has to learn to speak our language, to speak as we do, to try on the peculiar ways of knowing, selecting, evaluating, reporting, concluding, and arguing that define the discourse of our community. . . . [a student must learn] to work within fields where the rules governing the presentation of an example or the development of an argument are both distinct and (often), even to a professional, mysterious.
>
> (Bartholomae, 1985, p. 4)

Bartholomae pointed out that, while in introductory writing courses, students are concerned with university discourse in its most generalized form. Expertise in writing, in the longer term, requires students to locate themselves in disciplinary forms of discourse that are not immediately accessible. Those who can write reasonably coherent expositions in one domain, say, political science, may be incoherent when faced with crafting an essay in sociology or philosophy. This is not unlike the loss manifested by experts when they are required to operate outside of their disciplines.

Integrated Knowledge

Writing expertise requires substantial declarative and procedural knowledge. Students who are novice writers in a domain are not necessarily inept thinkers; they are rather insufficiently familiar not only with information about specialized topics but also with the specific conventions or techniques of expository discourse – the procedures for describing and arguing for an interpretation or for presenting claims and counterclaims. The patterns of reasoning that we expect in academic writing are not inherent in our thinking; they are conventional, learnable forms of argumentation and rhetoric.

For example, student writers must learn to support the generalizations on which their reasoning hinges. As novices, they may not be aware that they must explicate how examples and illustrations support generalizations. Proficient writing requires sophisticated forms of this sensitivity to grounding generalizations, interpretations, and claims. Writing knowledge also includes responsiveness to the intended audience; proficient writers shape their prose differently for specialists or for informed generalists.

These forms of writing knowledge are rather specific to the task and comprise the integrated knowledge that underlies proficiency.

Representation

In writing, the initial representation of the task is highly influential (Flower *et al.*, 1986). The individual's perceptions of the aims of a piece of writing largely determine the nature of subsequent revision, and revision, of course, is where the real work goes on. Perspectives on the task can be of a local and shallow nature or of a global and more meaningful nature. Consequently, inexperienced and experienced writers make different kinds of changes in the course of revision. Novices typically focus on the conventions and rules of writing, but more advanced students make many changes, including a significant number that affect the text's meaning. Here, again, surface as opposed to deeper problem representations characterize novices' performances: Novice writers work on surface features, using word and punctuation deletion and addition as important strategies; experienced writers conceptualize the task as a wholistic enterprise that may require elaborating the treatment of a point, insuring the effectiveness of argument structure, and estimating the utility of shifts in voice as well as checking grammar and punctuation.

As noted, expert/novice studies in various domains have shown that experts arrive at solutions quickly in problem-solving tasks, although they often appear to spend more time in the initial process of problem representation than novices. Studies of revision suggest that novice writers do not approach this task as a time-consuming, recursive one. They make little use of their drafts, making most of their changes as they produce the text; they hardly reread their papers before they begin a new version. Experts spend a significant portion of their time rereading their drafts in the attempt to develop more complete representation of the problems that must be attacked, and thus this aspect of revision is one to which instruction should attend (Bridwell, 1980; Flower *et al.*, 1986).

Representation of the problems to be attacked in revision can be accomplished in two ways. First, there is a monitoring and evaluation process that builds up a representation that carries with it information and strategies for solving the problem. Second, there is a more immediate categorization or pattern recognition process that occurs quickly. In the first kind of representation (Flower *et al.*, 1986), experienced writers monitor their progress; they observe the features of their draft, search the possible writing strategies in their repertoires, and focus on an appropriate goal, for example, decide whether to work at the level of the whole text or at a more syntactic proofreading level. A representation of the task is generated from this interplay between the analysis of text features and the student's store ·of knowledge about revision strategies and currently attainable goals.

The second kind of representation requires rapid categorization of a particular task to be accomplished. Like experts in other areas, the good writer must learn to recognize a wide array of patterns. Recognition of a familiar pattern brings forth the strategies and goals applicable to it, just as board patterns do for chess masters and x-ray patterns do for expert radiologists. Proficient writers, because of their stores of knowledge, employ problem classifications that go beyond superficial features to the deeper structure of text meaning and presentation. As noted, this rapid categorization of situations takes on the character of intuitive performance.

Task Monitoring and Goal Orientation

In carrying out revision, experts show a significant sensitivity to task demands and to features of prose; they match their performances to the goals entailed in their representation of the task. Sometimes, a subgoal at a particular level is chosen because a more complex or complete goal is not attainable at the moment. This may be done to simplify the task at hand, to get on with it, so that more complex goals can be eventually attained. At other times, the demands of a task are such that proficient writers see no reason for working at a complex level when a goal requiring less level of effort will suffice, and their technique is adjusted accordingly. Inexperienced writers are less facile in generating goals suitable to a portion of a task or in adjusting to the task required. Their subgoal analysis is superficial, with the result that changes appropriate to the text are never addressed. Thus, analysis of subgoals of revision should be a significant focus of instruction.

Writing competence, like other forms of expertise, probably ranges along a continuum from routine or conventional expertise to adaptive expertise. Routine experts are outstanding in terms of speed, accuracy, and automaticity of performance; they construct mental models convenient and efficient for performing their tasks, but they may lack adaptability when faced with new kinds of problems. Repeated application of a procedure, with little variation, can lead to routine expertise. Adaptive expertise requires variation and is encouraged by playful situations and educational settings and experiences where understanding and transfer are valued along with efficient performance (Hatano and Inagaki, 1986).

Implications for Teaching and Research

What do the accruing findings on expertise generally suggest for teaching and designing experiences for students that will enable them to attain high levels of competence in the various domains of knowledge? Four points seem essential: the nature of practice, the development of self-monitoring and of principled performance, and the social context of learning.

The Nature of Practice

Obviously, proficiency is a matter of experience and practice requiring highly motivated learners who spend long hours and do the hard work necessary. But there is more to practice than motivation. Practice, as it comes about in the usual course of training, is not necessarily very efficient. On the basis of our knowledge of the specific aspects of competence and expertise, we are now able to find ways to compress or shortcut experience, or at least to present experience in more systematic fashion so that its impact is optimized. These findings suggest that practice should focus on situations where there are complex patterns to be perceived, and where recognition of these patterns implies particular moves and procedures for solution. An organized sequence of increasingly complex forms of pattern recognition tasks, associated with their procedural meaning, might be developed in sequences of instruction. For example, such experiences have been designed for technical training, including components of the job of air traffic control (Schneider, 1985), for geometry (Anderson, *et al.*, 1985), and for electronic trouble shooting (Lesgold *et al.*, 1988).

A consideration in designing practice is its resulting in automaticity for some components of competence, that is, in the ability to perform certain actions with little conscious thought. If practice produces this automaticity, then an individual has greater memory processing capability available to engage in parts of the task that require conscious thought, such as re-representing a problem or self-monitoring performance. Automatic processes are very apparent in competent performers; skilled readers can decode words with little conscious thought and, as a result, have greater cognitive space left over for interpreting the meaning of a text. The point here is that practice must continue until certain aspects of behavior become effortless when carried on as part of a larger exercise. Situations that assess students' progress toward some proficient performance, therefore, must not test component skills separately because, although performed adequately when tested by themselves, taken in combination, some components might interfere with other aspects of the larger task (Glaser, 1981).

The value of practice can be increased, if we see it as something to be carefully designed. Much learning in elementary physics is thought to take place as students practise by solving the problems at the end of textbook chapters. These are usually done as homework assignments that may later be illustrated on the blackboard in the classroom. But, the opportunity for sustained, guided practice – practice in which the student sees the principles that relate groups of problems and links them to the procedures required for those problems – is rarely afforded. To optimize teaching, we need to design practice in which learners are encouraged to search for the important connections between principles and procedures (Chi, *et al.*, 1989).

Self-Monitoring

Because self-monitoring – the ability to observe and, if necessary, reshape one's performance – is a hallmark of expertise, this skill should be emphasized in instruction. The work of Alan Schoenfeld (1985) has opened up new ideas for teaching self-monitoring heuristics in the context of learning mathematical problem solving. Heuristics are taught in a contextualized way that makes contact with the students' mathematics knowledge base. One aspect of Schoenfeld's work involves the teaching and demonstration of control or management strategies that make explicit such processes as generating alternative courses of action, evaluating which course can be carried out and whether it can be managed in the time available, and assessing progress. The students learn to monitor and direct their activity by asking such questions as: What am I doing now? Am I making progress? What else could I be doing instead? Through demonstrations and practice, students focus on critical decisions and actions at strategic levels as well as on the rote specifics of the solution.

Furthermore, Schoenfeld has directly confronted the issue of imparting an appropriate belief system about the interpretive nature of mathematical problem solving. During the process of learning mathematics, students begin to realize that searches often come to dead ends; exploration of possible heuristics and different paths does not guarantee solution. He challenges his students to find difficult problems for him to solve, so they can observe his own struggles and floundering, which legitimate students' floundering as well. Students begin to realize that mathematics requires neither merely recognizing principles, nor merely applying procedures, but, rather, a creative interpretive process of exploration and reasoning. The student's adopting this view seems especially helpful when problem representations are not readily constructed, and revisions of equations and procedures are needed so that adequate solutions can be carried out.

Principled Performance

Education also must emphasize that the most salient and ubiquitous hallmark of expertise – whether in chess, writing, science, or mathematics – is principled performance. Performance takes place not only with well-learned procedural knowledge, but also in a space for thought – in the context of a model, a theory, or a principle that guides performance through constraints and structures for inference, and allows competent individuals to avoid disconnected trial and error (Greeno and Simon, 1988). This permits understanding of one's performance, the swift and graceful recovery from error, and the seizing of opportunities for more elegant and precise solution and discovery. Expertise then becomes more than a matter of sheer efficiency and, as it is acquired, knowledge becomes an object for questioning and learning from experience and, thereby, is reorganized to enable new thought and action. An essential aim of instruction and the design of curriculum materials should be to enable the student to acquire structured knowledge along with procedural skill. Too often the fragmented bits of information supplied by textbook and teaching presentations do not encourage students to construct organized knowledge usable for thinking and principled performance

The Social Context of Learning

A fourth aspect of cognition that should be emphasized as central to change in educational practice turns us away from internal cognition alone to the influence of the situation in which learning occurs. Cognitive activity in school and outside is inseparable from a cultural milieu. The acquisition of competent performance takes place in an interpersonal system in which participation and guidance from others influences the understanding of new situations and the management of problem solving that leads to learning. Certain theories of human development have emphasized the social genesis of learning (Vygotsky, 1978). Conceptual development involves internalizing cognitive activities experienced in social settings, and many studies have pointed out the motivational variables involved in shared responsibility for thinking that enhance learning in group settings (Brown and Campione, 1990; Brown and Palincsar, 1989).

From a cognitive perspective, a group can serve several roles. First, it extends the locus of self-monitoring activity by providing triggers for cognitive dissatisfaction outside the individual. An audience monitors individual thinking, opinions, and beliefs, and can elicit explanations that clarify points of difficulty. Moreover, the learner's exposure to alternative points of view challenges his or her initial understanding. In addition, with the help of advanced peers or a teacher who provide supportive scaffolding, the collaborative group maintains a mature version of a target task. By sharing it, a complex task is made more manageable, yet is not oversimplified. Each learner contributes what he or she can and gains from the contributions of those more expert. In this context, to use Vygotsky's term, a zone of proximal development is created where learners perform within their range of competence while being assisted in realizing their potential levels of higher performance.

A most salient aspect in a social context for learning is the elevation of thinking to an overt, observable status. As students participate in group roles, various problem-solving procedures, strategies of reasoning, and techniques for accomplishing goals become apparent. This reality is to be compared with classroom learning where thinking may be rarely an observable enterprise and opportunities for its shaping through external influences are limited. Thus, school instruction might well consider how teaching practice can make apparent the forms of student's thinking, in ways that can be observed, transmitted, discussed, reflected on, and moved toward more competent performance and dispositions for reasoning.

In conclusion, it should be emphasized that, for the most part, investigations of the nature of expertise have emphasized the characteristics of the performance system and not the learning and developmental processes through which performance is attained. Research must now turn to the study of conditions for learning. Undoubtedly, the significant contributions of the methods and the results produced by the analysis of complex human competence will contribute to this work. Investigation of learning processes in a pursuit of well-specified principles for instruction are accelerating (Glaser and Bassok, 1989). Significant studies are under way of instructional programs that facilitate the transition from declarative to more proceduralized functional knowledge (Anderson *et al.*, 1984; Lewis, *et al.*, 1988), the use of self-regulatory processes that foster learning and understanding (Brown and Palincsar, 1989; Collins, *et al.*, 1989), and the processes of knowledge interrogation that contribute to the development of the structured knowledge that enables expert problem solving (Clancey, 1986; White and Frederiksen, 1986). With the expansion of experimental programs that are grounded in well-articulated instructional principles, both theoretical and applied work on learning will gain in precision and effectiveness. With studies of expertise as the groundwork, a science of learning can make the path to proficiency one that is well marked and can be more readily followed than ever before.

Acknowledgement

Preparation of this chapter was sponsored in part by the national Center for Student Learning at the Learning Research and Development Center of the University of Pittsburgh. The national Center for Student Learning is funded by the Office of Educational Research and Improvement of the U.S. Department of Education.

References

Anderson, J. R., Boyle, C. F., and Yost, G. (1985) The geometry tutor. *Proceeding of the International Joint Conference in Artificial Intelligence*, pp. 1–7, Los Angeles.

Anderson, J. R., Farrell, R., and Sauers, R. (1984) Learning to program in LISP, *Cognitive Science*, 8, pp. 87–129.

Bartholomae, D. (1985) Inventing the university, in M. Rose (ed.) *When a writer can't write: Studies in writer's block and other composing-process problems* (pp. 134–165), New York: Guilford Press.

Bridwell, L. S. (1980) Revising strategies in twelfth grade students' transactional writing, *Research in the Teaching of English*, 14, pp. 197–222.

Brown, A. , and Campione, J. (1990) Communities of learning and thinking, or a context by any other name, in D. Kuhn (ed.) *Development Perspectives on Teach-*

ing and Learning Thinking Skills. Contributions to Human Development, Basel: Karger 21, 108–126.

Brown, A. L., and Palincsar, A. (1989) Guided, co-operative learning and individual knowledge acquisition, in L. B. Resnick (ed.) *Knowing and learning: Essays in honor of Robert Glaser* (pp. 393–451), Hillsdale, NJ: Lawrence Erlbaum Associates.

Chase, W. G., and Simon, H. A. (1973) Perception in chess, *Cognitive Psychology*, 4, pp. 55–81.

Chi, M. T. H., Bassok, M., Lewis, M. W., Reimann, P., and Glaser, R. (1989) Self explanations: How students study and use examples in learning to solve problems, *Cognitive Science*, 13, pp. 145–182.

Chi, M. T. H., Glaser, R., and Rees, E. (1982) Expertise in problem solving, in R. J. Sternberg (ed.) *Advances in the psychology of human intelligence* (pp. 7–70), Hillsdale, NJ: Lawrence Erlbaum Associates.

Clancey, W. J. (1986) From Guidon to Neomycin and Hercules in twenty short lessons: ONR final report 1979–1985, *AI Magazine*, 7, pp. 40–60.

Collins, A., Brown, J. S., and Newman, S. E. (1989) Cognitive apprenticeship: Teaching the crafts of reading, writing and mathematics, in L. B. Resnick (ed.) *Knowing, learning, and instruction: Essays in honor of Robert Glaser* (pp. 453–494), Hillsdale, NJ: Lawrence Erlbaum Associates.

Egan, D. and Schwartz, B. (1979) Chunking in recall of symbolic drawings, *Memory and Cognition*, 7, pp. 149–158.

Flower, L., Hayes, J. R., Carey, L., Schriver, K., and Stratman, J. (1986) Detection, diagnosis, and the strategies of revision, *College Composition and Communications*, 37, pp. 16–55.

Glaser, R. (1981) The future of testing: A research agenda for cognitive psychology and psychometrics *American Psychologist*, 36, pp. 923–936.

Glaser, R., and Bassok, M. (1989) Learning theory and the study of instruction *Annual Review of Psychology*, 40, pp. 631–666.

Greeno, J. G. and Simon, H. A. (1988) Problem Solving and Reasoning, in R. C. Atkinson, R. Hernstein, G. Lindzey and R. D. Luce (eds.) Stevens' *Handbook of Experimental Psychology* (pp. 589–672), New York: Wiley.

Hatano, G., and Inagaki, K. (1986) Two courses of expertise in H. Stevenson, H. Azuma, and K. Hakuta (eds.) *Child development and education in Japan* (pp. 262–272), New York: W. H. Freeman.

Larkin, J. H. (1979) Processing information for effective problem solving, *Engineering Education*, 70, pp. 285–288.

Larkin, J., McDermott, J., Simon, D. P. and Simon, H. A. (1980) Models of competence in solving physics problems, *Cognitive Science*, 4, pp. 317–345.

Lesgold, A., Rubinson, H., Feltovich, P., Glaser, R., Klopfer, D. and Wang, Y. (1988) Expertise in a complex skill: Diagnosing x-ray pictures, in M. T. H. Chi, R. Glaser, and M. Farr (eds.) *The nature of expertise* (pp. 311–432), Hillsdale, NJ: Lawrence Erlbaum Associates.

Lewis, M. W., Milson, R., and Anderson, J. R. (1988) Designing an intelligent authoring system for high school mathematics ICAI: The teacher apprentice project, in G. Kearsley (ed.) *Artificial intelligence and instruction: Applications and methods*, New York: Addison-Wesley.

McDermott, J. and Larkin, J. H. (1978) Re-representing textbook physics problems, in *Proceedings of the 2nd National Conference of the Canadian Society for Computational Studies of Intelligence* (pp. 156–164), Toronto: University of Toronto Press.

Paige, J. M., and Simon, H. A. (1966) Cognitive processes in solving algebra word problems, in B. Kleinmuntz (ed.), *Problem solving* (pp. 51–118), New York: Wiley.

Schneider, W. (1985) Training high performance skills: Fallacies and guidelines, *Human Factors*, 27, pp. 285–300.

Schoenfeld, A. H. (1985) *Mathematical problem solving*, New York: Academic Press.

Simon, D. P., and Simon, H. A. (1978) Individual differences in solving physics problems, in R. Siegler (ed.) *Children's thinking: What develops?* (pp. 325–348), Hillsdale, NJ: Lawrence Erlbaum Associates.

Simon, H. A. (1973) The structure of ill-structured problems, *Artificial Intelligence*, 4, pp. 181–201.

Voss, J. F., and Post, T. A. (1988) On the solving of ill-structured problems in M. T. H. Chi, R. Glaser, and M. Farr (eds.) *The nature of expertise* (pp. 261–286), Hillsdale, NJ: Lawrence Erlbaum Associates.

Vygotsky, L. S. (1978) *Mind in society: The development of higher psychological processes*, Cambridge, MA: Harvard University Press.

White, B. Y., and Frederiksen, J. R. (1986) *Progressions of quantitative models as a foundation for intelligent learning environments* (Tech. Rep. No. 6277), Cambridge, MA: Bolt, Beranek and Newman.

8

Knowledge at Work

Sylvia Scribner

The enterprise before us – understanding the functional role of knowledge in the everyday world – is haunted by a metaphysical spectre. The spectre goes by the familiar name of Cartesian dualism, which, in spite of its age, continues to cast a shadow over inquiries into the nature of human nature. Cartesianism conceives of mind and behavior as two distinctly different modes of life, each requiring its own terms for description and explanation, each demanding its own method of investigation. Within this philosophical framework, questions about knowledge are referred to specialists of the mind, not to students of behavior.

Most investigations of knowledge carried out in the cognitive sciences today reflect this mentalistic approach to the study of knowledge. Many researchers worry about what it is that people of a particular culture know and how such knowledge is represented in the mind. There is debate whether knowledge is best represented as a semantic network (Anderson, 1976), a script (Schank and Abelson, 1977), or a categorical structure (Rosch, 1975). Other researchers study how knowledge is used in intellectual tasks; for example, in speech understanding (Reddy and Newell, 1974) or story comprehension (Stein and Glenn, 1979). Still others try to characterize the mental models underlying complex behavior, such as in navigation (Hutchins, 1980) and chess-playing (Chase and Simon, 1973). These approaches to the study of knowledge have many accomplishments to their credit. But the dominant image they present of the human knower resembles closely that of a computer: This knower is an intelligent system with a storehouse of knowledge and a set of programs, performing tasks in isolation. The knower neither interacts with other people nor engages in transactions with the environment. The question we are addressing here – how knowers use their knowledge to get about the world and accomplish things – fails to arise as a central theoretical question.

It is clear that to address the relationship between knowing and doing we need another conceptual apparatus – one that offers a monistic framework in which to pose our questions. My work on the social organization of cognition has been guided by one such framework, known as activity theory (Leontiev, 1979). Activity theory was launched 50 years ago by the Soviet psychologist Lev S. Vygotsky and developed by his successors in

---

This chapter has been edited.

psychology and philosophy. This theory holds that neither mind as such, nor behavior as such, can be taken as the principal category of analysis in the social and psychological sciences. Rather, the theory proposes that the starting point and primary unit of analysis should be culturally organized human activities. Activities are enduring, intellectually planned sequences of behavior, undertaken in the service of dominant motives and directed toward specific objects. They represent a synthesis of mental and behavioral processes. They can be analyzed on a molar level – as, for example, artistic activities, work activities, play activities – and they also can be analyzed in terms of their lower levels – the goal-directed actions that comprise them or the specific operations by which actions are carried out.

This is not the place for a full exposition of activity theory nor of how knowledge can be conceptualized with it. The approach I have taken represents knowledge as an integral component of activities, along with technologies (tools and sign systems) and functional skills systems. Knowledge and action have a reciprocal relationship. Goal-directed action guides the selection of information from the environment and its organization for the task at hand. Organized knowledge in turn guides goal-directed action. In any segment of action, these two processes occur in parallel, but they can be separated analytically into moments when one or the other dominates.

To make these notions more concrete, I will draw on some of my recent research on work (Scribner, 1984a) for examples of knowledge-action relationships. The studies I describe are modest and are meant to serve primarily as illustrations of some propositions I want to advance.

The field site for this research was a milk processing plant – a dairy – employing some 300 people. For present purposes, we can think of this dairy as a bounded social system within American society as a whole. The various occupations employed in the dairy may be considered socially organized and culturally shaped activities. Specific work tasks required in these occupations are goal-directed actions. Our overall research aim was to analyze the relationship between cognitive operations and behaviors in some of the principal work tasks in the dairy, and to do so within an activity theory framework.

We conducted several studies, addressing specifically the question of how action guides the acquisition and organization of knowledge. Just as many anthropologists choose to investigate folk knowledge of things in the environment that seem important to cultural activities – for example, plants, or stars – we chose to investigate a domain of things central to the dairy's activities – the domain of dairy products. All of us, as members of a consumer culture and as supermarket shoppers, know what dairy products are and the names of a great many of them. It comes as a surprise to learn, though, that the dairy that functioned as our research site produces and/or distributes more than 220 items under this general category.

The dairy uses order forms listing these items. Products are divided into kinds – fluid milk, cheese, fruit drinks, and so on. Items within these kinds vary by size and by qualitative characteristics such as flavor or fat content.

We examined dairy knowledge comparatively across five groups. Two groups represented consumers – employees of a language research institute and students from a public junior high school. Three groups represented major occupations in the dairy, selected for study because their work involves them in different kinds of actions with dairy products. Office workers comprised one group; they fill out, compute, or file company forms that require them to read or write product names; they do not handle the actual products. Warehouse assemblers read order forms listing certain products, locate these products in the warehouse, and send them out to be loaded on delivery trucks. Drivers handle the products on their trucks and distribute them to customers; in addition, they check the products against order forms and truck inventories and prepare delivery tickets carrying product names. In short, office workers act only with symbolic representations of dairy products; warehouse assemblers and drivers interact with products in both their symbolic and material forms, but they do so for different purposes and in different settings.

Our first assay at product knowledge took the form of a simple recall task.[1] We asked each dairy worker to name the products the dairy sold, just as they came to mind; and we asked consumers to name as many dairy products as they could recall. As one might imagine, although we pressed each person to name at least 25 items and placed no upper limit, dairy employees retrieved the names of many more dairy products than consumers. But let us concentrate here on a less predictable aspect of product knowledge: How do people with different backgrounds relate one dairy product to another?

The universe of products in the dairy is rich with properties; the warehouse is a panoply of colors, sizes, shapes, and substances. Goods can be linked to each other in multiple ways. Consider a paper quart of chocolate milk. It may be associated with skim *milk* as a member of a common kind category. Or it may be associated with *chocolate* drink by shared qualities of flavor and color; or linked with a *quart* of orange juice through size; or with a *paper* half pint of yogurt by the material of its container. This by no means exhausts the possibilities. Do these objective properties of the dairy product universe impose common organizing principles on everyone who uses or works with dairy products? We thought not. If the actions we engage in with objects influence how we organize knowledge about them, we would expect to find different populations using different properties to organize their recall. To test this possibility we analyzed each person's recall list, using our knowledge of the dairy products to identify associative links between successive items. Were two adjacent items linked together by kind, quality, size, or a combination of these or other attributes?

Consider first the diversity of attributes that individuals used to link one dairy product with another (Table 8.1, top portion). The greatest difference arises in the performance of consumers as compared with dairy workers. Consumers have an impoverished product network; on the average, they restrict product relationships to three or four attributes, or attribute clusters, compared to twice that number among dairy workers. Note that

Table 8.1　*Recall organization by product attribute*

	Consumers		Dairy Occupations		
	Students	Institute Employees	Office	Drivers	Warehouse
Mean number of different or compound attributes	4	3	8	8	12
Percent associative links of principal attributes					
Kind (e.g. *milk*)	92	95	42	26	23
Quality (e.g. *chocolate*)	0	2	1	0	1
Size (e.g. *quart*)	0	0	5	7	9
Container (e.g. *carton*)	1	0	0	0	1
Compound (e.g. *chocolate milk*)	7	3	52	67	66
Total (percent)	100	100	100	100	100

warehouse assemblers – the group, by the way, with the lowest average amount of schooling – have the most diversified ways of associating products.

Carrying the analysis further (Table 8.1, bottom portion), we find that consumer groups relied almost exclusively on the category *kind of product* to organize their recall. In contrast, only 42 percent of office workers' associations, and roughly one fourth of driver and warehouse assemblers' associations, consisted of simple links by product kind. Overwhelmingly, workers' dairy product associations were of a complex nature, involving several dimensions at once, such as quality and kind: *chocolate* homogenized *milk* linked to *chocolate* lowfat *milk*; or size and kind: *gallon* homogenized *milk* linked to *gallon* skim *milk*.

Thus far we have distinguished members of the dairy group from members of society at large. Occupational distinctions within the dairy become clearer in a second study of product knowledge. In this task, we presented people with names of 25 products, using the company descriptors, and asked them to sort these products into groups of items that went together.

As Table 8.2 indicates, consumers (institute employees and students) relied mainly on kind of product to constitute similarity groups. Dairy office workers resembled them in this respect, but on a small number of occasions they also used size as a defining feature. Workers in the two blue-collar occupations made greater use of size as a grouping principle. Warehouse assemblers were exceptions. One third of the time they sorted by location – an attribute that we had not built explicitly into the product list. Location refers to the area of the warehouse in which various goods are stored – a critical thing to know about dairy products if you spend eight hours every night fetching them.

These results would seem to indicate that different work tasks provide opportunities for people to learn different things about the products. *What you learn is bound up with what you have to do*. This is certainly the case,

Table 8.2 *Sorting organization by product attribute*

| | Distribution of Sort (Percent) | | | | |
| | Consumers | | Dairy Occupations | | |
	Students	Institute Employees	Office	Drivers	Warehouse
Product Attributes*					
Kind	77	91	85	67	36
Size	2	0	11	22	31
Location	0	0	0	0	32
Other**	21	9	4	11	1
Total (percent)	100	100	100	100	100

*The average number of groups into which items were sorted was 5.1 (students), 5.4 (institute employees), 4.6 (office workers), 4.5 (drivers), 4.3 (warehouse).

** This category included groups organized by place of sale, season of greatest use, and idiosyncratic reasons.

but it is an incomplete explanation of the findings. Warehouse assemblers are not the only ones to know where products are located. Many of the drivers first started working in the warehouse, and all are familiar with the general layout, yet not one of them used location as a grouping principle. Consider size also. When office workers encounter product names on company forms, they often see them written with the size specified. They have considerable exposure to information about size, but they rarely single it out as a defining feature of product clusters on this task. Only those currently working with size in its physical embodiment employed it as an organizing principle.

What do these findings suggest? Even when we are concerned with a domain of common knowledge in our society, we cannot assume that the richness of such knowledge or the attributes by which it is organized are uniform across population groups. Even within one social subsystem – exemplified here in the dairy – the structuring of a domain of common knowledge takes different forms for groups that are related functionally to that domain in different ways.

Dynamic factors, not merely static structural factors, are at work in the organization of knowledge. What factors influence the selection and organization of knowledge? These studies offer two intriguing clues. One is that the modality in which objects are most frequently encountered – whether in symbolic or material form – makes certain properties more salient than others as organizing principles. The second clue has to do with purpose – what people aim to accomplish in their actions. Certain object attributes may be essential to the performance of a task, just as product location is to a warehouse assembler, whereas others may be peripheral, and essential attributes come into play when people are asked to think about how things go together.

Now let us reverse our perspective and consider the knowledge-action relationship from the point of view of how knowledge guides action. For

research illustrations, we go to the dairy warehouse and take a closer look
at the product assembly task. Two assemblers typically work as a team.
They consult a truck order form that is kept at a centrally located stationary point. Each then initials items to be fetched on a single trip, locates
them, and carries them to a common assembly area. This sequence is
repeated until all items on a particular order form are assembled and sent
out to the loading platform, whereupon the assemblers begin on a new
truck order form. In the course of a night's work, a team may go through 50
or 60 order forms and assemble over 1,000 items. Since the warehouse
measures 145 by 45 feet, they have a lot of ground to cover. And they are
interested, as they explained to us, in organizing their work to save their
own backs and feet. Management's motivation is to have the work done as
speedily as possible – an interest that overlaps, although only in part, with
the workers' interest in saving effort.

How does knowledge enter into the organization of this task? To approach this question, we need to make a distinction between accumulated
social knowledge and knowledge in the heads of individual product assemblers. Over generations, the experience of thousands of people in the
dairy business has produced an environment and instruments that support
intelligent organization of work. Social knowledge is incorporated in the
way dairy products are stacked in the warehouse: milk, cheese, and fruit
drinks are not distributed at random but are assigned particular locations
depending on such considerations as proximity to the area in the plant
where the item is packaged, proximity to similar items, and floor space. The
warehouse organization from night to night remains constant in certain
respects, yet it also changes in response to such factors as size of inventory,
amount of production, and other fluctuating conditions.

In addition to being in the physical environment, organized social knowledge is embodied in the load-out order form from which assemblers get
their instructions. This form does not list items at random, but tends to
group them according to gross divisions (bulk products versus others, for
example) and roughly according to kinds. So assemblers work in a partially
stabilized environment and with an imperfectly organized order list. To
determine how they use this reified social knowledge, we observed one
team getting items for 22 truck load orders.

The first thing we noticed is that although assemblers sometimes fetch
one item at a time, they frequently sign off to get 2, 3, or 4 items in a single
trip. As they rush around the warehouse, this requires them to remember a
set of products and the quantities attached to each – to engage in extra
mental effort.

Second, we noticed that some of these groups were not composed of
successive items on the order form but consisted of items separated from
each other by a number of lines. For example, one group started with one
item, '16 gallons of sour cream,' omitted the next three products, included
the next two, omitted two, and then included the last item on the list. We
have no reason to think that groupings and reorganizations are haphazard.

It seems evident that assemblers organize list items in the service of their overall goal of saving steps. If this is the case, the actual trips they made using their groups of items should represent a savings in travel distance over alternative ways of using the product list.

This proposition was tested by applying the principles of graph theory (Ore, 1963) to a scale map of the warehouse.[2] Travel distances were estimated for the two assemblers we observed, under assumptions of different trip organizing principles.

First consider the worst case, the distance the assemblers would have had to travel if they had passively accepted the list as given and gone for one item at a time: 20,016 feet, or roughly four miles. Next, consider the case of a grouping strategy that adheres rigidly to the list item order. Frequencies were computed for groups of various sizes organized by the assemblers in their actual trips. We then assigned randomly the same number of these various-sized groups to the items as they were given on the list, working from top to bottom. In other words, the lists were segmented into the same number of groups of the same sizes, but these groups, unlike the actual ones, were composed of items in sequential order. This procedure gave us a measure of the savings effect of item order on the list. We might consider it to measure the efficiency of the social knowledge embodied in the given organization of product names on the order lists. This sequential grouping procedure was applied to the lists five times, with the following results: the mean travel distance for the five generations of sequential groups was 13,279 feet. (Individual calculations for each generation ranged from 12,632 to 13,942 feet.) When we calculated the distance for the trips the assemblers *actually* took (including all their single items, groups, and reorganizations) it amounted to 10,922 feet (see Table 8.3). This was a little more than two miles of walking, a savings of approximately 2,500 feet over the random groupings on the socially ordered list.

Assemblers accomplished this feat speedily; they did not linger over the load-out order forms, nor did they engage in discussions with each other as to how they were going to divide the list. To work in such a coordinated and efficient manner, each assembler needed to have some internally represented knowledge of the spatial arrangement of the warehouse that could be used flexibly to organize the items on hand. Each also needed some knowledge of the customary sequence of items, and recurring chunks of items, on the load-out order forms. With such knowledge (and, of course, much more) they elegantly mapped one organization on to the other – the symbolic onto the spatial – to meet their own needs and to satisfy externally imposed task requirements. Product assemblers creatively

Table 8.3 *Estimated travel distance for different trip organizations* * *(in feet)*

One item at a time	Successive items in random groups	Assemblers actual groups
20,016	13,279 (Average)	10,992

* After Scribner, Gauvain, and Fahrmeier (1984)

synthesized several domains of knowledge as a means of organizing and regulating their own actions.

This is a small set of empirical observations. Their principal usefulness will be to stimulate new ways of thinking about knowledge and practice that avoid the old entrenched dualisms. What we discovered in the dairy are the complexities of working knowledge – its dependence on forms of action and its regulation of forms of action. In the dairy, social knowledge is differentiated from, but not opposed to, individual knowledge. If social knowledge organizes the dairy – its physical environment and symbolic forms – individuals use this social knowledge creatively to shape work that is better adapted to human needs. We can only regret that our social institutions – industrial workplaces – are so organized as to limit the ways in which the thought and action of individual workers can turn back, enrich, and humanize social knowledge and practice.

Notes

Acknowledgments. Research cited was supported by a grant from the Ford Foundation. My collaborator in these studies was Edward Fahrmeier. All our studies have drawn on an extensive ethnography of the dairy provided by Evelyn Jacob.
[1] Studies described here are reported in detail in Scribner, 1984b.
[2] Special thanks are due to Mary Gauvain who devised and applied this method of analysis (Scribner, Gauvain, and Fahrmeier, 1984).

References

Anderson, J. R. (1976) *Language, Memory and Thought.* Hillsdale, NJ: Lawrence Erlbaum Associates.

Chase, W. G., and Simon, H. A. (1973) Perception in Chess, *Cognitive Psychology*, 4, pp. 55–81.

Hutchins, E. (1980) *Culture and Inference.* Cambridge, MA: Harvard University Press.

Leonitev, A. N. (1979) The Problem of Activity in Psychology. In J. V. Wertsch (ed.) *The Concept of Activity in Soviet Psychology* (pp. 37–71). Armonk, NY: M. E. Sharpe.

Ore, O. (1963) *Graphs and their Uses.* New York: Random House.

Reddy, R. and Newell, A. (1974) Knowledge and its Representation in a Speech Understanding System. In L. W. Gregg (ed.) *Knowledge and Cognition* (pp. 253–286). Potomac, MD: Lawrence Erlbaum.

Rosch, E. (1975) Cognitive Representations of Semantic Categories, *Journal of Experimental Psychology*, General 104, pp. 192–233.

Schank, R. and Abelson, R. P. (1977) *Scripts, Plans, Goals and Understanding.* Hillsdale, NJ: Lawrence Erlbaum Associates.

Scribner, S. (1984a) Studying Working Intelligence. In B. Rogoff and J. Lave (eds.) *Everyday Cognition: Its Development in Social Context* (pp. 9–40). Cambridge, MA: Harvard University Press.

Scribner, S. (ed) (1984b) Cognitive Studies of Work, Special Issue *The Quarterly Newsletter of the Laboratory of Comparative Human Cognition*, 6 (1, 2).

Scribner, S., Guavin, M., and Fahrmeier, E. (1984) Use of Spatial Knowledge in the Organization of Work, *The Quarterly Newsletter of the Laboratory of Comparative Human Cognition*, 6 (1, 2), pp. 32–33.

Stein, N., and Glenn, C. (1979) An Analysis of Story Comprehension in Elementary School Children. In R. Freedle (ed.) *New Directions in Discourse Processing 2.* Norwood, NJ: Ablex.

9

Practical Knowledge: A View from the Snooker Table[1]

Robert McCormick

Editors' Introduction

Drawing on the kinds of ideas discussed in earlier chapters (e.g. Chapters 3, 7 and 8), McCormick explores the nature of knowledge. In particular he illustrates how knowledge is situated and how that, far from being only typical of how learners 'think', it is characteristic of expert knowledge.

Introduction

Let me begin by setting out my basic argument. I want to put the case for a greater role for the teaching and learning of practical knowledge in the curriculum of educational institutions, at whatever level. This case has two strands. The first is that expertise in the world outside schools and colleges is characterised by the use of such knowledge. The second strand lies in our views of learning and its relationship with knowledge. One of our premises as teachers is that we teach academic or theoretical knowledge because it is applicable in all situations, unlike practical knowledge that is limited to particular situations. We assume that theoretical knowledge is decontextualised, and therefore that it can be transferred from the classroom and used in practical situations outside schools and colleges. I shall argue that this is not so straightforward. None of this should be construed as an attack on the teaching of theoretical knowledge, but a plea that we should also teach practical knowledge. Although most of my examples will relate to science, mathematics and technology, I think the argument applies to other areas of the curriculum.

First, I need to explain what I mean by the first part of my title, *Practical Knowledge*. The role of practical knowledge was brought home to me most graphically early in my teaching career. As a physics teacher in Hong Kong, I was approached by two of my A-level students who wanted to enter the local science fair by producing a steam turbine. As I had trained in the design and manufacture of steam turbines, I thought I was well qualified to help them. I got out my steam tables and calculated the design of blades for an expansion turbine, and drew up the plans. They were very enterprising and managed to get a local workshop to manufacture the turbine. Needless to say it didn't work. My knowledge related to relatively high-pressure turbines, and it was obviously over-designed, being too heavy a construction to ever move. So what use was all my knowledge, not only from thermodynamics lectures in college, but from my experience within the design office in the factory?

Not only is this topic of interest in the particular curriculum area of technology or engineering education, but for me it lies at the heart of current debates about the relationship and relative value of vocational and academic education. The core of the issue for me is the extent to which academic education is of practical use in the world outside educational institutions, not whether it fits a particular occupational task. Employers have long been worried about students who come from schools and universities, but who cannot perform in the workplace. They are not asking for less theory, quite the opposite, nor that students should be taught particular vocational skills, but employers are concerned that educational institutions are not providing students with knowledge that can be used. This is of course an old debate about the theory-practice divide, but it is an issue that we should continually revisit as educators.

I hope that now you can see in what sense I am using the term 'practical knowledge'.

Well you may still be wondering about the second part of my title. I have chosen it because it provides all the features of what I have to say about practical knowledge. Snooker players are not only skilled at hitting a ball, but know a thing or two about the movement of balls about the table. They have to contemplate the arrangement of balls on the table, and make predictions about the effects of particular shots. This contemplative thinking in snooker is unique among ball games. I am interested in what it is that snooker players know and how that compares with the abstract knowledge of physicists and mathematicians. For these latter theorists the snooker table offers an unparalleled piece of reality, where motion is in two dimensions, friction relatively low, balls that impact with near perfect collisions, in short conditions that conform to the usual assumptions mathematicians and physicists like to make. The contrast between these theorists and snooker players provides, as I say, an illustration of the argument I want to explore in relation to practical knowledge and its contrast with the academic knowledge that is the basis of so much of our education.

The Snooker Table

Let me turn to the snooker table. The kind of knowledge about the movement of balls that is typical of an elementary level of snooker can be seen in the World Professional Billiards and Snooker Association *Basic skills* coaching video. Such videos, like many books on snooker, typically describe the various potting angles, how to hit the cue (white) ball to produce various kinds of spin, and the effect of that spin on the motion of the ball along the table and when it hits an object (coloured) ball or bounces off the cushion. The language of the commentary is quite unlike that of physics, and in particular the discussion of how to hit the ball and the resulting effects is carried out entirely in qualitative terms. For example:

- the angles of potting, described in terms of half-ball, three-quarter ball and full-ball (this is the amount of the object ball that can be seen when looking down the cue; for example, only half the object ball can be seen past the cue ball), rather than in terms of degrees;
- the clock positions used to describe where to hit the cue ball for various kinds of spin (hit the ball at six o'clock [at the bottom] to get bottom spin), and the resulting motion of it and the object ball.

Despite this, predictions can be made with considerable accuracy, and take in a number of features of a situation: the speed that the cue ball needs to be hit, the type of spin, the angle of the shot to ensure a pot, the distance of travel of the cue ball to the object ball, and for that ball to subsequently travel to the pocket, where the cue ball will then go for the next shot, and even, in the case of professional players, to help the two shots after that.[2] The margin for error can be quite small.

How does this compare with the mathematicians and physicists? In fact as early as the nineteenth century there were French and British texts that gave definitive accounts of the motion of balls on the snooker (or billiards) table (Coriolis, 1835; Hemming, 1899).[3] Hemming considers not only the mathematical equations to predict outcomes of ball interactions, but also indicates considerable empirical evidence from the motion of balls on a billiard table; he tries to relate all his findings to those of the billiard player. Let me consider how mathematicians, contemporary and past, deal with snooker, by considering a number of examples.

Example 1: Where the Cue Ball Goes after Impact

A recent statistical treatment of snooker ball potting started with the assumption that the path of the cue ball after impact was to be ignored, including the possibility of making foul shots (Percy, 1994). Percy derives a function that allows the probability of a successful pot to be combined with the gain of the score of that pot to compare the various shots that a snooker player could take. He concludes this derivation:

> The obvious gain from a successful pot is the score corresponding to the value of the object-ball. Often the cue-ball position after the shot is crucial in deciding longer-term and potentially more expensive gains and losses. Similarly, if the assumptions that foul strokes are avoidable is dropped, the possibility of losses

due to foul strokes must also be considered. Since the complexity of the problem increases substantially when cue-ball positioning and foul strokes are considered, it is simplest and most appropriate to use the object-ball value only as the gain function for each attempted pot.

(Percy, 1994, p. 590)

This treatment was aimed at helping players improve their predictions of whether a ball could be successfully potted. Indeed he suggests that players could take measurements at the table and with a graphical calculator could calculate the gain functions to decide which shot to make. However, what novice player would suggest making such assumptions, i.e. that what happens to the cue ball after it hits a red or a coloured ball does not matter? Perhaps that is why snooker players are paid more than mathematicians!

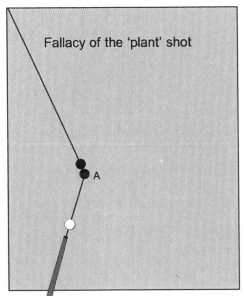

Figure 9.1   *Fallacy of the 'plant' shot*

Example 2: The Plant

Figure 9.1 shows a situation in which two object balls are in contact such that the line that joins their centres is in line with the pocket. If the cue ball is aimed directly at the object ball A (what players would call a 'full-ball shot'), the other object ball will pot every time. This is what is known as a 'plant' in the game. A contemporary mathematician, Mackie, using the typical diagram in his analysis deals with the error in potting (Figure 9.2), and makes the usual assumptions:

> If the balls are assumed to be smooth, thus creating no tangential component of impulse at impact the direction of the subsequent motion of B [the object ball] is that of the line of centres at impact.

(Mackie, 1982, pp. 82–3)

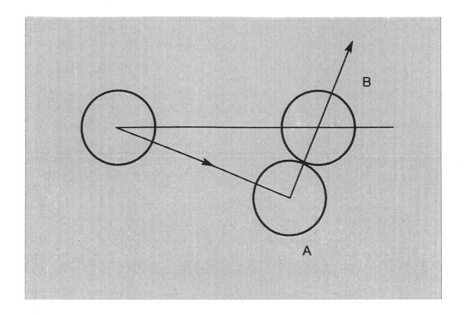

Figure 9.2 *A typical diagram of cue and object ball directions of motion*

The famous snooker player Joe Davis (1964, pp. 53–54) says that this plant will only work if the object ball is around 200–300 millimetres from the pocket or whenever the angle of the cue ball on the object ball is less than a three-quarter ball. Under these conditions the plant will work. Contrary to the basic science and mathematics theory assumption that with two smooth balls the force of impact acts in the line of their centres (no force can act perpendicular to this line because there is no friction), Davis' explanation is that the nap surface creates friction,[5] such that there is a 'squeeze' that diverts the object ball from the line that it would take 'if the angles were exact and according to Euclid' (p. 54). Indeed he makes quite a thing about the instincts of most novices and the theory of mathematicians both being wrong with respect to being able to choose the potting angle:

> you cannot trust yourself to a knowledge of geometry, or to any instinctive hunches about angles in snooker . . . trust only to your *knowledge* of an angle, based on experience and memory.
>
> (Davis, 1964, p. 54)

He relies on constant experimentation, noting after each attempt the error in the object ball at the pocket, to arrive at his 'knowledge'.

Example 3: Friction between the Balls

Hemming is more sensitive to the realities than some other mathematicians and scientists. For example, when trying to determine the effect of the

friction between balls he gives a demonstration of an action hitting the cue ball to send the object ball along the baulk line, but the object ball returning at an angle to the baulk line. In Figure 9.3, the (white) cue ball is hit towards the (red) object ball, such that the red ball goes along the baulk line. If the normal physicist's assumption of no friction between balls is borne out (the quote from Mackie, 1982, above), then the object ball would return along the baulk line. But it does not. This is the effect of transmitted or transferred spin (side). Contemporary mathematical treatments ignore this because, for most conditions, it does not matter (e.g. Mackie, 1982 and 1986). However, knowledge of this is crucial for cue ball positioning subsequent to its impact with the object ball.

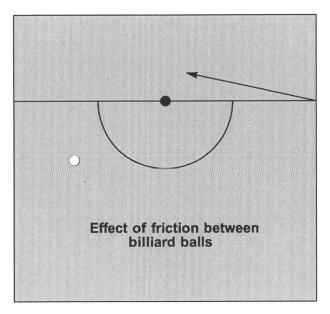

Effect of friction between billiard balls

Figure 9.3   *Effect of friction between billiard balls*

In reviewing these examples, what distinguishes the two contemporary scholars (Mackie and Percy) from Hemming is not their mathematical skill, but their purposes. Mackie and Percy are concerned to show that basic classical mechanics or statistical methods can be used to predict motion and snooker provides an illustration of theory.[4] Hemming, by contrast, clearly wants to treat mathematically the game of billiards, and he is careful to set his findings against what players expect, if necessary by empirical tests at the table (such as in Example 3). His focus is on the game and the particularities of the context, which he takes seriously. Mackie and Percy focus on the mathematics. Hemming is, however, convinced of the power of the theory and ends his account rather optimistically:

there is no one of the conclusions to which science has led us, . . . which has not
been arrived at by rule-of-thumb by players who have not professed any scientific
knowledge at all. It is interesting, however, to note that the conclusions from our
scientific inquiry are absolutely in harmony with the established rules of practice.
For comparatively untrained players, they have, moreover, some practical value.
A rule-of-thumb is as good as a scientific law to a man who has played often and
well enough to regard the rule-of-thumb as a necessary law of Nature. Amateurs
of less experience than this may find it much easier to obey a law, the reason of
which they have grasped, than to follow a rule merely because a highly-
developed billiard-maker has told them to do so.

(Hemming, 1899, p. 34)

While Hemming may have demonstrated the power of scientific knowledge to explain most of what professionals do (though I think there are
some limitations), his prediction about what will help novices is groundless.
As I will show, there is good reason to believe that much of the science
taught is not useful to amateurs (novices or learners) in the way he hopes.

Having shown that there are some limits to the mathematics, and that in
any case real snooker players follow a different approach to the theorists, I
want to draw out some general issues that I will then relate to research
findings. When taken together, these will give us some insight into the
nature of practical knowledge and lead to some important educational
implications. First, I indicated that snooker players, as experts about what
happens on the table, use considerable *qualitative knowledge*. This qualitative knowledge contrasts with that provided by the theory drawn from
mathematics and science. Not only does it contrast in style (e.g. references
to half-ball etc., rather than angles measured in degrees), but also in its
ability to deal with the complexity of reality (e.g. taking into account transmitted spin). Second, their knowledge is quite specific to the context and,
though that may reduce its generality (i.e. it may not apply to other situations), an understanding of this context is critical to make sense and use of
the theoretical and abstract knowledge of science. I will show later that this
identification of knowledge with a context is in fact a characteristic of
human learning, and that knowing 'abstractions' does not ensure that they
can be used in a particular situation. This assumption, commonly known as
'transfer', lies behind Hemming's assumption about the help that science
could give to novices.

I will examine these general issues in the next sections.

Qualitative Knowledge

Snooker players are not the only experts who use qualitative knowledge. It
is already well understood in the field of problem solving, for example in
physics, that experts always start to work on problems by thinking about
them in qualitative terms (Glaser, 1984; 1992). This stands in stark contrast
to how we start novices off on learning how to do such problem solving:

invariably with the figures and equations, working without much overall understanding of what they are doing. Chris Dillon, in his account of qualitative approaches used by experts, characterises them by the degree to which they reflect the device (that is to be controlled or understood) on the one hand, in contrast to the mathematics (or science) model that could be used to represent the device's operation on the other (Dillon, 1994). For example Joe Davis, on the effects of side spin, reasons qualitatively about the motion of a ball:

> Thus, if left-hand side is applied, the cue-ball is first of all pushed out to the right, and if right-hand side is used it starts its journey by going out to the left. How much to right or left it goes, and for what distance this drift is continued, depends on how much side is applied and at what speed . . . Given time and distance, the ball will recover; the driving force will fade, and the spinning ball will react to the nap[5] . . . and the ball will swing back.
>
> (Davis, 1967, p. 62)

This reflects the physical nature of the snooker table, and is in contrast to the sets of equations used by mathematicians, such as Hemming.

Even in the relatively simple world of the snooker table, theoretical knowledge is not adequate to cope with all situations; or at least is not worth the increased complexity that it creates in the solutions offered by the theory (e.g. in Percy's analysis). In more complex systems, such as those found in chemical or power-generation plants, the possibility of relying entirely upon theoretical knowledge to represent their operation is unrealistic, and beyond what is possible or at least sensible. Understanding the operational principles is necessary when automatic systems are required and so, in the field of artificial intelligence, researchers have turned to the qualitative reasoning of experts upon which to base the computer programs to run such plants. In complex systems that are to be controlled by computers, there is a need to recover the physical reality stripped away by scientific representations.

Let me illustrate the kind of complexity where qualitative approaches are useful, and do this in the context of a simple mechanism. As part of our research into problem solving in design and technology lessons in the first three years of secondary schools, Patricia Murphy and colleagues observed two 12-year-old girls working on a mechanism that was used to collect money for charity.[6] Figure 9.4 shows the mechanism, a woodpecker pecking when money is put in. The mechanism contains a number of components (Figure 9.5): a falling coin channelled (A) to hit a balanced beam (B) with an integral pendulum (C), with an off-set pivot (D) connected to a bird shape on the other side (E), that would rock to peck a tree trunk (F). The operational principle in this context is the overall mechanism; each of the components (e.g. the falling coin, the pendulum) could be understood with science, and made to operate successfully. For example, varying the distance of fall of the coin to allow enough momentum to be gained so that even a small coin would cause rocking; balancing the beam horizontally by altering the off-set pivot, such that the beam would move on impact. Now

Figure 9.4a　*A woodpecker money collection box (front view)*

Figure 9.4b　*A woodpecker money collection box (rear view)*

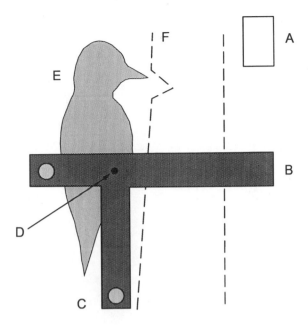

Figure 9.5   *The components of the woodpecker money collection box*

the science of this is well beyond children of this age, and it would be likely that even a professional engineer would be hard pushed to put down all the quantitative science and mathematics to represent the operation of such a system as a whole. Of course it wouldn't be worth it! Any engineer would use qualitative reasoning to ensure a working mechanism. There would be some experimenting with the size of coins on simple beams to determine the amount of fall necessary, and similarly with the counter weight on the beam (the beam size is a function of the overall size of the money box), and so on. It might look like trial and error, but in fact it would be qualitative reasoning supported by a knowledge of science. However, it would be a level of science at a much simpler level than required for the full explanation of the operation of individual components.

The qualitative reasoning is not just a feature of the way an engineer might work, but also of the two girls and their teacher. In our classroom research of this project we recorded their reasoning at three points. The first is at the beginning of the project when the students go to the teacher with their idea of a woodpecker that pecks a tree when money is put in the box. Figure 9.6 shows the teacher illustrating the rocking movement with his hand. As he does this he says 'Transmit movement [from lever[7] to bird] to the front . . .', and then tells the students that they must lock the pivot to the lever 'to make sure it runs . . . [with the lever]'. Neither of these statements draws on much conventional science and the wording is close to the physical nature of the mechanism.

Figure 9.6   *Teacher illustrating rocking motion with his hand*

The second point we observed was when, later in the first lesson, they started to model the mechanism in card, working from an example mechanism of a rocking boat. The girls try to decide on the positions of the components, including the bird, based on how much the beam moves for different size coins. At first one girl tries to locate the bird (cut out as a separate piece) relative to the tree trunk that she is trying to draw on the front cover sheet. She starts with the bird in its normal upright position and then rocks it, saying: 'It'll be in that position first of all, then it's going to go knock, knock.' The 'knock' is the sound of the bird pecking the tree. She then moves to the example mechanism and reasons about how it operates with different sized coins:

> P: It depends how much money they put in, because if it's a 50p, it's going to go 'dong' like that, so it's going to go really far.

> P: Then if it's a 5p . . . it will still move . . . but only a little bit . . .

The girl is using language that reflects the object ('dong' the sound a big coin makes), and it is qualitative in the way it describes the amount of movement ('really far', 'a little bit').

In the second week of the project, when they are making the actual mechanism the students went to the teacher for help and he said they had to balance the beam. This was done with BluTack as the counterweight on the left-hand end of the beam (Figure 9.5). He used phrases such as:

> Balance that [lever] up with a bit of BluTack . . . stick another bit on it . . .

The further over you get it [BluTack] . . . some more leverage . . . it's beginning to balance now.

There are some scientific ideas involved, but it is very qualitative, with language close to the operation of the mechanism.

Such qualitative reasoning could be improved if it was the focus of the learning, and I will return to this in the final part of the chapter. In the end they are working out the effect of dropping different sized coins, and the way that effect works its way through the mechanism, much as the effect of spin worked through the motion of the snooker ball in Joe Davis' explanation. This reflects the approach of the causal accounts that Dillon (1994) describes as one kind of 'qualitative reasoning' that is being formalised as a way of dealing with complex situations. He also notes that these are the kinds of explanations of electronic circuits found in undergraduate texts, and our researches on design and technology have indicated similar teacher explanations for circuits in secondary schools (Levinson *et al.*, 1997; Mc-Cormick and Murphy, 1994).

The usual way in which we think about explaining devices and systems, such as mechanisms or electric circuits, is to use knowledge from science. A number of assumptions underlie this. The first is that the science does indeed explain the devices. Layton (1993) has reminded us of Polanyi's idea of the *operational principle*, which according to Polanyi, determines how components in, say a machine, fulfil their functions and combine in an overall operation that achieves the function of the machine (Polanyi, 1962, p. 328). Layton contrasts this operational principle, as technological knowledge, with that of science; science he argues cannot contrive such a principle, but can explain the success and failure of it, and lead to improvement of it. This then sees science and mathematics in a supportive role, not a determining role, and the idea of technology as the 'appliance of science', as Zanussi uses in its advertisements, is a misrepresentation of the situation. This is evident in the case of the mechanism of the money-box. A second assumption is that when individuals are in a practical situation that typically occurs in technology, the science they have learned in science lessons (at whatever level) is usable in the practical situation. (Here I consider this science to have been taught in an abstract and theoretical way, as I characterised the approach science and mathematics adopts to the snooker table.) This second assumption itself has two parts: that the individuals understood the theory in the science lesson, and that they can 'transfer' it to another context. I am aware that even phrasing the assumption in these ways is to have a particular view about how people learn these kinds of abstractions, and so I want to turn to this next.

Problems with Learning Abstractions

The reason we teach Newton's laws of motion and not, for example snooker, in science lessons is that these laws are general and not bound by any particular context. It is assumed that the science knowledge is abstract and hence independent of context, in other words it is 'decontextualised knowledge'. I will indicate that this is not actually true, and contains a misunderstanding of the nature of knowledge. That we need abstract and symbolic knowledge such as science and mathematics is beyond dispute, but that people understand it in some abstract and symbolic form in their heads, is more difficult to sustain. First, let me examine the importance of context in learning.

The Importance of Context

The BBC television programme *Simple Minds* contained an examination of how science is learned, including some of the research of the Harvard Smithsonian Institute for Astrophysics, one part of which was video recordings of Massachusetts Institute of Technology graduates. As they came off the stage having been presented with their degree certificates, these graduates were asked what they thought a piece of wood was made of and in some cases if they could connect up an electrical circuit. In the case of the wood they did not know that its mass was the result of the photosynthesis of the carbon dioxide in the air, rather they thought it came from the soil. Indeed when they were told that it was made from carbon dioxide some thought it counter-intuitive; how could a gas that was light turn into a heavy piece of wood. When the graduates were given a bulb, wires and a battery they often could not connect it correctly, with one student saying 'I'm a mechanical engineer, not an electrical engineer!'

Now putting aside the fact that these students were caught on the hop, and no doubt thought that they would never again have to answer such questions, what explains their apparent misunderstanding of the most basic of science ideas? These students clearly can operate with complex science and mathematics, and if they can't, as graduates of the 'premier science and technology institution in the USA' (as the students are described in the programme), there would be little hope for the rest of us! The complex knowledge would have been learned within the specific context of the educational institution and geared to completing assignments and examinations that are peculiar to such institutions. Even where some of the tasks may have come from the real world, the context of understanding is quite specific. My personal story of designing the steam turbine for my students is an illustration of the same phenomenon. Others have shown by more systematic interviewing of university science students that they cannot provide adequate explanations of apparently simple situations such as throwing a ball up in the air and catching it (diSessa, 1996). In quite a different field of work Dahlgren (1984) has shown how economics undergraduates, when asked about the price of a bun from a bakery, gave replies that were typical of those ordinary citizens would give (e.g. relating it to the cost of materials and labour), and none used their economic knowledge (e.g.

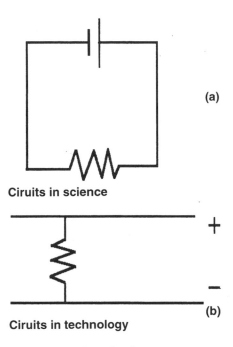

Ciruits in science

(a)

Ciruits in technology

(b)

Figure 9.7   *Circuits in (a) science (b) technology*

relating it to market forces). In all these situations the students have *not* been learning 'decontextualised knowledge', but knowledge tied to the problems and situations that they have faced within the educational setting.

The Harvard researchers showed more graphically how knowledge is linked to context in their work in high school science lessons. The programme showed a girl who had done some work on simple electric circuits using standard science lesson equipment (battery, bulb, bulb-holder, and wires). Prior to this work in science she was able to connect up a battery to light the bulb using only wires. When, in an interview, she was given the materials she had used in the science lesson, she drew a circuit diagram that would get full marks in a test, but, as she connected up the circuit, she insisted that the circuit needed the bulb-holder. Even when pressed by the interviewer, she said the circuit would not work without it, and was astounded when it did. Thus, when this girl learned about electric circuits she associated bulb-holders as a necessary part of the circuit. Imagine this girl before she had that misunderstanding corrected going into a technology lesson, where she will be confronted not with wires, bulbs and bulb holders but ceramic resistors and printed circuit boards. What is she to make of these, and how is she to 'transfer' the ideas from the science lesson to the technology lesson? Not only are the physical items different, but the representations can be different; in science she will see a circuit represented in an abstract form as a circular path (albeit in a the form of a square!), and its equivalent in technology would quite different (Figure 9.7). There is an enormous amount of research in science education that indicates the difficulties that children have with learning abstract science ideas (e.g. Driver *et al.*, 1985; Osborne and Freyberg, 1985). It is unlikely therefore that they will be able to use that knowledge in other situations, such as in the technology class, let alone outside school or college. This issue of context is at the heart of the difficulties with the 'transfer' idea, but before confronting this, I want to go back one step to our understanding of the nature of knowledge that comes from studies in situated cognition and learning, and also from traditional cognitive psychology.

Knowledge and Activity

Most of us no doubt assume that knowledge is in the head, and that we dig it out of our memory banks to use it for some task (whether that task is of the kind we find in schools or colleges, or ones that are part of daily life). There are a collection of approaches to cognition and learning that argue that knowledge is integrated with activity, along with the tools, sign systems and skills associated with the activity. In this sense knowledge guides action, and action guides knowledge. This is not just an individual affair, as some of the knowledge may be accumulated social knowledge. A classic study illustrating this inter-relationship of knowledge and activity was of dairy workers (Scribner, 1985). Each of the groups of dairy workers had their thinking organized by the kinds of activity they engaged in. But their knowledge also guided action. Looking at this from the point of learning (i.e. to be a dairy worker), Scribner (1985) concludes that 'What you learn is bound up with what you have to do.' (p. 203)

Transfer: The Wrong Metaphor?

Let me now return to the second part of the assumption about how abstract knowledge like mathematics and science is used in a practical context, such as would be found in technology, namely that of transfer. I have tried to show that there is an accumulation of evidence that relates knowledge to the social and physical context where that knowledge is used and learned. That being so, then the mathematics and science lessons in schools and colleges, and hence the knowledge learned there, are as much context-specific as that learned elsewhere. No doubt there is a level of abstraction that does allow it to be applicable elsewhere, but the evidence on both context-dependence and the link between activity and knowledge means that there are formidable obstacles to its transfer from these lessons to use in the world beyond. This is not the place to go into the literature on transfer, for the debates rage on to the extent that whole books and journal issues can be given over to the dispute.[8] It is hard to know whom to believe, when the most famous advocate of situated cognition, Jean Lave, can give a whole chapter of a book convincingly showing that most of the transfer studies have failed to show much evidence of transfer (Lave, 1988), only to have this dismissed by advocates of symbolic cognition (Anderson *et al.*, 1996), that is those who believe that we store in our minds symbolic representations that we recall for use in particular situations. I don't want to rehearse these debates here, but to draw attention to two points that the advocates of symbolic cognition make. The first is that the conditions under which transfer will take place depend on a match between the situation where the learning took place and the situation where the knowledge is used. This doesn't look much like transfer ('transportation' might be a better word). The second point Anderson *et al.* (1996) make is that we need to pay more attention to the cues that signal the relevance of skill (or knowledge).

In the second point lies the heart of the matter for me: where and what the cues are. Typically students learn some mathematical or scientific idea, and then move on to problems that require them to use it. The idea is for the student to strip out the context and 'see' the science or mathematics.[9] The salience, to use the technical term, lies in the science concepts, equations etc. This is the point I made much earlier about the way mathematicians treated snooker. Their concern was with the mathematics, not the snooker. On the other hand, the practical situation has salience located in the features of the context. Learners, like the girl who attributed salience to the bulb-holder in the electric circuit, need to come to understand where the salience is. In the science lesson it is in the stripped away situation; in the real world it is embedded in the context. Thus the shot to play in snooker needs to be considered in terms of the complex conditions in the table (the ball positions, the nap, the run of the table etc.). Under these circumstances learning the salience or the 'cues', as Anderson *et al.* (1996) describe it, is what should be the focus, not, in my view, transfer.

The Nature of Practical Knowledge

I hope that by now I have started to clarify the nature of practical knowledge. In the first section I tried to show how it was qualitative in nature and that this was not just to do with how situations are described, but how actions were reasoned about. This qualitative view reflects the context-specific nature of knowledge. But there is one hole in my jigsaw, that I have yet to fill. To do this I want to give another example from the research of some of my colleagues. We have developed our work on problem solving in design and technology projects to consider how children use mathematics in such projects. My colleague, Hilary Evens, observed several teachers teaching orthographic projection, a topic dealt with in 'technical drawing', although in mathematics it is called 'plans and views' (see Figure 9.8). In observations we have made of a teacher explaining how to make an orthographic projection we find, not surprisingly, that he focuses on procedures. Some of his words indicate this:

guidelines, all lined up
drop down (the vertical lines)
project the information round
transfers the sizes

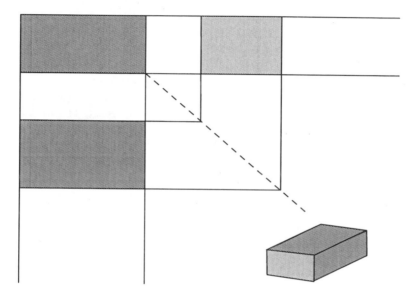

Figure 9.8   *Orthographic projection of a cuboid*

Hilary Evens has compared this kind of approach with that typical of mathematics classrooms, where the focus is on concepts.[10] Table 9.1 is a comparison of what the technology teacher says with the ideas a mathematics teacher might want to teach or use.

Table 9.1   *Comparison of terms used by technology and mathematics teachers in orthographic projection*

Technology teacher	Mathematics teacher
guidelines, all lined up	parallel lines
drop down (the vertical lines)	perpendicular lines
project the information round	reflection on line of symmetry
transfers the sizes	transformation

We have characterised this difference in terms of the technology teacher's concern with procedural knowledge and the mathematics teacher's concern with *conceptual knowledge*. Incidentally, it is also evident that one of the reasons that the technology teacher does not articulate concepts such as 'parallel lines' or 'perpendicular lines' is that these ideas are incorporated into the T-squares and set-squares that are the tools used in this kind of drawing (and not used in mathematics). This is another illustration of the way knowledge is bound in with context (in this case the tools), a central idea of those who argue for the situated nature of cognition.

Some cognitive scientists go as far as to define practical knowledge entirely in procedural terms (Sternberg and Carvso, 1985), but my concern here is to explore its nature not to create definitions. Nor is this the place to discuss conceptual and procedural knowledge, but research in a variety of fields indicates that it is necessary to link them both for effective action.[11] As I noted earlier, however, in the area of 'real-world' tasks it is *device* knowledge that makes procedural knowledge such as fault finding, for example, successful. As the complexity of devices increases so does the importance of the interaction of device knowledge and procedural knowledge (Gott, 1988, p. 120). Note here it is 'device' knowledge, not the conceptual abstractions of mathematics or science, though of course I am not implying that this conceptual knowledge is unimportant. Nor am I implying that abstract knowledge should not be part of education.

Educational Implications

I think my jigsaw is complete, so now let me draw lessons for education that try to take practical knowledge seriously. To do this I will return to the snooker table! The collision of snooker balls is a favourite 'context' for physics educators to illustrate such things as Newton's laws of motion (as Mackie (1986) was advocating). At secondary school level this use of snooker only extends to simple ideas about balls hitting cushions and being reflected. The Assessment of Performance Unit carried out research on assessment questions, and tried out different contexts for assessing the same kind of science.[11] Students aged 13 were given a series of drawings and asked which one was different or did not conform to the others (see Figure 9.9). Contexts included an abstract drawing (as shown in Figure 9.9), one that represented light rays reflecting off a mirror, and the other snooker balls bouncing off the cushion. Students do better when answering the question set in the snooker context than in the abstract situation, with boys doing very much better than girls except on the abstract situation (Assessment of Performance Unit, 1984a, p. 94). A consideration of the different pastimes of boys and girls surveyed by the APU, as shown in Figure 9.10, indicate why there may be this difference (APU, 1984a, p. 19).

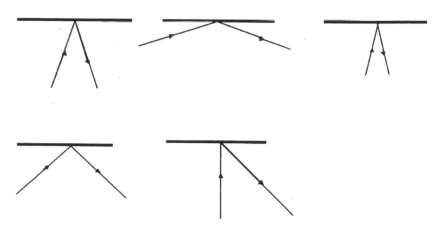

Figure 9.9   *Assessment of Performance Unit question of reflection*

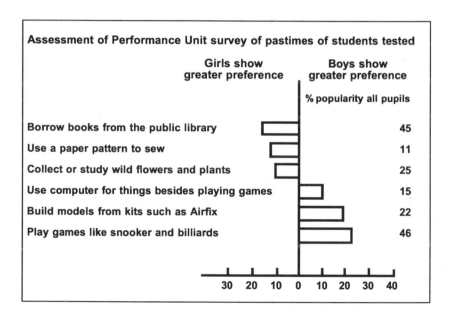

Figure 9.10   *Assessment of Performance Unit survey of pastimes on students tested*

Boys put snooker as their most popular pastime! When students were given diagrams that showed a spinning ball bouncing, they did better than when the question was about simple reflection (that is, when the balls were not spinning) and, interestingly, boys were no better than girls at answering this question (APU, 1984b, p. 168). But it is surprising that in this more complex situation students do better; it may be that the everyday ball games that all children play give them the insight to complete these questions correctly. The educational implication of this for me is the need to see

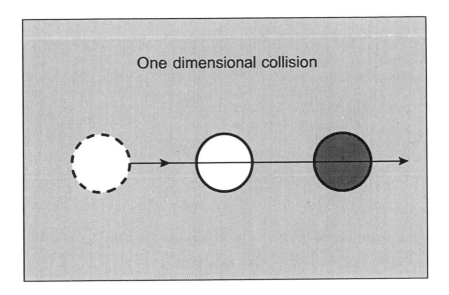

One dimensional collision

Figure 9.11   *A one-dimensional collision*

understanding from such everyday situations being the subject of mathematics and science, rather than just used as a 'cover' for the abstractions. Often context is introduced either as a motivational element or as part of some pretence that the mathematics and science are useful.

Undergraduates do get into the 'real' situation, but the engagement with the context is no more authentic. For example, they deal with snooker balls that don't roll (Open University, 1994). This leads to situations where even in simple one-dimensional motion (i.e. two balls colliding along a straight line joining their centres; Figure 9.11), the results of calculations fly in the face of the evidence from real situations. An example is given of a cue ball hitting a stationary black ball (a full-ball shot) and, to conform to the law of conservation of momentum, the cue ball stops dead and the black ball goes off with the same velocity as the cue ball had before impact (Open University, 1982). All snooker players know you usually have to apply slight back spin to stun the ball in this way. The physicist would of course say that there is an assumption of 'no friction' so the ball is sliding along the table not rolling; in snooker this is achieved if the cue ball is near enough to the object ball (or hit with enough power) for the cue ball to be still sliding when it hits the object ball. In fact the physicists are wasting an opportunity to explore the behaviour of balls in snooker *using physics*. Instead they are exploring physics *using snooker*, and in my view doing so in a way to guarantee that students will not have practical knowledge, knowledge that ·is usable. We have quite sophisticated theory being taught to students but, even in the relatively simple world of snooker, the average physics or mathematics undergraduate would not have the knowledge to deal with a situation that a moderately good snooker player could easily predict. The argument is not that the theory itself is inadequate; it clearly can cope with most of the practicalities, but with the purpose of teaching it when it is 'useless' in this simplest of worlds.

There are of course arguments for teaching such theory that are based on trying to represent and pass on to young people the ultimate achievements of human thinking that are part of our culture, but these arguments are usually not sufficient to sustain the depth of knowledge encountered at most levels of the education system. In any case they are usually accompanied by arguments about the utilitarian value of such knowledge. I am not advocating the abandonment of the teaching of theory. My point is a different one, and one that is tied up with trying to argue for the importance of practical knowledge. As I indicated with regard to the secondary school teaching, the use of practical contexts is important, even if it means that in some cases the treatment may be qualitative. The Open University physics course, S271, has produced an excellent television programme that looks at a number of ball games in a qualitative way. For example, snooker is examined from the point of view of rolling and sliding, in contrast to the theoretical and quantitative treatment in the printed course material. Such an approach is of course not new and most physics teachers will know the classic text *The Physics of Ball Games* (Daish, 1972), which deals with a variety of sports including snooker. What makes this an interesting text is that in the first half the various events that occur in ball games are described entirely in qualitative terms, leaving the quantitative mathematical treatment to a separate second section.

All these educational implications point to the need to value practical knowledge more highly, and to the importance of teaching it in its own right. Looking for qualitative models or qualitative reasoning that relate to practical situations are ways of matching to the world within which students exist (rather than the theoretical world of scientists and mathematicians). More attention needs to be paid, therefore, to the complexity of the world and to the fact that contexts have their own peculiarities and understandings, that stand apart from the theoretical world, an understanding of which is just as important to successful action. Students need to therefore spend some time in coming to understand these complexities, as they have an effect on the nature of knowledge they have to learn. To someone interested in technology education, these complexities and the associated knowledge are often more central than they would be to, say, the science educator. But students learning science or mathematics need to realise that the pure models at times make absurd assumptions, and that they therefore must pay attention to whether in the particular circumstances it really does matter, for example, where the cue ball ends up. Students need to learn where the salience lies in a situation, and that they need to be sensitive to the details of the context, not just treat it as 'noise' to be filtered out.

Central to my plea for the importance of practical knowledge is that we need to recognise its qualitative and procedural nature. This means that we must complement the formal conceptual knowledge of science and mathematics with qualitative and procedural knowledge that comes from the real world. I would even go as far as to say that perhaps we should try to teach students how to reason qualitatively about the world, using ideas that come from their own everyday life and that of experts who deal with the practicalities of that world.

Notes

1   A version of this was delivered as an inaugural lecture at The Open University, Milton Keynes, 10 December 1997.

2   I am of course ignoring all the skill elements to produce each of these effects. In fact there is no simple distinction between 'know how' and the ability to do.

3   I will not distinguish between the two games of billiards and snooker, as the basic motion of the balls on the table is the same.

4   The 'nap' is the way the cloth fibres of the table lie in one direction along its length.

5   In fairness to Mackie (1982), at a number of points in his analysis he does examine how his results accord with snooker players' experience, and he does examine a number of his assumptions. However, it remains true that his purpose is to illustrate theory and its power to analyse, not to particularly help the players. Percy can have no such defence. He claims to be both illustrating a mathematical technique and developing a method that in theory would help players, but in doing so makes assumptions that only the most novice of snooker players could use (e.g. that they don't care where the cue ball goes after the pot).

6   This research was funded by the Economic and Social Research Council (Grant number R00023445 *Problem solving in technology education: a case of situated learning?*).

7   The teacher refers to the 'beam' as a 'lever', reflecting the kind of science terms with which the students would have been familiar.

8   A recent book (Detterman and Sternberg, 1993) has as its first chapter 'The case for the prosecution: transfer as an epiphenomenon'. *Cognitive Science* gave over the whole of Volume 17, in 1993 to an argument between those who supported situated cognition and those who wanted to take a symbolic cognition view, central to which was the issue of transfer. More recently, Anderson, Reder and Simon (1996) gave a robust defence of transfer.

9   Patricia Murphy has shown how gendered this process is (Murphy, 1991; 1994). Here I would like to acknowledge Patricia's role in pointing out to me the importance of the concept of 'salience'.

10   We have reported this work more completely (Evens and McCormick, 1997).

11   I am obliged to Patricia Murphy for drawing my attention to this work.

References

Anderson, J. R., Reder, L. M. and Simon, H. A. (1996) Situated learning and education. *Educational Researcher*, 25 (4), 5–11.

Assessment of Performance Unit (APU) (1984a) *Science in Schools Age 13: Report Number 1.* London: Department of Education and Science, Department of Education for Northern Ireland and Welsh Office.

Assessment of Performance Unit (APU) (1984b) *Science in Schools Age 13: Report Number 2*. London: Department of Education and Science, Department of Education for Northern Ireland and Welsh Office.

Coriolis, G. (1835) *Theorie Mathematique des Effets Du Jeu de Billard*. Paris: Carilian-Goeury (Available in *Landmarks of Science: Monographs*. (microfiche) New York: Readex Microprint.)

Dahlgren, L-O. (1984) Outcomes of Learning. In F. Marton, D. Hounsell, and N. Entwistle, (eds.) *The Experience of Learning* (pp. 19–35). Edinburgh: Scottish Academic Press.

Daish, C. B. (1972) *The Physics of Ball Games*. London: The English Universities Press.

Davis, J. (1964) *How I Play Snooker*. London: Country Life Ltd.

Davis, J. (1967) *Advanced Snooker*. London: Country Life Ltd.

Detterman, D. K. and Sternberg, R. J. (1993) *Transfer on Trial: intelligence, cognition and instruction*. Norwood, N.J.: Ablex Publishing Corporation.

Dillon, C. (1994) Qualitative reasoning about physical systems – an overview. *Studies in Science Education*, 23, 39–57.

Driver, R., Guesne, E. and Tiberghien A.(eds.) (1985) *Children's Ideas in Science*. Buckingham: Open University Press.

diSessa, A. A. (1996) *Situated Cognition versus Cognitivism: a grounded debate*. American Educational Research Association annual meeting, April 8–12, New York.

Evens, H. and McCormick, R. (1997) *Mathematics by Design: An Investigation into Key Stage 3*. Report to the Design Council. Milton Keynes: School of Education, Open University.

Glaser, R. (1984) Education and thinking: the role of knowledge. *American Psychologist*, 39 (2), 93–104.

Glaser, R. (1992) Expert knowledge and processes of thinking. In D. F. Halpern (ed.) *Enhancing Thinking Skills in the Sciences and Mathematics* (pp. 63–75). Hillsdale, NJ: Erlbaum. (Chapter 7 in this volume.)

Gott, S. H. (1988) Apprenticeship instruction for real-world tasks: the coordination of procedures, mental models and strategies. In E. Z. Rothkopf (ed.) *Review of Research in Education 15 1988–89* (pp. 97–169). Washington DC: American Educational Research Association.

Hemming, G. W. (1899) *Billiards Mathematically Treated*. London: MacMillan and Co. Ltd.

Lave, J. (1988) *Cognition in Practice: Mind, Mathematics and Culture in Everyday Life*. Cambridge: Cambridge University Press.

Layton, D. (1993) *Technology's Challenge to Science Education*. Buckingham: Open University Press.

Levinson, R., Murphy, P. and McCormick, R. (1997) Science and technology concepts in a design and technology project: a pilot study. *Research in Science and Technological Education*, 15 (2), 235–255.

Mackie, A. G. (1982) The mathematics of snooker. *Institute of Mathematics and its Applications Bulletin*, 18, 82–89.

Mackie, A. G. (1986) Trajectories of spheres moving on a rough surface. *Institute of Mathematics and its Applications Bulletin*, 22, 105–108.

McCormick, R. (1997) Conceptual and procedural knowledge. *International Journal of Technology and Design Education*, 7 (1–2), 141–159.

McCormick, R. and Murphy, P. (1994) *Learning the processes in technology*. Paper presented at the British Educational Research Association Annual Conference, Oxford University, England, September.

Murphy, P. (1991) 'Gender and practical work'. In B. Woolnough (ed.) *Practical Work in Science*, Open University Press, Milton Keynes.

Murphy, P. (1994) *Teaching and Learning the Process of Science: messages for technology education?* Paper presented to the British Educational Research Association Annual Conference, Oxford University, England, 8–11 September.

Open University (1994) *S271: Discovering Physics. Block A: Newtonian Mechanics (Unit 3: Conservation of Momentum and Energy)*. Milton Keynes: The Open University.

Open University (1982) (MST204)*(Unit 17 The dynamics of many-particle systems)*. Milton Keynes: The Open University.

Osborne, R. and Freyberg, P. (eds.) (1985) *Learning in Science: The Implications of Children's Science*. London: Heinemann.

Percy, D. F. (1994) Focus on sport. *The Statistician*, 43 (4), 585–594.

Polanyi, M. (1962) *Personal Knowledge: Towards a Post-Critical Philosophy*. London: Routledge & Kegan Paul.

Scribner, S. (1985) Knowledge at work. *Anthropology and Education Quarterly*, 16 (3), 199–206. (Chapter 8 in this volume.)

Sternberg, R. J. and Carvso, D. R. (1985) Practical modes of knowing. In E. Eisner (ed.) *Learning and Teaching Ways of Knowing* (pp. 133–158). Chicago: National Society for the Study of Education.

10

Achievement and Theories of Knowing and Learning

J. G. Greeno, P. D. Pearson and A. H. Schoenfeld

Editors' Introduction

This is an extract from a study spelling out the implications of research on learning and cognition for the National Assessment of Educational Progress (NAEP). NAEP is responsible for testing in the USA to measure changes in educational attainments as well as to develop the technology of assessment. The authors examine theories of achievement that are derived from the cognitive and situative perspectives and then use these to examine what would count as achievement in mathematics and literacy. Only the latter is included in the extract below.

Theories of Achievement

NAEP attempts to provide an assessment of student achievement in selected subject-areas. The different perspectives on knowing and learning that have been developed in research each provide quite different characterizations of achievement. [. . .]

Aspects of Achievement in the Cognitive Perspective

[. . .] We organize our discussion using five aspects of knowing, similar to those in mathematics discussed by Schoenfeld (1985).

Elementary skills, facts, and concepts
Technical skills can be considered as resources in the knowledge structures that are described in cognitive models. These can be acquired and automated, and thereafter can be performed with little cognitive effort, allowing attention to be given to more complex aspects of performance.

This chapter has been edited.

Strategies and schemata

In every intellectual domain there are heuristic strategies – rules of thumb for making progress when the knowledge base does not in itself prove adequate for solving a problem. In mathematics and science these strategies are often formalizable; there are strategies such as 'exploit easier or analogous problems' or 'consider special or extreme cases'. Readers use various techniques to infer the meanings of words they do not know or to infer the biases of the authors whose works they read. Writers have rules of thumb for structuring paragraphs, for insuring continuity, for making sure the reader gets the point. The ability to use such strategies is an important aspect of competence in all content domains.

Aspects of metacognition, in particular self-monitoring and self-regulation

In any domain, an essential ingredient of competent performance is knowing how well you seem to be doing at any given moment – and acting on that knowledge. Poor problem-solvers will persevere on particular approaches long after those approaches have failed to yield results; in contrast, competent problem-solvers will truncate wild-goose chases. Good readers will realize they have lost the thread of an argument and will go back to the point where they lost it. Good writers will realize that the argument they are making is wandering and will go back to reconstruct it. Each of the above will check periodically to see if the work they have done is adequate to the task at hand.

Beliefs

Our sense of a discipline (our beliefs about it) shapes how we act – and those beliefs may vary from very productive (and very much like those of practitioners of the discipline) to very counter-productive. For example, many mathematics or science students believe (on the basis of their classroom and homework experience) that any problem can be solved in five minutes or less – and they thus give up on problems when they have not solved them in five minutes. People in many fields believe 'you either know it or you don't,' and simply give up when they face something unfamiliar, rather than trying to figure it out. In the case of reading, this means that such people fail to comprehend words or phrases whose meaning they could understand if they worked at it. Many students believe that 'writing is telling,' and thus that the appropriate (if not the only) strategy for writing is to sit down and let the words emerge in linear order. The results of such writing without planning and polishing are often rather dismal. In all of these fields, practitioners with opposite beliefs do rather differently. Those who believe that many problems will yield to sustained effort will work on them longer, often with more success. Those who believe they are capable of sense-making often do make sense of things that are not immediately familiar or understood. Finally, those who plan and polish their writing usually produce better prose than those who generate it 'on-line'.

Contextual factors
In the cognitive view, knowledge is acquired and held by individuals. Social interactions and other external conditions can have an effect on an individual's performance, and these contextual factors need to be understood in interpreting someone's performance.

Relations between aspects of achievement
According to some analyses, the elementary aspects of achievement – routine skills, facts, and concepts – are basic in students' knowledge and exist as prerequisites to learning more complex, 'higher-order' aspects of achievement. However, this is a disputed view. An alternative view is that strategic, metacognitive, and epistemic aspects of achievement are more fundamental than detailed procedures and routine skills to effective intellectual functioning. If students do not learn how to think about situations mathematically and believe that mathematical methods are not involved in sustained thinking, then any computational skill they have acquired will seldom be used. If students believe that the goal of reading is to recognize and pronounce the words and do not have strategies for understanding the meanings of texts, then their abilities to decode text will not support their learning from text. A plausible view is that aspects of knowing at multiple levels are all necessary for effective achievement.

Aspects of Achievement in the Situative Perspective

In the situative perspective, knowing is viewed as sustained participation in practices of a community. This leads to a different understanding of relations between various aspects of achievement.

Basic aspects of participation
In the situative view, engaged participation in practices is basic to a person's achievement, and other aspects of achievement are dependent on being engaged and participating in ways that others find appropriate. Practices are the conventional activities of a domain in which participating members engage. Members of the community of readers or mathematicians engage in typical patterns of sense-making, of inquiry, of production; such patterns are readily identifiable and recognizable. These actions are both individual and communal: book groups getting together to discuss works read individually, or members of any intellectual community discussing ideas 'live' at meetings and in colloquia, in one another's offices, as well as via e-mail. For students, being engaged in the practices of classroom activities provides a necessary substrate for successful learning and performance.

Following extended experience in a discipline and membership in a community of people who practice it, we pick up certain practices – ways of perceiving (the self, the discipline, and the world) and of acting. Mathematically-minded people tend to mathematize – to model things mathematically, to symbolize, to analyse. They tend to demand analytic proof of assertions: if something is claimed to be true, there should be a comprehensible and communicable reason as to why it is true, and they feel comfortable interacting with others who do the same. Readers read – and they would not be caught without reading material, just in case they get stuck somewhere with nothing to do. Writers or artists reflexively translate their experiences into their media. They think and communicate in such terms. The common stereotypes of doctors, lawyers, etc., also make the point: when we get embedded in a field, we pick up the practices and perspectives of the people who inhabit the field. Those practices and perspectives are a part of our competence and a sign of our membership in the community of practitioners of that field.

Identity and membership in communities
There is a duality between membership in a community and issues of self-perception and identity. Community memberships contribute to aspects of people's sense of self and influence individuals' values and standards in the domains of community activity. Readers see themselves as readers, for example, and define themselves (and others) by whether or not they belong in this particular group. This sense of self, in general, includes having various dispositions (habits of mind, predilections to view the world in particular ways), a certain kind of self-confidence and competence, and feelings of entitlement and empowerment. Note that there is no simple one-to-one mapping between individuals and communities: among those who consider themselves readers are those who consider themselves mathematicians, educators, food and wine connoisseurs, etc.

Formulating problems and goals and applying standards
Problem and solution formulation derive from the notion of 'seeing the world in a particular way' as a member of a particular community – of having particular means of sense-making. It has to do with the way we frame and evaluate problems and goals, and how we evaluate proposed solutions and progress. Community membership entails (to some degree) taking on, and participating in, the perspectives, values, and focal interests of the community. Mathematicians are interested in 'hot problems'; they talk about them, work on them, interact over them. Those with an interest in literary criticism compare and contrast alternative approaches to text, constructing (or deconstructing) meanings and interpretations.

Of course, there is a participatory dialectic related to community membership: individuals' problem formulations and goals are shaped by those of the community and individuals shape the goals and perspectives of the community. For example, one mathematician noted, after seeing express lanes in some supermarkets that allowed a maximum of 15 packages per purchase and express lanes in other supermarkets that allowed a maximum of six, that the supermarket owners 'didn't understand the problem': there had to be a 'right number,' more or less, and the variation between six and 15 was too large. He then posed (and answered) the question of what that right number might be. Similarly, a sophisticated reader may wish to understand the 'deeper' meaning of a text (i.e., its psychological properties or what it reveals about the author) or may wish to understand more about the author's biases in order to develop a more 'objective' reading of the content.

Constructing meaning
Here is where the tools of the trade come into play. In mathematics, we formulate and evaluate conjectures, build models, use a variety of mathematical techniques, and evaluate evidence according to mathematical norms. In reading, we do likewise: we construct meaning by situating pieces of writing within various genres, by making and applying various assumptions about the text, and by recognizing various conventions and interpreting the text thereby.

Fluency with technical methods and representations
The meaning-making in 'Constructing meaning' uses the foundation of knowledge and skills that comprise the knowledge base. To build a mathematical model, we must have the relevant mathematical tools at our disposal; to work our way through a problem, we must have facility with a wide range of tools, techniques, and representations. We draw upon all of these while doing mathematics. Similarly, making sense of text depends on knowledge of genres, basic reading skills, and factual knowledge against which the text can be interpreted. It has been noted in various spheres of activity (e.g., for graduate students entering academic professions and for doctors during their periods of hospital residency) that coming to be a member of a particular community involves picking up the language and terms of reference used in that community – and that the meanings and entailments of such terms are developed as individuals become more deeply embedded in the community.

Assessment in Different Perspectives

This section discusses issues of assessment, as these are framed by the different research perspectives on cognition and learning. [. . .]

Literacy Achievement and Assessment in the Cognitive Perspective

Elementary Literacy Skills

Describing the knowledge base relevant for literacy is, from one perspective, impossible because everything students learn in or out of school affects their reading and writing competence. After all, the 'stuff' of texts (both those students read and those students write) is, or ought to be, the stuff of life. One of the central contributions of the cognitive revolution to literacy theory and practice was to validate the centrality of prior knowledge in the comprehension process. Nonetheless, in addition to knowledge about the world and how it works, there are some critical knowledge bases.

Cognitive models of literacy have been developed and used in basic reading instruction (Kintsch and van Dijk, 1978; Lesgold and Perfetti, 1978; Perfetti 1985). Words are recognized; phrases are converted to propositions that are integrated into a text base and a model of the situation that the text describes.

Knowledge about language

The most important understanding for success with printed language is that everything students have learned about oral language can be applied to written language – all of the implicit, and later explicit, knowledge students have acquired about the phonological, semantic, and syntactic structure of English is helpful in rendering written language sensible and accessible. The semantic and syntactic cues that students discover as they recode printed messages into oral messages provide information they can use to confirm, disconfirm, or revise their hypotheses about meaning. These cues can, but do not necessarily, help them make predictions about upcoming letters, words, and meanings; there is substantial evidence, for example, that highly competent readers are more likely to avail themselves of these sources of contextual information to decode words.

As the texts students encounter become more sophisticated and more technical, the semantic aspects of language growth, especially as they are indexed by knowledge of vocabulary, become more important to their comprehension and writing. But since vocabulary tends to expand in direct proportion to growth in general world knowledge, it is not clear whether vocabulary in and of itself – or the world knowledge to which it is indexed – is the critical factor in facilitating or impeding comprehension and writing. Suffice it to say that one or the other is crucial to both reading and writing development. Through these linguistic mechanisms, readers cope with written language in much the way they cope, as listeners, with oral language. They engage their knowledge of syntax and semantics to ascribe meaning to the messages they decode while reading.

Yet, something is missing. Written language is not well suited for conveying subtle aspects of meaning; it conveys literal meaning but not authorial intention. Written language conveys what authors mean but not how authors intend readers to regard their messages. What is missing, of course, is clear representation of the suprasegmental phonemes that account for intonation (the rising and falling patterns that distinguish statements from questions from commands), stress (the differential amplitude that signals which word in a sentence contains the core meaning or, within words, whether we are encountering RECord or reCORD). Granted punctuation and special fonts point readers in the right direction, but they do not eliminate ambiguity altogether. Readers are forced to use context and knowledge about that text.

Knowledge about the conventions of written English

Students learn the conventions of our written language. They learn to manipulate symbol systems, the print to speech codes of our alphabetic writing system, and the structural, rhetorical, and literary conventions of increasingly sophisticated texts. In order to learn to read and write, students, even at an early age, must understand the symbolic nature of written language – that print is a code that represents yet another code, oral language. Children develop an intuitive understanding of this idea long before they can explain it. For example, a three-year-old child, upon sighting the golden arches of McDonald's shouts, 'Hamburger!' This approximation may not be 'right' in the conventional sense, but it is certainly a symbolic act of reading and a very important step along the way to becoming a reader. The child reads the sign for meaning, bringing to bear knowledge, purpose, and, more importantly, an emerging understanding that symbols can 'stand for' thoughts and words.

Because English orthography is alphabetic, beginning readers also gain two additional understandings. First, they learn a specific set of mappings between the basic units of oral and written language – what we commonly refer to as symbol-sound correspondences or phonics knowledge. Second, they learn the general principle of the cipher – that letters represent sounds in a more or less systematic fashion. Their discovery of the symbolic nature of print and its power in conveying meaning is mediated in many ways in their home and school environments. The models provided by older siblings and adults are an important form of mediation. From a young age, children are surrounded by print symbols that are meant to convey meaning. As children explore their worlds, they interact with adults and older children who serve as 'models' by engaging in everyday acts of reading and writing. Over time, as they observe and begin to participate in symbolic activities, they learn to attach meaning to the symbols they see in books and those they create in scribbles and drawings. Gradually, they take on the reading-like and writing-like behaviors of their models. As suggested earlier, oral language is a second important source of mediation as students discover how oral language can be used to assist in the prediction and verification process. In school settings, mediation also takes the form of intentional instruction provided by teachers (and other students) and information emerging from discussions and conversations about print with teachers and peers.

As students encounter more sophisticated written texts, they encounter more sophisticated conventions. Within both expository and narrative traditions of text, they learn prototypic structures and frames for different genres. History tends toward causal and synchronically ordered structures; biology tends toward descriptions and explanations, and the like. They learn about the tools of the author's craft, how authors use those tools to achieve literary and rhetorical effects, and the ways in which writers manipulate typographic and visual effects to clarify and support normal textual displays.

Genres and rhetorical structure

The structural aspects of language do not end with the sentence. Students also acquire substantial knowledge about how texts are written and structured. As their experience with oral and written texts grows, so does their knowledge. Even with preschoolers, it is not uncommon for them to abstract features of stories, such as, 'Once upon a time,' or 'They all lived happily ever after.' By middle and high school, students can often distinguish among several different genres of narratives, poetry, and expository text, and they are aware of various types of rhetorical structure (causation versus description versus comparison versus attribution) in expository text. More impressively, they often demonstrate control of at least some of these text structures in their own writing.

Tools of understanding and interpretation

They also develop rich knowledge about the tools that authors use as they ply their craft. They learn about the nature and function of figurative language as a specific instance of the more general practice of indirection – saying one thing while meaning another. They learn the distinction between the denotative and connotative character of words and how authors select words to convey mood and to give shape and life to their characters. They learn a host of specific techniques, such as foreshadowing. When they acquire this knowledge, they are able to use it as both readers (to read with a critical eye in order to discover the tricks that authors are trying to play on readers) and writers (when they try to shape the views their ideal readers will take from their texts). They learn, in the words of Frank Smith (1988), how to read 'like a writer'.

World knowledge

It is impossible to provide a full characterization of the knowledge base underlying reading and writing without addressing the role of world knowledge (often referred to as background knowledge or prior knowledge) in the reading and writing process. Since the advent of schema theory in the mid-1970s, theory and research about literacy have posited a central role for background knowledge in the comprehension process. Most revealing is the consistent characterization of comprehension as a process of relating the new (novel information coming from texts) to the known (knowledge currently stored in long-term memory). The research base documenting the powerful effect of knowledge on comprehension is impressive (see, for example, Anderson and Pearson, 1984). The reader's existing knowledge base is also a key factor in metacognitive activity; for example, when a reader monitors her reading to determine whether it 'makes sense,' the criterion for sense-making is whether or not her current model of meaning is consistent with her existing knowledge base.

Strategies and Schemata

Students understand and appreciate what they read, and they develop the competence to demonstrate their understanding and appreciation by constructing responses appropriate to their reading purpose, the genre and tradition of the text, and the social context of their reading. Significant aspects of the knowledge needed to accomplish this are considered in theories of macrostructures of texts (Kintsch and van Dijk, 1978). Texts do not 'present' themselves for comprehension. At every stage and moment, students at all levels build (and constantly revise) their models of what the text means. The knowledge base that students bring to the text is the most critical tool in this building process. This reservoir of knowledge ranges from the broad social understandings that are widely shared by members of a culture to narrower bodies of knowledge unique to particular subgroups to highly local, even personal bodies of knowledge. It is this range of knowledge, taken as a whole, that serves both to constrain and liberate the reading of text for individuals. Once students have made an initial interpretation of even a small segment of a text, they use their knowledge to evaluate the appropriateness of that interpretation. They ask themselves how well it 'fits' within their current knowledge base. New information based upon new interpretations of additional text provide an occasion to re-evaluate the model constructed thus far and, if necessary, to revise it. The process is truly reciprocal, and the accountability works both ways. New and evolving interpretations of the text are accountable to the learner's knowledge base, and that knowledge base is accountable to the new information emerging from the text. This accountability exchange arises again and again in the reading-writing process – in discussions, conversations, writing activities or personal reflections. Often, during one of these exchanges, students are called on to revisit the text to support or evaluate their current interpretations, thus continuing the reciprocal cycle of accountability to knowledge and text.

Current theories of language use emphasize the central role played by the learner in creating and responding to text, including printed and auditory texts, as well as information in events that students experience. Students bring an extensive background of knowledge and experience to each language event. Part of this reservoir is knowledge that we possess because we belong to a range of cultural groups. Equally important, however, is the idiosyncratic knowledge and experience each reader brings to a text. This idiosyncratic knowledge accounts for our individuality and the inevitability of multiple interpretations, both across readers and across time for the same reader.

The active nature of literacy is also apparent in the many and multiple stances that readers can choose to take at different points in the process of reading a text. Readers can read to gain an overall impression or an initial understanding – a sort of 'getting the gist' process. They can also get more 'inside the text' and focus on developing interconnected interpretations of the ideas in the text. They can respond personally, comparing the experiences or feelings of characters with their own experiences or situations, or they can read with a critical eye, to try to get inside the author's shoes to understand the motive for or impact of a particular authorial choice, or to challenge the author's credibility or effectiveness.

Metacognitive Processes

As students use written language strategically, they monitor reading and writing for communicative adequacy; they ask themselves questions such as, 'Does the text I have written or the meaning I have created satisfy my current purpose?' They also know how to access and use resources (from their own knowledge repertoire, texts they read, and members of their learning community) to revise texts and meanings when initial attempts to construct meaning fall short. To become strategic is to move from an automatic to a deliberate level of analysis and action. Readers use a wide range of repair strategies once they recognize a comprehension or communication failure; they predict, ask questions, reread, sound out words, seek additional information, consult dictionaries, consult other members of their literacy communities, and use reference materials to solve problems they encounter as they read and write.

In the process of monitoring/evaluating comprehension or composition and allocating resources to improve communication, they come to understand themselves as learners. They learn their particular profile of strengths; they know what they can do automatically and what they must place under deliberate control. So one individual might not concern herself with paragraph organization because it 'just happens'; for another, it becomes a matter for special attention, including deliberate rehearsal and practice. One individual might require a very specific plan to get into the writing of an essay; another might begin the planning with a free write that continues until the topic takes a shape of its own.

Metacognitive knowledge arises in many situations during literacy activities:

1. *While reading and writing.* Students monitor and evaluate the communicative adequacy of their language use. They can articulate when a text they are reading or writing is or is not serving its communicative purpose.

2. *When students recognize a miscommunication and attempt to resolve it.* Students access and employ resources to improve communication. They engage in a wide internal and external search for resources – from their own knowledge repertoire, their own repertoire of strategies, the texts they read, and members of their learning communities.

- They question, reread, predict, seek additional information, skim, think about context, sound out words.
- Students use the language of explanation and questioning to advance their own learning and to be supportive of other members of one's literacy community.

3. *When students evaluate themselves.* Students understand themselves as learners. They know their particular strengths and learn how to allocate their strategic energies to different activities.

- Students are able to 'size up the task' based on probable difficulty and goals, and create and initiate plans for handling the task.
- Students know how goals, activities, and texts influence their own decisions about strategy use and regulation.

Beliefs and Dispositions

All students acquire beliefs about literacy in response to the instruction we offer in our schools. But they may acquire beliefs that are at odds with our curricular intentions and certainly at odds with a constructivist view of learning. We might like students to develop a set of beliefs consistent with the view that reading is a meaning making process involving purpose, interpretation, social negotiation, and cultural grounding. Interviews with students at various ages, however, indicate that most students believe that reading consists of pronouncing the words correctly, that the meaning is *in* the text, and that questions do have right answers (which the teacher and/ or the test makers possess).

Consistent with advances in cognitive development and constructivist views of language learning, we want students to develop a set of beliefs that place themselves as meaning-makers at the center of the reading and writing processes. We certainly want them to believe that they can, through concerted effort, careful analysis, and the flexible application of strategies, satisfy their personal goals in reading and writing. We also want them to believe that reading and writing are tools for learning, enjoyment, insight, and communication.

Inextricably interwoven with beliefs are habits of minds and dispositions; these are, in a sense, the cognitive and conative mechanism for putting one's beliefs to work. Consistent with the model of the active, strategic reader, several 'habits of mind' are essential to effective literacy practice: seeking connections, taking multiple perspectives, monitoring, persisting, and accepting responsibility.

Seeking connections
Language users seek connections between ideas, processes, and events. They look for and find relationships among texts and explanations of how ideas are alike and different. They also seek to understand the similarities and

differences among the processes and strategies they use. For example, they learn that summarizing the gist of an article as a reading activity is 'like' writing a summary of a class event. Or that a summary for a speech is not unlike an outline for a text. Processes and strategies for constructing meaning in reading are like those they use in writing, speaking, listening, and viewing. They find that the reverse is also true. They see that all language is connected and inter-related. As students make more connections, it becomes easier to find connections and to understand language and literature.

Taking multiple perspectives

Accomplished language users view things from multiple perspectives. Students find multiple and alternative pathways from which to reflect on the issues that evolve from literature. As they read and write, they become aware of their own perspectives, the perspectives of different characters, and the perspectives of the author. For instance, as students read a work of literature, they may first take the perspective of Character A, then re-examine the work by taking the perspective of Character B. In writing and speaking, students are also aware of multiple perspectives, especially those of audiences who might read their pieces. Students may write a persuasive piece for one audience and then rewrite the piece from a different perspective for an audience with a differing point of view on the topic. Students see how perspectives change with different purposes for using language.

Monitoring

The habit of monitoring, the hallmark of metacognition, facilitates all aspects of language use. Students monitor understanding by checking new information with what they already know. Language and literature make sense when there are strong connections between old and new knowledge. They test and match incoming information with their prior knowledge. If there is a good fit, they know that it makes sense. If the fit is poor and there are discrepancies between incoming knowledge and prior knowledge, the student will employ strategies to reconcile the difference, sometimes by rechecking a word or phrase in a text and sometimes by searching in the mind for a more appropriate set of information with a better fit. Students make meaning as they find connections between their knowledge framework and what they are perceiving in language. As students gain new information by participating in language activities, their initial interpretations may change. They can use this new knowledge to monitor their understanding of texts that they subsequently encounter.

Persisting

Persistence in literacy activities is a key feature of active, confident language users. Instead of throwing in the towel when a text is not yielding or an interpretation seems beyond their grasp, persistent individuals search their repertoire of fix-up strategies for approaches which will take them over the humps they encounter in the complexities of language use.

Taking responsibility
Successful language users have the disposition to take responsibility for their own learning. They are engaged in self-evaluation and monitor their own growth. They are reflective about their language use. Students gain confidence as they see the quality of their writing improve, the fluency of their speaking increase, and the depth of their engagement with literature intensify. They seek to become independent learners in a society of language users.

Knowledge-like beliefs
The beliefs delineated thus far are dispositional in character; they delineate the actions that literate individuals are likely to take in support of their own literacy. But students acquire other sorts of beliefs, beliefs that are closer to knowledge than to dispositions. For example, students learn that literature is a means to learn about themselves and others. Students use literature to learn about themselves, their values, assumptions, and beliefs through reading, discussing, and writing about literature. In the process, their ideas both shape and are shaped by these encounters. They learn, in particular, that literature is the medium in which they encounter the big ideas of life – love, hate, growth, death, ecstasy, disappointment, success, failure – the gamut of experiences that account for our humanity. Students use literature to learn about others, including those in their classrooms and communities, and about people of other cultures, other places, and other times. Literature can provide access to knowledge and experience that may be available in no other medium. It can take students well beyond the experience defined by the school curriculum or even by their own cultural worlds. Similarly, they come to understand the role and function that informational texts play in their school lives and in their everyday lives. They also come to understand the social, cultural, and political faces of literacy. They learn about the uses to which literacy can be put, what literacy is good for, how it can be used to achieve personal goals, how it functions in communication, and how it can be used politically, either to emancipate or control groups of people.

Literacy in Contexts

People whose literacy abilities are well developed are able to use and construct texts successfully in the wide range of settings where those abilities are appropriate and useful. This is illustrated in examples [. . .] such as Hull's (Hull *et al.*, 1994) study of workplace literacy which included construction of reports by the work team and Moll's (Moll *et al.*, 1993) study of classroom activities in which students used text to contribute to class discussions from different cultural perspectives. [. . .]

The Situative Perspective: Assessing Achievement in Literacy

In this section we discuss a view of achievement and assessment in [. . .] reading based on research in the situative perspective. We organize this discussion in terms of the five aspects of achievement:

1. Basic aspects of participation in the literary practices of communities;
2. Personal identity and membership in communities;
3. Formulating and evaluating problems and solutions according to literary standards of quality;
4. Participation in construction of meaning; and
5. Fluency in technical representations and meanings. [. . .]

Literacy Achievement and Assessment in Situative Perspective

Basic Aspects of Participation in Literary Practice

In the situative perspective, the most basic aspects of knowing involve abilities to engage in activities that use text, including discourse about text. Literacy communities can exist inside or outside of schools. Within classrooms, teachers can help students learn to be active members of the classroom club. The best part about a classroom literacy community is that it is filled with real live peers with whom students can exchange oral and written communications that render their activities authentic. In such communities, students and their teachers read and write regularly to, with, and for one another. Thus the question of the relevance and functionality of literacy activities never arises because the community itself provides the incentives that make literacy an everyday event. They also provide occasions for us to celebrate and honor individual and collective accomplishments.

What makes the classroom community both powerful and different is its basic assumption that, instead of preparing students to use literacy skills 'out there' in the 'real' world, the classroom community and its curriculum must provide the rationale and incentives for literate behavior within its walls and its instructional programs. Teachers are not getting kids ready to do the real stuff; instead they are providing occasions in which the real stuff matters so much that students can, perhaps must, engage in literacy as a part of living their everyday lives and conducting their everyday work in classrooms. If this occurs in a genuine way, then the transfer from school-based literacy to work-based literacy will be completely transparent. In fact, the goal of classroom literacy communities should be to make their literacy activities as indistinguishable from everyday literacy events as is humanly possible.

In such community environments, students and teachers do all of the things they do when they are behaving literately: they participate in the discourse of literacy, they evaluate the claims of others; they agree and disagree with others; they appropriate the ideas of others to inform and extend their own; they share ideas with others; they read and write regularly to move the work of the community along. [. . .]

As students mature and build more connections with other parts of their worlds, the idea of community becomes more complex. For now, students belong to multiple communities, some with identities and practices that are likely to be at odds with the literate community of their elementary and middle school classrooms. But the expansion of community membership can be supportive of, as well as competitive with, literacy. Membership in new communities can provide even more reasons for reading and writing.

At some point, the classroom literacy community must be extended into the cultural communities in which the students live, and those communities must be extended into the classroom. If this does not occur, the classroom community will lose its capacity to honor and celebrate the cultural and interpretive diversity of its constituents (Moll *et al.*, 1993).

Personal Identity and Community Membership

First and foremost, to belong to a literacy community is to identify with it in the sense that part of our identity is framed by membership in that community. Frank Smith captured this sense of literate identity in a powerful 1983 piece in which he talked about what happens to students when they begin to think of themselves as members of the *literacy club*. They begin to think of themselves as competent, literate individuals. They expect reading and writing to make sense. When what they read, for example, does not make sense, they tend to question the author or the particular reading they gave the text instead of blaming the communication failure on themselves as so many unsuccessful readers are likely to do (Johnston and Winograd, 1985). They begin to 'read like a writer' in the sense that they can examine a text from an author's perspective, asking questions such as, 'I wonder why the author used those particular phrases to describe this character?' or, 'I wonder what the effect would have been if X rather than Y had been responsible for the collapse of Z?'

To think of ourselves as members of a literacy community, as literate individuals, is to accept a whole set of dispositions and habits of mind. A literate identity would certainly entail habits such as seeking connections, taking multiple perspectives, monitoring, persisting, and accepting responsibility. To this list, others would be added. A belief in the credibility of our ideas would be present, but it would be balanced against the expectation that changing our mind is part of the responsibility that comes with community membership. Community membership also entails being prepared to tolerate, perhaps even to try to understand, interpretations that contradict our own.

Formulating and Evaluating Goals and Accomplishments According to Literacy Standards

If the community established in a classroom meets the test of authenticity, the process of formulating problems and setting goals becomes very different from most school-based literacy activities. As learners in schools, the problems we encounter are determined by others, usually the teacher or the curriculum designer, and these problems are nothing but reflections of the goals that motivated their design and implementation in the first place. If classroom communities are genuine communities, then the goals and problems of the literacy curriculum will have a very different genesis. They will arise from life and work in that community, from the business of using literacy to achieve other ends in the community. Thus, if the community wants to put on a play, then script writing, oral reading, the study of the prosodic (intonation, stress, and juncture) features of speech, program (what gets handed out) production, committee meetings and decision-making, town meetings, and the like become the literacy curriculum. But notice that the goal (the play) and the problems (getting things done to ensure its production) are not driven by any notion of a literacy curriculum. Instead the curriculum is event-driven and completely situated within the community's broader set of goals and activities. Literacy becomes completely functionalized, a means to a broader set of ends. If this discourse seems to hearken back to the ideas of Dewey, it should not be surprising; even though he did not use the term situativity or situatedness to describe his notions of curriculum, he is clearly the forerunner of modern theories of situativity.

The community can proceed and do its work in a completely functional manner – just engaging in activities in which literacy plays a major role. But community members can also become more analytic about their work and examine it in terms of literacy constructs, asking decidedly literate questions: How are these two stories alike? What is the point of the piece? What intentions could the author have had in mind in crafting this section in this manner? How would this piece have been different if it had been written by Maugham rather than Hemingway?

In the first instance (putting on the play), the problems and goals are outside the realm of literacy, but literacy skills are involved in solving or completing them. In the second instance (answer all of the literary questions), they are inside the realm of literacy, and they are addressed by employing more general thinking and analytic skills.

Participating in the Construction of Meaning

Most of the concepts presented in the section on schemata and strategies of the cognitive perspective ('Aspects of Achievement in the Cognitive Perspective' above) apply equally well within situativity theory. In other words, within a situated perspective on developing literacy skills, many of the cognitive outcomes remain the same. We would still expect students to use their cultural, social, and individual reservoirs of knowledge to construct evolving models of text meaning. We would still expect students to be able to assume multiple stances (inside, outside, impressionistic, reflective, critical) toward a text.

A few aspects of the learning, and perhaps the assessment, process would differ, however. First, situativity theory has a more distinctively social focus than does cognitive theory. Hence both the learning and assessment of comprehension would lean toward the employment of social resources. This is not to imply that the cognitive view expressed in 'Aspects of Achievement in the Cognitive Perspective' excludes a social dimension; to the contrary, it is an important feature of most modern theories of cognitive development, including the current presentation. Rather the situated perspective is more inclined to begin by describing and analyzing the social features of the learning environment, making them figure rather than ground.

Fluency with Literary Methods and Representations

As with the previous section, the difference between this aspect and the cognitive view of the knowledge base for literacy ('Elementary Literacy Skills') is more contextual than substantive. Again, the expectation is that individuals would surely develop a knowledge base – including elements such as knowledge of language, text, the world, and written language conventions, but these would seldom, if ever, be presented in a curriculum as independent goals or objects of study and examination. Instead, they would be viewed as the knowledge resources that individuals would need to develop and employ to achieve more situated, contextualized goals emanating from everyday life in classroom literacy communities – presenting the play, influencing a community policy, sending a letter, reading a favorite book. They become highly functional – the means to other ends such as communicating with others, acquiring information, developing personal insights, and gaining control over our environment and place within it.

Thus the point of possessing this sort of knowledge is its functionality. In such a setting, issues of relevance (or rather the perceived irrelevance of doing 'school') and authenticity are minimized because the point of learning such knowledge is usually transparent. As with constructing meaning, within situativity theory such knowledge is best assessed when it is at work in the service of other problems or goals, not when it is conceptualized and presented as an end unto itself. [. . .]

References

Anderson, R. C., and Pearson, P. D. (1984) A schema-theoretic view of basic processes in reading comprehension, in *Handbook of reading research*. Ed. P. D. Pearson. New York: Longman.

Hull, G., Jury, M., Ziv, O., and Schultz, K. (1994) *Changing work, changing literacy? A study of skill requirements and development in a traditional and restructured workplace* (Interim Report Two). National Center for the Study of Writing and Literacy, University of California, Berkeley.

Johnston, P. H., and Winograd, P. N. (1985) Passive failure in reading. *Journal of Reading Behavior* 17: 279–301.

Kintsch, W., and van Dijk, T. (1978) Toward a model of text comprehension and production. *Psychological Review* 85: 363–394.

Lesgold, A. M., and Perfetti, C. A. (1978) Interactive processes in reading. *Discourse Processes* 1: 323–336.

Moll, L. C., Tapia, J., and Whitmore, K. F. (1993) Living knowledge: The social distribution of cultural resources for thinking, in *Distributed cognitions: psychological and educational considerations*. Ed. G. Salomon. Cambridge: Cambridge University Press.

Perfetti, C. A. (1985) *Reading ability*. New York: Oxford University Press.

Schoenfeld, A. (1985) *Mathematical problem solving*. New York, NY: Academic Press.

Smith, F. (1988) *Joining the literacy club*. Portsmouth, NH: Heinemann.

11

Meaning and Values in Test Validation: The Science and Ethics of Assessment

Samuel Messick

Editors' Introduction

To validate a test (or any assessment) the meaning and the implications for action are important. Messick argues that therefore a unified concept of validity is required, based on construct validity. This unified validity is concerned with the appropriateness, meaningfulness and usefulness of any inferences made on the basis of any scores or grades etc., produced by the assessment procedure. These inferences are therefore judgements both about the knowledge itself (the construct) and the understandings of it on the part of the learner.

On the basis of what sort of evidence may we interpret test scores to be indications of verbal reasoning, for instance, or of achievement motivation? How do we know what an achievement test score means if different response processes are engaged by alternative styles or strategies of performance or as a function of varying levels of experience or expertise? On what evidence may we justify using a purported measure of subject-matter knowledge to select or license teachers? Or a purported measure of clerical skill to select office workers? On what basis may we sustain the valuations inherent in score interpretations, say, of competence versus incompetence or of flexibility versus rigidity? And how may we justify implementation of the attendant evaluative implications for action, as in selection on the basis of competence, for example, or in training for flexibility? As a final instance, should tests demonstrably predictive of dire academic failure be used to place children in special education programs without explicitly weighing the intended and unintended consequences of such use?

At their core, these are all questions of test validity. And although many other such questions could be posed, they may all be considered to be exemplars of four interrelated aspects of the basic validity question, which might be phrased as follows: To what degree – if at all – on the basis of evidence and rationales, should the test scores be interpreted and used in the manner proposed? The four interrelated aspects of this question ask:

This chapter has been edited.

- what balance of evidence supports the interpretation or meaning of the scores;
- what evidence undergirds not only score meaning, but also the relevance of the scores to the particular applied purpose and the utility of the scores in the applied setting;
- what rationales make credible the value implications of the score interpretation and any associated implications for action;
- and what evidence and arguments signify the functional worth of the testing in terms of its intended and unintended consequences?

It must be emphasized that this basic, four-faceted question exemplifies a consolidated, four-pronged attack on the problem of validity. It is by no means to be taken to suggest four distinct *types* of validity, a kind of quadriform variation on the erstwhile trichotomy of content, criterion, and construct validities. On the contrary, validity is an integrated evaluative judgment of the degree to which empirical evidence and theoretical rationales support the *adequacy* and *appropriateness* of *inferences* and *actions* based on test scores or other modes of assessment (Messick, 1988).

The term 'test score' is used generically here in its broadest sense to mean any observed consistency, not just on tests as ordinarily conceived but also on any means of observing or documenting consistent behaviors or attributes. This would include, for instance, any coding or summarization of observed consistencies on performance tests, questionnaires, observation procedures, or other assessment devices. This general usage also subsumes qualitative as well as quantitative summaries and applies, for example, to protocols, clinical interpretations, and computerized verbal score reports.

Broadly speaking, then, validity is an inductive summary of both the existing evidence for and the actual as well as potential consequences of score interpretation and use. Hence, what is to be validated is not the test or observation device as such but the inferences derived from test scores or other indicators–inferences about score meaning or interpretation and about the implications for action that the interpretation entails.

To validate an interpretive inference is to ascertain the extent to which multiple lines of evidence are consonant with the inference, while establishing that alternative inferences are less well supported. This represents the fundamental principle that both convergent and discriminant evidence are required in test validation. To validate an action inference requires validation not only of score meaning but also of value implications and action outcomes, especially of the relevance and utility of the test scores for particular applied purposes and of the social consequences of using the scores for applied decision making. Thus the key issues of test validity are the meaning, relevance, and utility of scores, the import or value implications of scores as a basis for action, and the functional worth of scores in terms of the social consequences of their use.

The term 'interpretive inference' is used deliberately in this formulation even though it blurs conventional usage in philosophy and science.

Technically speaking, the terms 'induction' and 'inference' refer to formal processes grounded in logic and probability theory. On the other hand, the term 'interpretation,' being less constrained, is ordinarily applicable to situations in which there may be a mix of verified and unverified (possibly even unverifiable) considerations. In this usage, the term 'inference' would be reserved for conclusions derived from empirical evidence bearing on score meaning, whereas 'interpretation' would refer to the possible ramifications of the inferred score meaning. In contrast, by speaking of 'interpretive inferences' and 'action inferences,' we mean to imply that score interpretations and proposed score-based actions should, to the extent possible, be viewed as tested or testable inferences – that is, as theoretically grounded hypotheses supported by or derived from empirical evidence. Such usage also helps to underscore the point that test validation is fundamentally both theory driven and data driven.

Although there are different sources and mixes of evidence for supporting score-based inferences, validity is a unitary concern. Validity always refers to the degree to which empirical evidence and theoretical rationales support the adequacy and appropriateness of interpretations and actions based on test scores. Furthermore, although there are many ways of accumulating evidence to support a particular inference, these ways are essentially the methods of science. Inferences are hypotheses, and the validation of inferences is hypothesis testing. However, it is not hypothesis testing in isolation but, rather, theory testing more generally because the source, meaning, and import of score-based hypotheses derive from the interpretive theories of score meaning in which these hypotheses are rooted. Hence, test validation embraces all of the experimental, statistical, and philosophical means by which hypotheses and scientific theories are evaluated. What follows amplifies these two basic points – namely, that validity is a unified though faceted concept and that validation is scientific inquiry into score meaning.

Ways of Configuring Validity Evidence

The basic sources of validity evidence are by no means unlimited. Indeed, if we ask where one might turn for such evidence, we find that there are only a half dozen or so main forms. The number of forms is arbitrary, to be sure, because instances can be sorted in various ways and categories set up at different levels of generality. But a half dozen or so categories of the following sort seem to provide a workable level for highlighting similarities and differences among validation approaches.

● We can appraise the relevance and representativeness of the test content in relation to the content of the domain about which inferences are to be drawn or predictions made.

- We can examine relationships among responses to the tasks, items, or parts of the test – that is, the internal structure of test responses.
- We can survey relationships of the test scores with other measures and background variables – that is, the test's external structure.
- We can directly probe the ways in which individuals cope with the items or tasks, in an effort to illuminate the processes underlying item response and task performance.
- We can investigate uniformities and differences in these test processes and structures over time or across groups and settings – that is, the generalizability of test interpretation and use.
- We can see if the test scores display appropriate variations as a function of instructional and other interventions or as a result of experimental manipulations of content and conditions.
- Finally, we can appraise the value implications and social consequences of interpreting and using the test scores in particular ways, scrutinizing not only the intended outcomes but also unintended side effects.

One or another of these forms of evidence, or combinations thereof, have in the past been accorded special status as a so-called 'type of validity.' But because all of these forms of evidence fundamentally bear on the valid interpretation and use of scores, it is not a type of validity but the relation between the evidence and the inferences to be drawn that should determine the validation focus. The varieties of evidence are not alternatives but rather supplements to one another. This is the main reason that validity is now recognized as a unitary concept (American Psychological Association, AERA, and NCME, 1985).

Historically, not only were distinctions drawn among three types of validity, but each type was related to particular testing aims (American Psychological Association, 1954, 1966). This proved to be especially insidious because it implied that there were testing purposes for which one or another type of validity was sufficient. For example, content validity was deemed appropriate to support claims about an individual's present performance level in a universe of tasks or situations, criterion-related validity for claims about a person's present or future standing on some significant variable different from the test, and construct validity for claims about the extent to which an individual possesses some trait or quality reflected in test performance.

However, for reasons expounded in detail elsewhere (Messick, 1989) and reviewed in bare outline shortly, neither content nor criterion validity alone is sufficient for any testing purpose – with the possible exceptions of test samples that are truly domain samples observed under naturalistic conditions and of predictor tests having very high correlations with uncontaminated complete criteria. Even in these rare instances, however, the legitimacy of the domain sample and of the criterion measure ultimately needs to rest on construct-related evidence and arguments. Nor may the integrative and summary power of construct validity be invoked to justify a particular score interpretation or test use on the basis of just any pieces of construct evidence. Rather, the construct evidence accrued should be attuned to supporting the interpretive and action inferences to be drawn and to undercutting alternative interpretations and actions.

In instances of test use, this construct-related evidence would include specific appraisals of the relevance, utility, and consequences of the scores in the applied setting. Thus, because test use is or should be based on the action implications of score meaning, general evidence supportive of the construct interpretation of scores needs to be buttressed in areas of test use by specific evidence of relevance, utility, and consequences contributing to the construct validity of the action implications. In short, construct validation entails evidence supportive of (or counter to) not only the substantive or theoretical implications of score meaning but also the value implications.

Neither Content nor Criterion Validity Suffices

Let us first underscore some critical limitations of the traditional 'types' of validity and then consider other ways of configuring validity evidence to highlight major facets of meaning and values in a unified validity conception. By comparing these three so-called validity types with the half dozen or so forms of evidence outlined earlier, we can quickly discern what evidence each validity type relies on as well as what each leaves out.

Content Validity
In its perennial form, content validity is based on expert judgments about the relevance of the test content to the content of a particular behavioral domain of interest and about the representativeness with which item or task content covers that domain. Content validity as such is not concerned with response processes, internal or external test structures, performance differences across groups and settings, responsiveness of scores to experimental intervention, or with social consequences. Thus, content validity provides judgmental evidence in support of the domain relevance and representativeness of the content of the test instrument, rather than evidence to sustain inferences made from test scores. Response consistencies and test scores are not even addressed in typical accounts of content validity. To be sure, some test specifications do make reference to desired cognitive levels or response processes. But validity in these instances, being inferred not from test content but from consistencies in test responses and their correlates, is patently construct related.

In a fundamental sense, then, so-called content validity does not qualify as validity at all, although such considerations of content relevance and representativeness clearly do and should influence the nature of score inferences supported by other evidence. Furthermore, the ubiquitous problem of irrelevant test variance, especially method variance, is simply not confronted in the content validity framework, even though irrelevant variance serves to subvert judgments of content relevance. For example, experts may judge certain ostensible items of knowledge and skill to be highly relevant to domain performance, but the items themselves might instead tap reading comprehension or contain such transparent distractors that they primarily reflect merely testwiseness or common sense. Indeed, irrelevant test variance contributes, along with other factors, to the ultimate frailty of classical content validation, namely, that expert judgment is fallible and may imperfectly apprehend domain structure or inadequately represent test structure, or both. The way out of this bind is to evaluate (and inform) expert judgment on the basis of other evidence about the structure of the behavioral domain under scrutiny as well as about the structure of test responses. This other evidence, in actuality, is construct-related evidence, which will be discussed shortly.

Criterion Validity

In contrast with content validity, criterion-related validity is based on the degree of empirical correlation between the test scores and criterion scores. As such, criterion-related validity relies on selected parts of the test's external structure. The interest is not in the pattern of relationships of the test scores with other measures generally, but rather is more narrowly pointed toward selected relationships with measures deemed criterial for a particular applied purpose in a specific applied setting. As a consequence, there are as many criterion-related validities for the test scores as there are criterion measures and settings, and the extent to which a criterion correlation can be generalized across settings and times has become an important and contentious empirical question (Schmidt *et al.*, with commentary by Sackett *et al.*, 1985).

Thus, in its pure form, criterion-related validity is not concerned with any other sorts of evidence except specific test-criterion correlations or, more generally, the regression system linking the criterion to predictor scores. But criterion scores are *measures* to be evaluated like all measures. They too may be deficient in capturing the criterion domain of interest and may be contaminated by irrelevant variance – as in supervisors' ratings, for example, which are typically distorted by selective attention and by halo or other biases. As another example, consider the use of a written exit examination in a job-training program for mechanics, which gives short shrift to manipulation skills and at the same time is burdened by intrusive verbal variance. Consequently, potentially deficient and contaminated criterion measures cannot serve as the unequivocal standards for validating tests, as is intrinsic in the criterion-oriented approach to validation. The way out of this paradox is to evaluate the criterion measures, as well as the tests, in relation to construct theories of the criterion domain. Once again, such a resolution portends the potential power of construct validity, to which we now turn.

Comprehensiveness of Construct Validity

Construct validity is based on an integration of any evidence that bears on the interpretation or meaning of the test scores. The test score is not equated with the construct it attempts to tap, nor is it considered to define the construct, as in strict operationism. Rather, the measure is viewed as just one of an extensible set of indicators of the construct. Convergent empirical relationships reflecting communality among such indicators is taken to imply the operation of the construct to the degree that discriminant evidence discounts the intrusion of alternative constructs as plausible rival hypotheses. The two major threats to construct validity are *construct underrepresentation* – that is, the test is too narrow and fails to include important dimensions or facets of the construct – and *construct-irrelevant variance* – that is, the test contains excess reliable variance, making items or tasks easier or harder for some respondents in a manner irrelevant to the interpreted construct. In essence, construct validity comprises the evidence and rationales supporting the trustworthiness of score interpretation in terms of explanatory concepts that account for both test performance and score relationships with other variables.

Almost any kind of information about a test can contribute to an understanding of its construct validity, but the contribution becomes stronger if the degree of fit of the information with the theoretical rationale underlying score interpretation is explicitly evaluated. Historically, primary emphasis in construct validation has been placed on internal and external test structures – that is, on the appraisal of theoretically expected patterns of relationships among item scores or between test scores and other measures. Probably more illuminating of score meaning, however, are studies of expected performance differences over time, across groups and settings, and in response to experimental treatments and manipulations. Possibly most illuminating of all are direct probes and modeling of the processes underlying test responses, an approach becoming both more accessible and more powerful with continuing developments in cognitive psychology.

Construct validity also subsumes content relevance and representativeness as well as criterion-relatedness, because such information about the range and limits of content coverage and about specific criterion behaviors predicted by the test scores clearly contributes to score interpretation. In the latter instance, as anticipated earlier, correlations between test scores and criterion measures – viewed in the broader context of other evidence supportive of score meaning – contribute to the joint construct validity of both predictor and criterion. In other words, empirical relationships between predictor scores and criterion measures should make theoretical sense in terms of what the predictor test is interpreted to measure and what the criterion is presumed to embody (Gulliksen, 1950).

In one way or another, then, these three traditional types of validity, taken together, make explicit reference to all but one of the forms of validity evidence mentioned earlier. This occurs in spite of the ad hoc singularity of reference of both content and criterion-related validity, but because of the comprehensiveness of reference of construct validity. The only form of validity evidence bypassed or neglected in these traditional formulations is that which bears on the social consequences of test interpretation and use.

It is ironic that little attention has been paid over the years to the consequential basis of test validity, because validity has been cogently conceptualized in the past in terms of the functional worth of the testing – that is, in terms of how well the test does the job it is employed to do (Rulon, 1946; Cureton, 1951). To appraise how well a test does its job, we must inquire whether the potential and actual social consequences of test interpretation and use are not only supportive of the intended testing purposes, but at the same time are consistent with other social values. However, this form of evidence should not be viewed in isolation as a fourth validity type, say, of 'consequential validity.' Rather, because the values served in the intended and unintended outcomes of test interpretation and use both derive from and contribute to the meaning of the test scores, appraisal of social consequences of the testing is also seen to be subsumed as an aspect of construct validity (Messick, 1964, 1975, 1980).

In viewing the three traditional types of validity, we discern that the touchstone in content validation is expert judgment specifying the relevance and representativeness of the test content vis-à-vis domain content. The touchstone in criterion-oriented validity is the criterion measure, which serves as the standard for evaluating the relevance and utility of the test scores. As we have seen, the basic problem is that these touchstones are not only fallible or subject to error, but possibly bogus. In contrast, the touchstone in construct validation is convergent and discriminant evidence corroborating score meaning and discounting plausible rival interpretations. Although any piece of evidence may be fallible and some may be spurious, the continuing construct validation process attempts to appraise, and take into account, the nature and extent of such distortion in the evolving validity judgment.

Indeed, such convergent and discriminant evidence provides a rational basis for evaluating the other two, suspect touchstones in particular instances. In other words, construct-related evidence is critical in the very delineation of content domains and in the conceptualization and measurement of applied criteria – that is, in precisely those aspects of domain coverage and criterion prediction that are at the heart of traditional content- and criterion-oriented validities. From this standpoint, the construct validity of score interpretation comes to undergird *all* score-based inferences – not just those related to interpretive meaningfulness but including the content- and criterion-related inferences specific to applied decisions and actions based on test scores.

Thus, the validity of score meaning and of the action and value implications derived therefrom – that is, the construct validity of both the substantive or trait connotations and the value connotations of the score interpretation – is central to all test validation. This means that, fundamentally, all validation is construct validation, in the sense that all validity evidence contributes to (or undercuts) the empirical grounding or trust-

worthincss of the score interpretation. And the validity of score interpretation provides the main rationale sustaining inferences and actions
based on test scores. We turn now to a brief examination of some of the
scientific and ethical implications of this unified view of validity.

Science and Ethics in Test Interpretation and Use

The unified concept of validity integrates considerations of content, criteria, and consequences into a construct framework for testing rational hypotheses about theoretically relevant relationships. These hypotheses
relate to data patterns expected not only on the basis of provisional score
meaning but on the basis of the relevance and utility of the scores for
particular purposes, on the basis of value implications of the score interpretation, and on the basis of the presumed relative import of intended and
unintended outcomes of score use. Thus, the unified concept of validity
embraces not only scientific hypotheses but applied hypotheses as well.
Furthermore, the source of these hypotheses, apart from empirical seren-
dipity, is basically the same in both scientific and applied instances –
namely, the hypotheses derive from construct theories of the scientific or
applied domain of interest.

The bridge or connective tissue that sustains this unified view of
validity is the meaningfulness or trustworthy interpretability of the test
scores, which is the goal of construct validation. In other words, the
essence of this unified view is that the appropriateness, meaningfulness,
and usefulness of score-based inferences are inseparable and that the
integrating power derives from empirically grounded construct
interpretation. Hence, construct validity is a sine qua non in the
validation not only of test interpretation but also of test use, in the sense
that relevance and utility as well as appropriateness of test use depend, or
should depend, on score meaning. To act otherwise is not just dubious but
dangerous. Using test scores that 'work' in practice without some
understanding of what they mean is like using a drug that works without
knowing its properties and reactions. You may get some immediate relief,
to be sure, but you had better ascertain and monitor the side effects. And
although evaluation of side effects – or more generally, of the social
consequences of the testing – contributes to score meaning, it is a weak
substitute for score meaning in the rational justification of test use.

Facets of Unified Validity

To speak of validity as a unified concept is not to imply that validity cannot
be differentiated into facets to highlight issues and nuances that might
otherwise be downplayed or overlooked. But this, too, is simply a manner

of speaking, and a complicated manner of speaking at that. For example, the distinctions introduced may seem fuzzy because the facets of validity are not only intertwined but overlapping, which derives from the fact that we are trying for purposes of clarification to cut through what indeed is a unitary concept. Nonetheless, these distinctions provide us with a means of addressing functional aspects of validity that help disentangle some of the complexities inherent in appraising the appropriateness, meaningfulness, and usefulness of score inferences.

As we have seen, traditional ways of configuring validity evidence have led to three major categories of content-related, criterion-related, and construct-related evidence. However, because content- and criterion-related evidence contribute to score meaning, they have come to be recognized as aspects of construct validity, as has the appraisal of social or value consequences of testing. In a sense, then, this leaves only one category, namely, construct-related evidence. But being left with a single global category including almost any kind of information about a test that contributes to an understanding of score meaning is not very helpful. Various facets of validity attuned to the inferences drawn and to the discounting of rival inferences need to be introduced to help decide when the balance of evidence is sufficiently comprehensive and on target to justify, at least provisionally, the proposed inferences and actions.

For example, in scientific uses of tests, evidence bearing on the value implications of score interpretation is rarely even sought as opposed to that bearing on the substantive or trait implications. Thus, when there are multiple sources of inference underlying the score interpretation, one needs multiple sources of pertinent evidence to fully firm up the validity argument. Appeal to general construct validity evidence of whatever sort may not be sufficient in covering the various bases, thereby allowing imbalances such as that between trait-relevant and value-relevant evidence just alluded to. The problem is that an undifferentiated view of construct validity evidence provides no framework for detecting or redressing such imbalances. Attention must also be directed to important *facets* of validity, especially those of value as well as of meaning.

This is not a trivial issue, because the value implications of score interpretation are not only part of score meaning, but a socially relevant part that often triggers score-based actions and serves to link the construct measured to questions of applied practice and social policy. Consider, for example, the evaluative implications of just the construct label itself. As a case in point, envision a performance measure that at one extreme reflects continual changes in strategy in attacking successive problems and at the other extreme reflects the repeated application of a single strategy. The evaluative implications of score interpretations would be very different if the construct being measured were conceptualized as 'flexibility versus rigidity,' say, as opposed to 'confusion versus consistency.' Similarly, a construct and its associated measures interpreted as 'inhibited versus impulsive' would have different implications if it were instead labeled 'self-controlled versus self-expressive,' and distinctly different yet if labeled 'inhibited versus expressive.' So would a variable like 'stress' if it were relabeled as 'challenge.'

The point is not that a concept like 'stress' is converted from something bad to something good by renaming it but, rather, that the name has implications of good or bad valuations that can be supported or contravened by evidence. More important, by evaluating the extent to which stress is good or bad, we would be more likely to investigate a broader range of consequences, facilitative as well as debilitative. Thus, appraisal of the value implications of construct interpretation contributes to the scientific probing of score meaning as well as to clarification of the action implications of score meaning.

As with scientific uses of tests, being left with only one undifferentiated category of construct-related evidence is not very helpful in applied uses of tests, either – unless facets of construct evidence relevant to applied decision making are taken into account. This is the case because, in practical testing applications, there needs to be some means of assuring that *general* evidence supportive of construct validity includes *specific* evidence of the relevance of the test to the applied purpose and of the utility of the scores in the applied setting. Cutting validity evidence into three categories that are then folded into one does not illuminate these nuances in the roles of specific content-and criterion-related evidence as ad hoc adjuncts to construct validity in justifying test use.

Furthermore, the continuing reference to three categories of validity evidence perpetuates, no less than did reference to three types of validity, the temptation to rely on only one (or, worse still, any one) category of evidence as sufficient for the validity of a particular test use. What is needed is a way of configuring validity evidence that forestalls undue reliance on selected forms of evidence, that highlights the important though subsidiary role of specific content- and criterion-related evidence in support of construct validity in testing applications, and that formally brings consideration of value implications and social consequences into the validity framework.

Both Meaning and Values in Score Interpretation and Use

These needs may be met by distinguishing two interconnected facets of the unitary validity concept. One facet is the source of justification of the testing, being based on appraisal either of evidence supportive of score meaning or of consequences contributing to score valuation. The other facet is the function or outcome of the testing, being either interpretation or use. If the facet for source of justification – that is, either an evidential basis for meaning implications or a consequential basis for value implications of scores – is crossed with the facet for function or outcome of the testing – that is, either test interpretation or test use – we obtain a fourfold classification highlighting both meaning and values in both test

Table 11.1   *Facets of validity as a progressive matrix*

	Test Interpretation	Test Use
Evidential Basis	Construct Validity (CV)	CV + Relevance/Utility (R/U)
Consequential Basis	CV + Value Implications (VI)	CV + R/U + VI + Social Consequences

interpretation and test use, as represented by the row and column headings of Table 11.1. The four cells thereby generated correspond to the four interrelated aspects of the basic validity question, with which we began. These four aspects, it will be recalled, bear on the empirical grounding of score interpretation, on score meaning as a rational basis for test use, on the value implications of scores as a basis for action, and on the functional worth of the testing in terms of social consequences.

Let us briefly consider in turn each of the cells in this fourfold crosscutting of unified validity, beginning with the evidential basis of test interpretation. Because the evidence and rationales supporting the trustworthiness of score meaning is what is meant by construct validity, the evidential basis of test interpretation is clearly construct validity. The evidential basis of test use is also construct validity, but with the important proviso that the general evidence supportive of score meaning be enhanced by specific evidence for the relevance of the scores to the applied purpose and for the utility of the scores in the applied setting.

The consequential basis of test interpretation is the appraisal of value implications of score meaning, including value implications of the construct label itself, of the broader theory that undergirds construct meaning, and of the still broader ideologies that give theories their perspective and purpose. A central issue is whether or not the theoretical implications and the value implications of the test interpretation are commensurate, because value implications are not ancillary but, rather, integral to score meaning. However, to make clear that score interpretation is needed to appraise value implications and vice versa, this cell for the consequential basis of test interpretation needs to comprehend both the construct validity as well as the value ramifications of score meaning. Finally, the consequential basis of test use is the appraisal of both potential and actual social consequences of the applied testing. And once again, in recognition of the fact that the weighing of social consequences both presumes and contributes to evidence of score meaning, of relevance, of utility, and of values, this cell needs to include construct validity, relevance, and utility as well as social and value consequences.

Thus, construct validity appears in every cell, which is fitting because construct validity is the integrating force that unifies validity issues into a unitary concept. At the same time, by distinguishing facets reflecting the justification and function of the testing, it becomes clear that distinct aspects of construct validity need to be emphasized, in addition to the general mosaic of evidence, as one moves from appraisal of evidence for the construct interpretation per se, to appraisal of evidence supportive of test use, to appraisal of the value consequences of score interpretation, and, finally, to appraisal of the social consequences – or, more generally, of the functional worth – of test use. As different foci of emphasis are added to the basic construct validity appearing in each cell, this movement makes what at first glance was a simple fourfold classification appear more like a *progressive matrix,* as portrayed in the cells of Table 11.1. One implication of this progressive-matrix formulation is that both meaning and values, as well as both test interpretation and test use, are intertwined in the validation process.

In contrast, some measurement specialists maintain that test interpretation and test use are separate issues, so they should be treated more independently than is done in the unified validity framework. From this standpoint, construct validity is usually accepted as the validity of test interpretation, but the validity of test use is appraised in terms of relevance or utility, or both. But judgments of relevance and utility as well as of appropriateness depend, or should depend, on the meaning of the test scores. Hence, construct validity binds the validity of test use to the validity of test interpretation, as is made explicit in the unified validity view.

Others contend that value implications and social consequences of testing are policy issues separate from test validity as such, so that they too should be treated as something different from or independent of validity evidence. But a social consequence of testing either stems from a source of test *in*validity or else reflects a valid property of the construct assessed, or both. For example, adverse impact against females in the use of a quantitative test for admission into science programs might stem from undue reliance on spatial geometric items, on which males typically outperform females, or might instead reflect a consistent gender difference in quantitative performance more broadly on an array of tasks representative of that cognitive domain. In the former case, the adverse consequence bears on the meaning of the test scores and, in the latter case, on the meaning of the construct – as would further evidence on the source and determinants of the gender differences in quantitative performance. In both cases, therefore, construct validity binds social consequences of testing to the evidential basis of test interpretation and use, as the progressive-matrix formulation makes explicit.

Still others argue that test validity should not bear the additional burden of value judgments. Their main objection is that the occurrence of contending values with respect to score meaning and testing outcomes would make it difficult, if not impossible, to determine whether a proposed test interpretation or use were valid or not. But validity, except in extreme cases, is not an all-or-none question. On the contrary, it is a question of the *degree* to which evidence and rationales support the adequacy and appropriateness of interpretations and uses of scores. And an integrated evaluative judgment of the adequacy and appropriateness of a particular score interpretation and use includes a weighing of the possibly conflicting value implications and social consequences of the testing. That is, the question of validity is addressed by appraising the weight or balance of the evidence and arguments, including conflicting arguments.

Furthermore, it is simply not the case that values are being added to validity in the unified view. Rather, values are intrinsic to the meaning and outcomes of the testing. For example, information about the utility of scores for a particular purpose is both validity evidence and a value consequence. As opposed to adding values to validity as an adjunct or supplement, the unified view instead exposes the inherent value aspects of score meaning and outcome to open examination and debate as an integral part of the validation process. This makes explicit what has been latent all along, namely, that validity judgments *are* value judgments.

Accordingly, the validity of test interpretation and test use, as well as the evidence and consequences bearing thereon, are highlighted in this unified faceted framework, because of a conviction that the commonality afforded by construct validity will in the long run prove more powerful and integrative than any operative distinctions among the facets. None of this is meant to imply, however, that value implications and social consequences are not issues of social policy but, rather, that they are not *only* issues of social policy. To be sure, the determination of social policy falls beyond the pale of validity theory. But the interpretation of test scores and, more dramatically, the use of test scores in the implementation of social policy falls well within the realm of validity inquiry, because the import of scores for action depends on the validity of their meaning and their value implications. This is why validity and values are one imperative, not two, and why validation implicates both the science and the ethics of assessment.

Social Consequences as Signs of Validity or Invalidity

Social consequences, being a form of evidence bearing both on the meaning of scores and on their action import, clearly have implications for both the science and the ethics of assessment. But so may all the other aspects of unified validity highlighted here. It will be recalled that the basic validity question was cast not in a logic of indicatives but in a logic of imperatives – '*Should* the test scores be interpreted and used in the manner proposed?' This was done deliberately as one means of raising consciousness about the ethical and not just the scientific underpinnings of testing and test validation. For similar reasons, the term 'appropriateness' was consistently used along with 'adequacy' in characterizing the validity of inferences and actions based on test scores. Indeed, consciousness would be raised even further on this point by asking what the consequences would be if a given scientific judgment about the validity of test interpretation and use also had the status of an ethical judgment and were routinely treated as such (Singer, 1959; Churchman, 1971).

It is important to recognize, however, that the appraisal of consequences depends not only on their valuation but on their origins or causes. What matters is not only whether the social consequences of test interpretation and use are positive or negative, but what source and determinants engendered the effect. In particular, it is not that adverse social consequences of test use render the use invalid but, rather, that adverse social consequences should not be attributable to any source of test invalidity such as construct-irrelevant variance. If the adverse social consequences are empirically traceable to sources of test invalidity, such as undue reading comprehension requirements in a purported test of knowledge or of reasoning, then the validity of the test use is jeopardized, especially for less proficient readers. If the social consequences cannot be so traced – or if the validation process can discount sources of test invalidity as the likely determinants, or at least render them less plausible – then the validity of the test use is not overturned. Although adverse social consequences associated with valid test interpretation and use implicate the attributes validly assessed as they function under the existing social conditions of the applied setting, such as authentic group differences in knowledge or skill, they are not in themselves indicative of test invalidity.

In general, the best protection against adverse social consequences as threats to valid score interpretation and use is to minimize in the measurement process any potential sources of test invalidity, especially construct under-representation and construct-irrelevant variance in the test. Thus, the watchword for educational and psychological measurement is to maximize empirically grounded interpretability and minimize construct irrelevancy in the test scores.

The role of social consequences, and of values more generally, in test validation is becoming increasingly visible. For example, in his treatment of validation as persuasive argument, Cronbach (1988) stresses that '*the argument must link concepts, evidence, social and personal consequences, and values*' (p. 4). Furthermore, he maintains that 'the bottom line is that validators have an obligation to review whether a practice has appropriate consequences for individuals and institutions, and especially to guard against adverse consequences. You . . . may prefer to exclude reflection on consequences from meanings of the word *validation*, but you cannot deny the obligation' (p. 3). But we would prefer a somewhat stronger phrasing, because the meaning of validation should not be considered a preference. On what can the legitimacy of the obligation to appraise social consequences of test interpretation and use be based, we argue, if not on the only genuine imperative in testing, namely, validity?

References

American Psychological Association. (1954). Technical recommendations for psychological tests and diagnostic techniques. *Psychological Bulletin, 51*(2, Part 2).

American Psychological Association. (1966). *Standards for educational and psychological tests and manuals.* Washington, DC: Author.

American Psychological Association, American Educational Research Association, & National Council on Measurement in Education. (1985). *Standards for educational and psychological testing.* Washington, DC: American Psychological Association.

Churchman, C. W. (1971). *The design of inquiring systems: Basic concepts of systems and organization.* New York: Basic Books.

Cronbach, L. J. (1988). Construct validation after thirty years. In R. L. Linn (ed.), *Intelligence: Measurement theory and public policy* (Proceedings of a symposium in honor of Lloyd G. Humphreys. Manuscript copy). Urbana: University of Illinois Press.

Cureton, E. E. (1951). Validity. In E. F. Lindquist (Ed.), *Educational measurement* (1st ed., pp. 621–694). Washington, DC: American Council on Education.

Gulliksen, H. (1950). Intrinsic validity. *American Psychologist, 5,* 511–517.

Messick, S. (1964). Personality measurement and college performance. *Proceedings of the 1963 Invitational Conference on Testing Problems* (pp. 110–129). Princeton, NJ: Educational Testing Service. (Reprinted in A. Anastasi (Ed.). (1966). *Testing problems in perspective* (pp. 557–572). Washington, DC: American Council on Education.)

Messick, S. (1975). The standard problem: Meaning and values in measurement and evaluation. *American Psychologist, 30,* 955–966.

Messick, S. (1980). Test validity and the ethics of assessment. *American Psychologist, 35,* 1012–1027.

Messick, S. (1988). Validity. In R. L. Linn (Ed.), *Educational measurement* (3rd ed., pp. 13–103). New York: Macmillan.

Rulon, P. J. (1946). On the validity of educational tests. *Harvard Educational Review, 16,* 290–296.

Schmidt, F. L., Hunter, J. E., Pearlman, K., and Hirsh, H. R., with commentary by Sackett, P. R., Schmitt. N., Tenopyr, M. L., Keho, J., and Zedeck, S. (1985). Forty questions about validity generalization and meta-analysis. *Personnel Psychology, 38,* 697–798.

Singer, E. A., Jr. (1959). *Experience and reflection.* Philadelphia: University of Pennsylvania Press.

SECTION 3
LEARNING IN DOMAINS

12

On Understanding the Nature of Scientific Knowledge

Susan Carey and Carol Smith

[. . .]

One important curricular goal of science education is to help students understand the nature of the scientific enterprise itself. This goal is important for several reasons. First of all, students can master only a small fraction of scientific knowledge in the course of their schooling, but as citizens they must adopt positions on public issues that turn on controversial points. Hence, the successful science curriculum will have fed an interest in science that underlies lifelong learning, a valuing of the kind of knowledge that is acquired through a process of careful experimentation and argument, as well as a critical attitude toward the pronouncements of experts. Involving students in the process of doing science and talking with them explicitly about its nature are thought to be central to cultivating these interests, values, and attitudes.

In addition, another quite different reason for teaching students about the nature of science has recently come to the fore. Because students come to science class with theories and concepts that are different from the scientists', the successful science curriculum will have involved students in making difficult conceptual changes. An open question is the relation between student understanding of the nature of scientific knowledge and student success in learning from curricula designed to foster conceptual change. Making students aware of the process of conceptual change may help them succeed at it.

Exactly what view of the nature of science do we wish to give to students? It is common practice for current textbooks to portray scientists as engaged in a process that depends on careful observation and experiment and to teach students some of the skills involved in careful experimentation. However, overlooked in these accounts is any discussion of the role of the scientists' theories in this process. Instead, mention is only made of scientists' specific hypotheses or beliefs about the world. In some accounts, these hypotheses are seen to be a simple consequence of unbiased observation and experiment, whereas in others it is acknowledged that scientists may have hypotheses that motivate their doing a particular experiment. However, in both cases, these hypotheses are thought to be tested in unproblematic and straightforward ways by the data of critical experiments, and scientific knowledge is portrayed as the steady accumulation of a set of confirmed hypotheses. As Hodson (1985, 1988), Nadeau and Desautels (1984), and Strike and Posner (1985) claimed, such a view is essentially an inductivist or empiricist view: the origin of scientific knowledge lies solely in data about the world.

We argue (along with the just-mentioned authors) that it is important to present students with a more constructivist epistemology of science: one in which students develop an understanding that scientists hold theories that can underlie the generation and interpretation of specific hypotheses and experiments. We want them to come to understand that our knowledge of regularity in nature is a consequence of successful conjecture, rather than its precursor, and that an adequate theoretical perspective is essential to both observation and experimentation. Thus, without challenging students' faith that theories may ultimately reflect reality, we may be able to help them see that theories are large-scale intellectual constructions that constitute the scientists' understanding and guide the day-to-day activities of scientists. Such an understanding would help students understand why scientists do experiments, why there can be legitimate controversies in science, and even why learning science is difficult.

In this article, we first review the evidence that seventh-grade students come to science class with an epistemology that is at odds with the constructivist epistemology we wish to teach. We then go on to consider how that epistemology is changed as a consequence of an explicit attempt to teach them about the constructive nature of science.

Student Epistemology

Hodson (1985, 1988) and Nadeau and Desautels (1984) assumed that the existing science curricula reinforce students' own common sense views about the nature of scientific knowledge: one that sees knowledge acquisition driven solely by the data at hand. But what is the evidence for this assumption? Surprisingly, most of the evidence regarding this point is indirect. In this section, we review the evidence from three quite separate literatures that potentially can bear on this issue.

Common Sense Epistemology

The first literature concerns common sense epistemology in general, not particularly an epistemology of science. Several authors have used clinical interviews to probe adolescent and adult views of the nature of knowledge and its source and justification (e.g., Broughton, 1978; Chandler, 1987; Kitchener and King, 1981; Kuhn *et al.*, 1988; Perry, 1970). Emerging from these clinical interview studies is some consensus on the stages ordinary people go through in developing their epistemological views, although the exact number of stages and the timing of transitions has been subject to some dispute. In reviewing this literature, we focus on two related developments that we regard as important: a conception of a theory or interpretative framework and an appreciation that theoretical knowledge is acquired through indirect arguments from evidence.

Relating to the first theme, some have claimed that young children begin with a common sense epistemology in which they see knowledge arising unproblematically (and directly) from sensory experiences and see knowledge as simply the collection of many true beliefs (e.g., Chandler, 1987; Kitchener and King, 1981; Kuhn *et al.*, 1988). At this point, there is no notion that beliefs themselves are organized in intuitive theories or interpretative frameworks or that one's intuitive theory can influence one's beliefs and observations.

A study by Kuhn *et al.* (1988) provides support for this claim. They presented subjects with two accounts of a fictitious war called the Fifth Livian War, told by a historian from each of the different sides. In each account, the two historians, among other things, each claimed victory for their side. Subjects were then asked to describe in their own words what happened in the Fifth Livian War, whether the two historians' accounts were different in any important ways, and whether both accounts could be right.

Responses were coded into six stages: all sixth graders and over three quarters of the ninth graders were at the lowest three stages. A key feature of the lowest stages is that students show no awareness of 'theoretical interpretation as having played a role in the construction of the accounts and as a vehicle for reconciling them' (Kuhn *et al.*, 1988, p. 213). Instead they deal primarily on the level of objective fact, at most seeing the accounts as differing in the facts chosen for presentation. This may be due to the historians being in different places at different times or having had different motives or purposes (i.e., they may have lied or exaggerated to make their side look good). However, students at this point still assume there is a simple truth to the situation which can be known to a careful impartial observer.

In contrast, older adolescents, college, and graduate students tended to be at the highest three stages. At these stages, students are increasingly aware that the two historians have different points of view and that determining the reality of the situation is not so simple as determining who lied and who told the truth. Some believe there may in fact be multiple individual realities, whereas others acknowledge an elusive objective reality that can only be known approximately.

At the same time children are moving from a common sense epistemology that sees knowledge arising unproblematically from observations to one that sees a role for interpretative frameworks in knowledge acquisition, they are also developing more complex conceptions of how beliefs are justified. This point is nicely illustrated in Kitchener and King's (1981) studies. Like Kuhn *et al.* (1988), Kitchener and King presented students with dilemmas about differences of opinion; one difference was that they then probed students about how they would decide what to believe. They found that the younger adolescents justified beliefs primarily in terms of perceptual experiences or what they were told by authorities. Sometime in late adolescence (especially for students who go to college), students become aware of genuine differences in the interpretation of the same facts and, consequently, that even authorities may disagree. This leads to an epistemological crisis, a period in which students are radical relativists and hold there is no true knowledge and everybody is free to believe whatever they want. Finally, in the college years, some people reach a mature epistemology that not only recognizes the relativity of belief to interpretative frameworks, but also recognizes that there are canons of rational justification of belief. Beliefs need to be justified in terms of arguments from patterns of data, and some beliefs are better justified than others.

Although these data certainly indicate likely differences between the epistemological beliefs of young adolescents and adults, other data indicate that these authors may not have done full justice to the complexity of the beliefs of young adolescents. For example, in Kuhn *et al.*'s (1988) earliest stage, it is asserted that students fail to make a distinction between the account of an event and the event itself; similarly, in Kitchener and King's (1981) earliest stage, there is no awareness that one's own beliefs can be false or different from an expert's. Both of these stages are thought to characterize a number of young adolescent children. Yet, there is now very good evidence (using a different methodology that calls for less formal and verbalized understandings) that even 3-year-olds can make distinctions between their beliefs about reality and reality itself and understand that people can have false beliefs (see, e.g., the work of Wellman, 1990).

Another example of an oversimplification in Kitchener and King's (1981) account of early adolescent epistemology concerns their claims that students view perceptual experience and expert testimony as the sole sources of belief and that students do not realize that the same facts can be given different interpretations or that there can be legitimate differences in opinion. Again, however, there is now good evidence that even 6-year-olds understand that inference is a genuine source of knowledge (Sodian and Wimmer, 1987). In addition, Taylor *et al.* (1991) showed that by age 6, children are beginning to understand that the same visible stimulus might be interpreted differently by different people, depending on their background knowledge. (Although presumably only one interpretation is right; the other interpretations are wrong due either to misinformation or ignorance.) Finally, Flavell *et al.* (1990) demonstrated that even 3-year-olds are aware that people can have differences of opinion especially about questions of value.

An adequate characterization of young students' epistemology must integrate findings from these diverse methodologies. Appendix A sketches our preliminary attempt to give a richer account of students' early epistemology and to contrast it with a later epistemology which makes clear use of a notion of theory. Both are constructivist epistemologies in the sense that they acknowledge that one's present beliefs can affect one's observations and subsequent knowledge. And both are realist in the sense that both assume the existence of an objective reality. However, in the first (dubbed *knowledge unproblematic*), it is assumed knowledge of reality can be obtained with enough diligent observation, whereas in the second (dubbed *knowledge problematic*), reality can be known only through successive approximations via a process of critical inquiry. We offer these, tentatively, as the beginning point and one relatively sophisticated possible endpoint for school-aged children's epistemologies. Clearly, there are many intermediate steps between these two points.

Process Skills

The second literature that bears indirectly on students' epistemology of science concerns attempts to construct scientific arguments. These are studies of the so-called science process skills (e.g., Dunbar and Klahr, 1989; Inhelder and Piaget, 1958; Kuhn *et al.*, 1988). Many studies show that preadolescents and young adolescents do not appreciate the logic of argumentation from experimental results. Dramatic deficiencies in designing experiments and/or drawing conclusions from experimental evidence are amply documented in Inhelder and Piaget's (1958) classic work exploring the development of scientific reasoning and in more recent work by Kuhn *et al.* (1988) and Dunbar and Klahr (1989).

There may be at least two distinct deficiencies underlying children's problems on such tasks. On the one hand, students may genuinely lack knowledge of aspects of the logic of hypothesis testing. For example, Kahneman *et al.* (1982) documented errors in statistical reasoning that are made even by quite sophisticated adults. On the other hand, students' difficulties may in part reflect their commitment to a naive epistemology that makes no clear distinction between theory, specific hypothesis, and evidence. Such an epistemology leads them to expect a more direct relation between hypothesis and experiment than exists, to overlook the role of auxiliary assumptions in testing hypotheses, and to reach more certain conclusions from their data than the data in fact allow. In this way, some of the literature on deficiencies in process skills may indirectly support the existence of the knowledge unproblematic epistemology of young children.

Kuhn *et al.* (1988) reported a series of studies in which they looked at students' abilities to modify their initial theories (e.g., about the causes of colds) in light of experimental evidence that was presented to them. Subjects of all ages, even adults, found their tasks difficult. That is, even lay adults were poor at drawing proper conclusions from patterns of statistical evidence. However, Kuhn *et al.* (1988) also argued that the way young children responded indicated that they did not have a clear notion of theory which they distinguished from evidence. In particular, they noted that fewer than one third of the sixth graders spontaneously referred to evidence when answering whether the scientist's data showed that a given variable makes a difference to some outcome. What subjects did, instead of referring to the evidence, was to restate their theory or elaborate it with a mechanism. When the evidence was at odds with their theory, only graduate students were likely to distinguish what they thought from what the scientists' evidence showed. Instead subjects changed their hypotheses and only later mentioned evidence. When their theory was compatible with the evidence, Kuhn *et al.* (1988) described the subjects as regarding the evidence as 'equivalent to *instances* of the theory that serve to illustrate it, while the theory in turn serves to explain the evidence . . . . The two meld into a single representation of "the way things are"' (p. 221).

We believe Kuhn *et al.*'s (1988) findings are consistent with young adolescents' knowledge unproblematic epistemology: one in which they do not yet distinguish between theory and belief and one in which they do not yet see the importance of indirect, multistepped arguments in specific hypothesis testing. At the same time, note that the kinds of findings just presented, although consistent with this hypothesis, do not provide strong evidence for it, for two reasons. First, it is hard to disentangle how much of their difficulty is with the specific statistical inferences they are asked to draw and how much is because of their holding the more limited epistemology which makes it hard for them to appreciate what it means to test a hypothesis. Second, note that the studies do not assess a concept of 'theory' in the sense of an interpretative framework; the theories tapped by these studies are simply beliefs about causal relations among single variables.

Epistemology of Science

A third literature derives from more direct study of students' verbalizable epistemology of science. Two of the most ambitious standardized tests (Test of Understanding Science, Klopfer and Carrier, 1970; the Nature of Scientific Knowledge Scale, Rubba and Anderson, 1978) probe for an understanding of science as a set of theories built up through a process of critical inquiry. Results reveal that young adolescents have much to learn about science in this regard but make steady progress toward such understanding throughout secondary school and college, especially as a result of specific instruction (Rubba and Anderson, 1978). However, these standardized tests were not designed to probe for the existence of an alternative epistemology in students. To remedy this limitation, two clinical interviews of seventh-grade students' epistemology of science were conducted.

In the first study, students were asked about the nature and purpose of science, the role of experiments in a scientist's work, and the relations among ideas, experiments, and results/data (see Carey *et al.*, 1989, for further details). Interview questions were divided into six sections, and students' responses on each section were coded into categories that reflected three general levels of understanding. Appendix B summarizes the three general levels that were coded in this study, ranging from Level 1, in which the goal of science is seen simply in terms of gathering specific facts about the world, to Level 3, in which the goal of science is seen in terms of a process of generating ever deeper explanations of the natural world.

Twenty-seven of the seventh-grade students were interviewed prior to their curriculum unit on the nature of science, and the overall mean level was 1.0. Only 4 students had an overall mean score over 1.5. Perhaps the most critical feature of Level 1 is the absence of an appreciation that ideas are distinct, constructed, and manipulable entities that motivate the scientist's more tangible experimental work. In Level 1 understanding, nature is there for the knowing. Accordingly, scientists 'discover' facts and answers that exist, almost as objects 'out there.' Scientists' ideas themselves, however, are never the object of scrutiny.

In the second interview study (Grosslight *et al.*, 1991), researchers probed students' conceptions of science in quite a different manner, but the results were quite similar. Students were asked questions such as, 'What comes to mind when you hear the word *model*, What are models for?, What do you have to think about when making a model?, How do scientists use models?,' and 'Would a scientist ever change a model?' In addition, a number of physical items such as a toy airplane, a subway map, and a picture of a house were presented, and the students were asked to explain whether these could be called models. As in the nature of science interview, three general levels in thinking about models were identified. These differ in how students talk about the relation of models to reality and the role of ideas in models. Appendix C gives a characterization of the dominant ideas at each level, ranging from a Level 1 understanding, in which models are seen as little copies of reality, to a Level 3 understanding, in which models are seen as tools used in the construction and testing of scientists' theories about the world.

In this study (Grosslight *et al.*, 1991), both seventh and eleventh graders were interviewed. Levels were assigned based on six separately scored dimensions (the role of ideas, the use of symbols, the role of model makers, communication, testing, and multiplicity of models). Each student was given six scores, corresponding to each dimension. A student scoring at the same level across five or six dimensions was assigned that level; all students with mixed levels straddled two adjacent levels and were assigned mixed levels (e.g., Level 1/2). Using this scheme, Grosslight *et al.* found that the majority (67%) of seventh graders were at Level 1. Only 12% of the seventh graders were at Level 2, and 18% had Level 1/2 scores. Turning to the eleventh graders, Grosslight *et al.* found that only 23% were pure Level 1s. The rest were split evenly between Level 1/2 (36%) and Level 2 (36%).

Overall, the reliability in scoring the levels was moderate in Study 1 (74%) and quite high in Study 2 (84%). One problem in the first study was that the interview was not designed to clearly probe the difference between Level 2 and Level 3 understandings. In retrospect, this is a significant shortcoming, because both Level 1 and 2 understandings may fall within the knowledge unproblematic epistemology (described in Appendix A), whereas Level 3 calls for a more mature constructivist epistemology, closer to the knowledge problematic epistemology (described in Appendix A). Currently, revisions are being made to the interview and scoring system to handle these shortcomings. Although in both studies no students gave evidence of a Level 3 epistemology, some validation of its existence came from interviews of a group of expert scientists using the nature of models interview. All the scientists clearly showed Level 3 understanding.

Certainly further work is needed to clarify the nature of these levels and to determine how consistent student epistemology is, both within and across domains. For example, it is possible that students may be more advanced in their common sense epistemology than in their epistemology of science. Yet the results from the three different literatures are all consistent with the claim that seventh-grade students have an alternative epistemology that they bring to science class that is at odds with the constructivist epistemology that we wish to teach.

Levels and Development

Suppose that we have correctly characterized the junior high school students' common sense epistemology of science. Two questions of urgent importance to educators now arise. First, in what sense are these levels developmental? Is there something else we know about 12-year-olds that would help us understand these levels? Second (and distinctly), do these levels provide barriers to grasping a constructivist epistemology if such is made the target of science curricula?

We do not believe these levels reflect stages in Piaget's sense (see Carey, 1985a, for a review of these issues). That is, they are unlikely to reflect some other, more abstract, cognitive failing of the child. The approach we favor is to characterize knowledge acquisition and knowledge reorganization within cognitive domains. So, for example, we have characterized changes in the child's intuitive biology (Carey, 1985b) and in the child's intuitive theory of matter (Carey, 1991; Smith *et al.*, 1985). We see epistemology as part of one such domain – an intuitive theory of mind – that has a specific developmental history (e.g., Wellman, 1990). Understanding why junior high school students have these particular epistemological views consists of understanding their construction of a theory of mind, a process that begins in infancy.

That the levels probably do not reflect stages in Piaget's sense does not mean that they do not provide important constraints on student understanding. Domain-specific knowledge acquisition often involves large-scale reorganization and genuine conceptual change (Carey, 1985b, 1991). It is an open question whether a transition from Level 2 to Level 3 epistemology requires such a reorganization. The levels are not yet well enough characterized to even hazard a guess. One source of evidence relevant to the issue is the success of curricula designed to foster this transition. Insofar as the curricular ideas are sound, the students' failure to grasp Level 3 ideas would suggest that Level 1 and Level 2 epistemologies provide constraints on understanding Level 3 points.

Effects of Curricular Intervention on Student Epistemology

At the junior high school level, curricular interventions concerning meta-conceptual lessons about science have focused primarily on process skills. Although such skills are an important component of scientific inquiry, their mastery constitutes only a small part of the goals for student understanding of scientific knowledge just outlined. In this section, we first contrast two approaches to teaching seventh-grade students about the nature of science: a traditional approach with its emphasis on teaching process skills out of context and our approach with its emphasis on teaching these skills in the context of genuine scientific inquiry. We argue that only the latter approach has a chance at challenging the entrenched knowledge unproblematic epistemology that students bring with them to science classes. Then we discuss briefly the results of using this more innovative unit with seventh graders and raise a series of questions that need to be addressed in subsequent research.

The Standard Curricular Approach to Teaching about Inquiry

Much of current educational practice grows out of curriculum reform efforts that have emphasized the teaching of the process skills involved in the construction of scientific knowledge with such diverse skills as observation, classification, measurement, conducting controlled experiments, and constructing data tables and graphs of experimental results. These skills are typically covered in the junior high school science curriculum, beginning with the introduction of the scientific method in the seventh grade. The standard curricular unit on the scientific method, for example, contains many exercises to teach students about the design of controlled experiments, such as identifying independent and dependent variables in experiments and identifying poorly designed experiments in which variables have been confounded. Although in the best of these curricula, students go on to design and conduct controlled experiments, typically, the possible hypotheses and variables for a given problem are prescribed by the curriculum. Indeed, because students are testing disembodied hypotheses, this curriculum would be expected to move students toward Level 2 understanding on the nature of science interview (i.e., toward an understanding of the role of experimentation in testing hypotheses) but not toward Level 3 understanding with its notions of theory and indirect argument.

Certainly, process skills are important elements of a careful scientific methodology. Junior high school students do not spontaneously measure and control variables or systematically record data when they first attempt experimental work. Yet the standard curriculum fails to address the motivation or justification for using these skills in constructing scientific knowledge. Students are not challenged to utilize these process skills in exploring, developing, and evaluating their own ideas about natural phenomena. Rather, instruction in the skills and methods of science is conceived outside the context of genuine inquiry. Thus, there is no context for addressing the nature and purpose of scientific inquiry or the nature of scientific knowledge.

A Theory-Building Approach to Teaching about Inquiry

We assume, but at present have no evidence for our assumption, that process skills will be more easily and better learned if they are embedded in a wider context of metaconceptual points about the nature of scientific knowledge. Such metaconceptual knowledge is important in its own right, and it can be gained only by actively constructing scientific understanding and reflecting on this process. These assumptions motivate a curricular approach that emphasizes theory building and reflection on the theory building process. Carey *et al.* (1989), therefore, developed and tested an instructional unit to replace the typical junior high school unit on the scientific method.

This instructional unit begins with the question of what makes bread rise and ends with designing a research program aimed at discovering why combining yeast, sugar, and water produces a gas, and, ultimately, the nature of yeast. The metaconceptual points in this curriculum concerned how scientists decide what experiments are worth doing, how the answer to each question we ask raises still deeper questions, how one's theories of chemistry and biology constrain the experiments one does and the interpretations of results, and how unexpected results require changes in those theories.

As a result of the yeast unit, seventh-grade students' overall mean score on the nature of science clinical interview increased from 1.0 on the pre-instruction interview to 1.55 on the postinstruction interview ($p < .001$, Wilcoxon Signed Ranks Test). Every student improved, and improvement averaged one half a level. Now 16 of the 27 students achieved overall scores of 1.5 or better (as opposed to 4 students on the preinterview), and 5 scored Level 2 or better – a score nobody achieved on the preinterview. Although these results are certainly in the right direction, movement was toward consolidating Level 2 responses; there was little evidence that students appreciated the Level 3 metaconceptual lessons included in the curriculum that called for a notion of theory and indirect argument.

The results of curricular interventions aimed at changing students' conceptions of models are even more discouraging. At Harvard's Educational Technology Center, Smith and Wiser have developed curricula using computer-implemented interactive models to foster conceptual change in two domains: the theory of matter, especially weight/density differentiation (Smith *et al.*, 1992); and thermal theory, especially heat/temperature differentiation (Wiser *et al.*, 1988). Although conceptual change in the respective domains of physics was the purpose of these model-based curricula, discussion of various metaconceptual points about the nature and use of models in science was included in each of the curricular units: in particular, the ideas that models can be used to develop and test ideas, that multiple models are possible, and that models are evaluated in terms of their usefulness or how well they serve a given purpose. There was no noticeable effect of this discussion on the postinstruction clinical interviews about models. The seventh grades scored the same on the postinstruction interviews as on the preinstruction interviews. And although the eleventh graders improved significantly to a solid Level 2 understanding, the improvement was just as great in a control group that did not have the modeling curriculum. Apparently, simply having thought about the issues as a result of the preinterview was sufficient to lead eleventh graders to better articulate their views on the postinterview.

Conclusions and Further Questions

It may be that it would be impossible for junior high school students to attain Level 3 understanding of the nature of scientific knowledge. Such understanding may have to await developments in more general epistemological beliefs and may require confronting head-on the relativism that characterizes the transition between the first and second senses of constructivism in the normal, untutored course of development. However, we do not take our failures to date as warranting this conclusion. We feel it is possible that scientific knowledge could well be an arena in which young adolescents could acquire some aspects of a constructivist epistemology in the knowledge problematic sense, in an optimal curricular environment. The curricular interventions we tried so far are far from optimal. They were both designed before we had fully appreciated the differences between students' starting epistemology and the epistemology we wished to teach, and the modeling curriculum had much less metaconceptual content than it would be possible to include. We take it to be very much an open question whether junior high school students can grasp the more sophisticated constructivism depicted in Appendix A.

Another extremely important issue for exploration is the relation between students' epistemiological beliefs and conceptual change in science content. Although many have speculated that students' epistemological beliefs interfere with successful learning of science and mathematics, there is little empirical evidence on this point. We know of no studies, for example, that show that changes in students' epistemological views affect their success in learning content. Of course, such studies will not be possible until the research program just outlined is brought to further fruition. That is, we will need accurate and detailed descriptions of student epistemology, as well as curricula that advance their epistemological views, before such studies will be possible.

Acknowledgments

The preparation of this article was supported, in part, by grants to Marianne Wiser, Carol Smith, and Susan Carey from the McDonnell Foundation (Grant No. 87–38, Clark University) and to Carol Smith and Susan Carey from the National Science Foundation (Grant No. 8955381).

References

Broughton, J. M. (1978). Development of concepts of self, mind, reality, and knowledge. In W. Damon (Ed.), *Social cognition: New directions for child development* (Vol. I, pp. 75–100). San Francisco: Jossey-Bass.

Carey, S. (1985a). Are children fundamentally different thinkers and learners from adults? In S. F. Chipman, J. W. Segal, and R. Glaser (Eds.), *Thinking and learning skills* (Vol. 2, pp. 485–517). Hillsdale, NJ: Lawrence Erlbaum Associates, Inc.

Carey, S. (1985b). *Conceptual change in childhood.* Cambridge, MA: Bradford Books/MIT Press.

Carey, S. (1991). Knowledge acquisition: Enrichment or conceptual change? In S. Carey and R. Gelman (Eds.), *Epigenesis of mind: Studies in biology and cognition* (pp. 257–291). Hillsdale, NJ: Lawrence Erlbaum Associates, Inc.

Carey, S., Evans, R., Honda, M., Jay, E., and Unger, C. M. (1989). 'An experiment is when you try it and see if it works': A study of grade 7 students' understanding of the construction of scientific knowledge. *International Journal of Science Education, 11,* 514–529.

Chandler, M. (1987). The Othello effect: Essay on the emergence and eclipse of skeptical doubt. *Human Development, 30,* 137–159.

Dunbar, K., and Klahr, D. (1989). Developmental differences in scientific discovery processes. In D. Klahr and K. Kotovsky (Eds.), *Complex information processing: The impact of Herbert A. Simon* (pp. 109–143). Hillsdale, NJ: Lawrence Erlbaum Associates, Inc.

Flavell, J., Flavell, E. R., Green, F. L., and Moses, L. (1990). Young children's understanding of fact beliefs versus value beliefs. *Child Development, 61,* 915–926.

Grosslight, L., Unger, C. M., Jay, E., and Smith, C. (1991). Understanding models and their use in science: Conceptions of middle and high school students and experts. *Journal of Research in Science Teaching, 28,* 799–822.

Hodson, D. (1985). Philosophy of science, science and science education. *Studies in Science Education, 12*, 25–57.

Hodson, D. (1988). Toward a philosophically more valid science curriculum. *Science Education, 72*, 19–40.

Inhelder, B., and Piaget, J. (1958). *The growth of logical thinking from childhood to adolescence.* New York: Basic.

Kahneman, D., Slovic, P., and Tversky, A. (Eds.). (1982). *Judgment under uncertainty: Heuristics and biases.* New York: Cambridge University Press.

Kitchener, K. S., and King, P. M. (1981). Reflective judgment: Concepts of justification and their relationship to age and education. *Journal of Applied Developmental Psychology, 2*, 89–116.

Klopfer, L. F., and Carrier, E. D. (1970). *TOUS: Test of Understanding Science (Form JW).* Pittsburgh: Learning Research and Development Center, University of Pittsburgh.

Kuhn, D., Amsel, F., and O'Loughlin, M. (1988). *The development of scientific thinking skills.* Orlando, FL: Academic.

Nadeau, R., and Desautels, J. (1984). *Epistemology and the teaching of science.* Ottawa: Science Council of Canada.

Perry, W. G. (1970). *Forms of intellectual and ethical development in the college years.* New York: Academic.

Rubba, P., and Anderson, H. (1978). Development of an instrument to assess secondary students' understanding of the nature of scientific knowledge. *Science Education, 62* (4), 449–458.

Smith, C., Carey, S., and Wiser, M. (1985). On differentiation: A case study of the development of size, weight, and density. *Cognition, 21*(3), 177–237.

Smith, C., Snir, J., and Grosslight, L. (1992). Using conceptual models to facilitate conceptual change: The case of weight-density differentiation. *Cognition and Instruction, 9*, 221–283.

Sodian, B., and Wimmer, H. (1987). Children's understanding of inference as a source of knowledge. *Child Development, 58*, 424–433.

Strike, K. A., and Posner, G. J. (1985). A conceptual change view of learning and understanding. In L. West and A. L. Pines (Eds.), *Cognitive structure and conceptual change* (pp. 211–231). New York: Academic.

Taylor, M., Cartwright, B., and Bowden, T. (1991). Perspective taking and theory of mind: Do children predict interpretive diversity as a function of differences in observer's knowledge? *Child Development, 62*, 1334–1351.

Wellman, H. (1990). *The child's theory of mind.* Cambridge, MA: MIT Press.

Wiser, M., Kipman, D., and Halkiadakis, L. (1988). *Can models foster conceptual change? The case of heat and temperature* (Tech. Rep. No. TR88–7). Cambridge, MA: Harvard Graduate School of Education, Educational Technology Center.

Appendix A

Two Contrasting Constructivist Epistemologies

Knowledge unproblematic

Knowledge consists of a collection of true beliefs. The sources of beliefs are perception, testimony, and one-step inference. Individuals may draw different conclusions from the same perceptual experience due to differences in prior knowledge or motives; individuals may have different opinions in matters of value and personal taste. Individuals with this epistemology believe there is only one objective reality that is knowable in a straightforward way by making observations. Hence, when individuals disagree about reality, it is possible for only one of them to be correct. Ultimately, ignorance, misinformation, or deceit are the causes of having false beliefs.

Knowledge problematic
Knowledge consists of theories about the world that are useful in providing a sense of understanding and/or predicting or explaining events. Individuals actively develop their theories through a process of critical inquiry. Conjectures derived from interpretative frameworks merit testing; the results constitute evidence for or against the interpretative framework and associated specific beliefs. Different people may draw different conclusions from the same perceptual experiences because they hold different theories that affect their interpretation of evidence. Reality exists, but our knowledge of it is elusive and uncertain. Theories are judged to be more or less useful, not strictly right or wrong. Canons of justification are framework relative. in addition to false beliefs due to ignorance and misinformation, beliefs can be in error for much deeper reasons: Theories can be on entirely the wrong track, positing incorrect explanations of accurate beliefs and positing entities and causal mechanisms that do not even exist.

Appendix B

Three Levels of Understanding in the Nature of Science Interview

Level 1
The students make no explicit distinction between ideas and activities for generating ideas, especially experiments. A scientist tries 'it' to see if it works. The nature of 'it' remains unspecified or ambiguous; 'it' could be an idea, a thing, an invention, or an experiment. The motivation for an activity is the achievement of the activity itself, rather than the construction of tested ideas. The goal of science is to discover facts and answers about the world and to invent things.

Level 2
Students make an explicit distinction between ideas and experiments. The motivation for experimentation is to test an idea to see if it is right. There is an understanding that the results of an experiment may lead to the abandonment or revision of an idea. However, an idea is still a guess; it is not a prediction derivable from a general theory. (Indeed, students may not yet have the general idea of a theory.) There is yet no appreciation that the revised idea must now encompass all the data, the new and the old, and that if a prediction is falsified, the theory may have to be revised.

Level 3
As in Level 2, students make a clear distinction between ideas and experiments, and they understand that the motivation for experiments is verifica-

tion or exploration. Added to this is an appreciation of the relation between the results of an experiment (especially unexpected ones) and the theory leading to the prediction. Level 3 understanding recognizes the cyclic, cumulative nature of science, and identifies the goal of science as the construction of ever deeper explanations of the natural world.

Appendix C

Three Levels of Understanding in the Nature of Models Interview

Level 1
Models are thought of as either toys or as simple copies of reality. Models are considered to be useful because they can provide copies of actual objects or actions. If students acknowledge that aspects or parts of objects can be left out of the model, they do not express a reason for doing so beyond the fact that one might not want or need to include it.

Level 2
The student now realizes that there is a specific, explicit purpose that mediates the way the model is constructed. Thus, the modeler's ideas begin to play a role, and the student is aware that the modeler makes conscious choices about how to achieve the purpose. The model no longer needs to match the real world object exactly. Real world objects or actions can be changed or repackaged in some limited ways (e.g., through highlighting, simplifying, showing specific aspects, adding clarifying symbols, or creating different versions). However, the main focus is still on the model and the reality modeled, not the ideas portrayed. Tests of the model are thought of as tests of the workability of the model itself, not of the underlying ideas.

Level 3
At Level 3 understanding is characterized by three important factors. First, the model is now constructed in the service of the development and testing of ideas, rather than as serving as a copy of reality itself. Second, the modeler takes an active role in constructing the model, using symbols freely and evaluating which of several designs could be used to serve the modeler's purpose. Third, models can be manipulated and subjected to test in the service of informing ideas.

13

Medical Education; Or the Art of Keeping a Balance between Science and Pragmatics

H. P. A. Boshuizen

The Aims of Education

One of the aims of scientific education is that we want that our graduates will be versatile generalists that may successfully apply for a wide range of jobs. Another thing we would like to achieve is that our education is not a sort of higher professional training, but rather a more or less practical scientific one. We expect our students and graduates that, not only do they know a lot of things, but that they are also able to do something with that knowledge. However, what they must be able to do precisely is not always very well known.

In this context we often encounter the terms 'expertise' or 'scientific expertise'. People who talk about that, and who say that we should try to instil expertise in our students, actually mean that the university or the polytechnic should take care that graduates do not enter the work force with a head full of knowledge, while they still have to learn to know the daily practice and reality of their domain. But even if we formulate the aim of education in this way, an important question remains, and that is: which reality and which daily practice of a domain do students have to train for?

It will be evident that the answer to this question is not always very easy to provide. For instance, a school in industrial product design (Haagse Hoge School) will have more problems in answering that question than a medical school, and a school of management will probably have more problems than a technical faculty. The answer to our question will always depend on whether we know in which jobs our graduates will enrol. Again an example: in Nijmegen, The Netherlands, there is a new school of policy studies. Students can specialize in several subjects including political sciences, urban and rural planning, business-oriented environmental studies, etc. Graduates may come to work in a wide variety of jobs for a wide variety of employers, e.g., they could come to work as a specialist in environmental law and regulations for a political party or a consultancy firm, or as a urban planner for a city council or an architect's firm. Things become even more complicated if we bear in mind that the reality our graduates will have to work in is an ever changing reality. Take for instance the changes that must occur due to the European integration process (will it still be allowed to sponsor the national film makers or not; how about fishing quotas?), or the ever changing regulations that are meant to protect the environment. A very different situation is found in a Dutch school of aviation and aerospace technology. Due to the economic situation in that branch in my country, only a very few of the recent graduates of that school are employed in a job they are specially trained for: aircraft or space ship design. Yet, unemployment is rare in this group, because they are sought for their skill in construction with and knowledge of modern, light-weight materials. Designing a consistent educational policy is difficult in such situations. Other schools like medical schools seem to have an easier job, but this appearance is deceptive. These schools train their students for the reality of at least 10 years after enrolment, maybe even later (depending on the educational system of the country), and dramatic changes are expected in national and international health policies, as a result of changing insights in the role of the doctor in care, treatment and prevention and of the changing population characteristics: a strong increase of the ageing population in Europe and North America, and a growing proportion of people under 18 in Africa and Asia. Even a traditional domain like medicine has to deal with uncertainty about the daily practice its graduates have to be prepared for.

From my rather remote perspective, it is difficult to see how the situation is in the different branches in engineering sciences, but I guess that they have to deal with the same problems: changing laws and regulations, changing materials, production processes, new views on organization principles, logistics, economic decline, etc. If that is so, teachers and educationalists in schools of engineering are also working in a domain in which it is hard to indicate exactly for which expertise students have to be prepared.

Yet, it is worthwhile spending some time on the question of what expertise is in general – how experts deviate from non-experts – and on the question of how expertise develops. For that reason I want to analyse how the ugly duckling of a high school graduate gradually turns into an experienced, expert professional. I take the domain of medicine, not only because that is my research domain (I do research about accountancy expertise as well), but also because medicine has a sort of prototype value. One might say that medical students and physicians are the fruit flies of expertise research, because of their relatively rapid, clear and uniform development and training, and because there are so many of them.

So in the next paragraphs I will deal with expertise in general, keeping in mind that it is not always easy to tell beforehand what kind of expertise a person will be supposed to develop. I'll come back to that aspect later. Then I will spend some attention on educational means for reaching the goal of expertise development, and will address special aspects of the human intellectual set up that further confines the possibilities available when I try to construct an expertise curriculum.

What is Expertise?

Several years ago I did a small informal survey asking people in my lab what came to their minds first when they thought of experts and expertise. This is what they came up with: experts are good problem solvers; they arrive at the solution without much thinking and without many detours; they can do things in a fraction of the time that it would take a layperson to fulfil the same task, if a layperson could do it; the outcome of the expert's approach is much better than a layperson's; experts have a special talent; they know a lot of their domain; you have to rely on them (this is a somewhat emotional reaction which again emphasizes the gap between laypeople and experts; it says that you are at their mercy) etc. Research on expertise corroborates many of these ideas, especially the speed and correctness of experts' reactions and their knowledge and skill. It adds that experts do not only know a lot, they also know what they do not know; they also know what is and what is not known in the field; they are often able to oversee all aspects of a problem, and if they are not able to do that in one glance, then they take time to analyse all aspects of the problem. Beginners do not do that; they attack the problem from the moment they see something that suggests a clue for an solution, eventually ending up solving the wrong problem.

For instance, suppose there is a couple, somewhere in their sixties, all children have left home, except for one son who has a physical handicap that is increasingly affecting his physical abilities. This son is home only for the weekends. Now suppose that this couple has a big house, that is however rather inconvenient, both for themselves and for their son who is no longer able to climb the stairs and use a normal bathroom. This couple want to build a new house that can accommodate them as an ageing couple for at least 10–15 years and that has a facility for their son's coming over at the weekends. Furthermore, the price of the house should not exceed the price of a normal house with the same volume. A student of architecture may design a very nice little house for an ageing couple with an attractive guest house that can harbor all children and grandchildren, completely forgetting that this guest house should be suitable in the first place to accommodate the handicapped son who cannot move around freely. Or the other way round, come up with a design that has special toilets, broad doors, ramps etc. all over the place, forgetting the financial consequences of these features. This is typical of beginners. Experts on the other hand typically spend much time on analyzing what the constraints given really imply and how they can be combined.

Despite their broad orientation, experts are fast. Experts can be fast because their knowledge of different subject areas is integrated and easily accessible. On top of that, experts have at their disposal abstract solution patterns (scripts) that can be filled in once the problem has been analyzed satisfactorily and that suggest how the solution of the problem can be

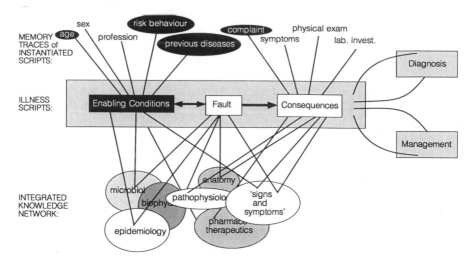

Figure 13.1 *An illness script*

found. These scripts tell experts that if they meet a problem of type X, with features A and B, then method M has to be applied. The same scripts tell them what the result will be, more or less, and where complications can be expected. Students do not have those scripts. They have to design a problem-solving strategy from bits and pieces of knowledge from different domains. This is a time consuming and error-prone process. Finally, experts can re-use (parts of) solutions of earlier look-alike problems.

The question is of course how did experts come that far?

When we turn toward medicine, we see that students first acquire a great deal of what is called basic (science) knowledge. The problems they will deal with later in medical practice will hardly ever relate to only one scientific domain. Therefore, knowledge about these different domains has to be integrated. But that is only part of the story.

By solving patient problems students learn how to translate what patients tell them about their disease and the signs and symptoms they show into theoretical medical terms. On top of that, by solving patient problems on a daily basis, physicians have developed a special sort of ready-made abstract problem-solving scripts: the illness scripts (Feltovich and Barrows, 1984). These illness scripts tell them that, if someone is in these or those circumstances and complains about so and so, the problem is probably caused by X or Y, and that it should be approached by treatment A or B (see Figure 13.1). Illness scripts contain knowledge about the conditions in the patient of his or her environment (the enabling conditions) that may lead to a fault in the patient's body such as alterations due to toxic matter, trauma or infection. They also contain knowledge about the consequences of the fault, the signs and symptoms of the disease. These three components tell 'the story' about how and why a patient got his or her present complaints.

These scripts connect conceptual, perceptual and strategic knowledge. One can imagine that someone who has a great deal of experience with a specific kind of problem has scripts that are very detailed, while the same person has also more global scripts on problems that he sees less frequently. Parts of these script are learned from books or journal articles, but the scripts themselves are not. They are formed through practical experience. Finally, we remember quite a lot of what we experience: e.g., the bluish nails and lips of the cardiac patient, or the situation in which we nearly overlooked a dangerous problem. These remembered episodes can be applied when we solve new problems. Someone with a lot of experience will have myriads of episodes in memory to build on. I will illustrate this process of expert knowledge application with a clinical case:

A 45 year old lawyer complains about a nagging pain in the upper abdomen since some months. He attributes this to stress due to a decline in his clientele and to his divorce, two years ago. He pays occasional visits to a prostitute, but the last time he appeared impotent. He admits substantial alcohol consumption and to smoke a lot (40 cigarettes/day). There is no evident food intolerance.
Physical examination revealed a somewhat extended abdomen, but no shifting dullness. The liver can be palpated, and has an irregular surface; the spleen cannot be palpated. At the ankles a little edema is found. The testes are rather small. The thorax shows a spider naevus.
Laboratory tests showed an ESR of 44 mm/h (normal: < 12 mm/h) and a hemoglobin-level of 8.0 mmol/l (normal: 8.5–11.0 mmol/l). Sodium 138 mmol/l (normal: 132–142 mmol/l), potassium 3.6 (normal: 3.6–5.0 mmol/l), ALT (SGTP) 120 U/l (normal: < 40 U/l), AST (SGOT) 84 U/l (normal: < 40 U/l), LDH (LD) 800 U/l (normal: 200–450 U/l), GTT 250 U/l (normal: < 50 U/l), alkaline phosphatase 200 U/l (normal: 30–125 U/I) an bilirubin 25 umol/l (normal: < 17 umol/l).

In order to fully comprehend this case one must have knowledge of very divergent domains: of psychology and psychosomatics, of internal medicine, of the epidemiology of diseases associated with high alcohol and cigarette consumption, of the normal and abnormal anatomy and physiology of the liver and the surrounding organs (especially the supplying veins of the liver), of the procedures required to get information about physical signs and symptoms and of processes at the cellular level resulting in specific laboratory findings. And this knowledge should be organized and available in such a format that it can be easily activated and applied during clinical reasoning: the illness script.

After having read the first paragraph of the case description there are two candidate scripts: liver and stomach problems, because of the location of the pain, the alcohol and cigarette consumption and the stress. The stomach is less plausible, because there is no relation of the pain with food. Furthermore, substantial alcohol consumption is highly correlated with

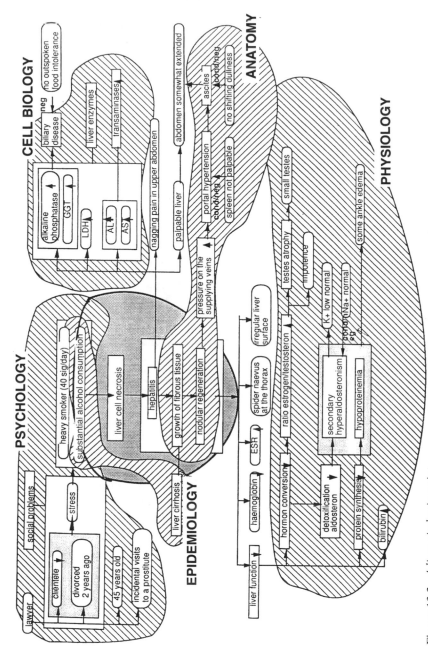

Figure 13.2 *A liver cirrhosis script*

liver disease. Instantiating these scripts soon shows that this patient has indeed liver cirrhosis, as is shown in Figure 13.2.

This figure represents a liver cirrhosis script that is instantiated with the details of patient case described above. This figure not only shows you what such a script may look like, and how it connects the different parts of circumstances in and of the patient, but also the fault that has arisen from these circumstances and the physical consequences of that fault. Maybe even more importantly, it also shows that this script integrates the distinct knowledge domains listed before. The left hand corner is the domain of psychology, the relation between alcohol consumption and liver cirrhosis is the domain of the epidemiology. The relation between hepatitis and the lab findings is mediated by knowledge at the cellular and intracellular level (concepts at that level like destruction of the cell wall and release of cellular enzymes are not included in the script because experts will no longer use them when explaining a case; they are however required at the earlier stages of the learning process). Below (starting from 'nodular regeneration') is the domain of the anatomical changes that have taken place. The lower part that is connected to the decreased liver functioning describes the physiological changes that have taken place.

Lower Levels of Expertise

When we ask an expert to diagnose and explain this case to us we will hear a story that comes close to the script depicted in Figure 13.2. Experts will cover most of the aspects of the case: the circumstances, and the changes in liver function and anatomy, and they will use a few of these theoretical terms to explain how it came to be that way in this patient. Students who do not have these versatile ready made scripts show different behavior and often a different outcome of their problem-solving process. They will have to access the relevant domains of their knowledge one by one and activate the relevant concepts in order to comprehend the information given in the case description and to come to a diagnosis. In doing so students have to actively build up complicated lines of reasoning, often consisting of the tiny biomedical concepts derived from the basic sciences. Hence, students apply concepts at a more detailed level than experts. For instance, experts may say in our example that nodular regeneration of the liver results in portal hypertension leading to ascites and spider naevi. Students may come up with details about infection and destruction of the liver cell, how the fibrous tissue that is formed instead cannot perform the same function as the intact liver cells, that fibrosations may result in strictures leading to anatomical changes leading to pressure on the supplying veins of the liver that ·may lead to the development of collateral veins, exertion of lymph fluids and hence ascites, etc.

Students also need auxiliary reasoning, like 'the normal situation is . . ., so if there is disturbance at this or that level, then . . . may occur.' A student who applies such a line of reasoning starts by stating the normal situation and then runs a qualitative simulation of a disturbance that may have taken place. In this way the student tries to explain why certain findings have been found. This is a powerful aid for students (and experts when they are dealing with a new and difficult problem) in case of absence of direct knowledge. The problem with this kind of reasoning is, however, that it has a high level of uncertainty due to the assumptions that have to be made about the presumed fault and how it will affect the normal situation. People who have immediate knowledge about certain findings and how they relate to diseases evidently have a great advantage over those who need such ancillary reasoning.

Another striking phenomenon is that, despite (or maybe because of) their long and detailed lines of reasoning, important parts of the case that are covered by the script are not included. Many students, even advanced ones, happen to 'forget' an important part of the case, the physiological changes.

These differences between experts and intermediates not only lead to differences in time needed, but also the quality of the outcome and the solver's certainty about the quality are affected by having to apply knowledge that does not really fit the problem to be solved. In situations where it matters a great deal whether a task is performed with speed, quality and certainty, which is the case in real time tasks with high personal, societal and economical consequences, these aspects of expertise come to the fore. So, depending on the domain, a certain level of expertise is required in our graduates. This conclusion implies that the level of expertise required in graduates will depend on the characteristics students are training for.

Teaching for Expertise

How can we organize a curriculum in such a way that graduates acquire such a degree of problem solving and hence a knowledge structure that allows these fast and accurate lines of reasoning? In the previous sections it was concluded that knowledge of different domains and subject matters should be integrated and abstract problem-solving schemas should be developed. Conceptual knowledge acquisition and integration is the first key process. When we think of the knowledge that students need to have, we often think in terms of the sciences that the students should learn. In our medical example it will be sciences like internal medicine, anatomy, physiology, epidemiology, psychology, and cell biology. In architecture it might be things like spatial and material structure of buildings, architectonical design, construction, building physics, mathematics and drawing.

There are as many ways of structuring these subjects into a curriculum as there are ways leading to Rome. For instance, we can think of semester-like structure in which we have basics first, later followed by the applied sciences. The rationale behind this approach is that the basic sciences provide insights into the relations that are described or applied by the applied sciences. For instance, one has to know the anatomy of the liver and its supplying veins before one can understand how liver cirrhosis may lead to ascites. Or you'll first have to learn everything about building physics before you can understand the principles of construction. A further advantage of this curriculum principle is that understanding is an important aspect of learning: people are better at remembering things they understand than things they do not understand. Having to learn construction without having dealt with building physics first will require longer study times. This may sound like common sense to you, but there are students and teachers who deny the relation. Some even say that it is easier to learn things by heart than to try to understand first. Psychological research shows, however, that information acquired by rote learning soon decays. A curriculum set-up like this also has disadvantages. One of them has to do with motivation.

Students first have to learn all the details of the basics which they are often not really interested in, before they can start doing the things they actually came for. Another problem is that by the time the interesting applied sciences are introduced, students may have forgotten the procedures and the principles learned in the basic science classes. These two problems are aggravated by the way the basic sciences are usually taught in such a curriculum set-up. The leading thread of the introductions is usually the principles of these sciences per se, not the question of what is important for the students to know in order to understand the applied sciences taught in the next semester. An example is statistics. In most curricula students first have to learn the fundamentals of statistics including probability, populations and sample distribution, while the same courses hardly ever touch on subjects like how a research question is transformed into a statistical question. Since most basic sciences teachers do not know how exactly their domain is (mis)used in the applied sciences, it is very hard to make an acceptable selection that satisfies both sides: basic and applied sciences.

This problem might be avoided if basic and applied sciences could be taught and learned simultaneously. This can be done in many ways: by giving priority to the basic sciences, in which case the applied sciences are only used as points of illustration of the practicality of the basics, or the other way round, when the applied sciences are the leading thread and the basics only come up if needed to deepen or explain something that is met in the lectures on the applied sciences. To students a curriculum set-up like this one is more attractive than the previous structure. The content of their learning seems more relevant since they now know why they are learning this. On the other hand, for teachers it is very difficult to teach these integrated courses. The domains themselves are not so integrated as one might hope, and the handbooks are often written from a completely different perspective.

Part of the solution to this problem may be to give primacy not to teaching but to learning. Without further explanation it may be hard to see what the consequences of this suggestion may be. I postpone that for some time and first go into schema formation, our second ingredient of expertise formation.

No abstract problem-solving schemas are formed without the repeated active application of the knowledge acquired. Knowledge alone, even integrated knowledge, is not enough; it has to be made applicable and tuned to practical situations. This is shown by an example from the domain of economics by Mandl, *et al.* (1994). These authors found a rather counter-intuitive phenomenon in an economic business-management simulation study. In this study they compared graduate students of economics with students of psychology and education who had virtually no knowledge of economics. Their task was to optimalize the profits of a simulated jeans factory. The novices, especially in the first planning period, were apparently not hindered by any knowledge, outperformed the more knowledgeable subjects. This phenomenon was not due to lack of knowledge but rather to the impracticality of the knowledge applied. The advanced students contemplated hypotheses that were far too complicated, and tried to run models of the firm that were in themselves correct, but lacked an adequate hierarchical organization. As a consequence they were unable to integrate all relevant aspects under consideration and could not come to a sound decision. Another problem with Mandl's advanced subjects was that they made assumptions that were theoretically true, but irrelevant in the present context, and that they were too cautious in their manipulations of the variables (selling price, production, etc.). For instance, after deciding that they wanted to get rid of stocks, they lowered the price, but only by DM .50 per pair, which did not have the desired result (of course). Schemas that were too complex were not tuned to the characteristics of real life practice and were detrimental to these subjects' performance. I have no examples of research from the domain of engineering, so it is hard to say whether the same problems will be found in those graduate students, but there is no reason to assume that the situation there is better than in economics, mathematics, physics or medicine, where similar phenomena were found. Engineering students' schemas will probably be as unrealistic, incomplete, and badly implemented in the whole knowledge structure as in these other domains.

There is only one way out of this problem and that is to let students practise their knowledge and skill by solving as many problems as possible. These problems should be real-life problems or realistic simulations in order to tune the knowledge to the characteristics of reality (what was missing in the economics students). In problems like the jeans factory simulations immediate feedback should be given in terms of information about the consequences of decisions made. Feedback should also be given on the approach taken and the knowledge applied. This is the only way to show students that the models applied were too complicated or otherwise defective, although reflection by the student on his or her own problem solving may work as well. As was already shown before in a medical example, schemas integrate knowledge from different domains. That is another reason to give problem solving a prominent place in a curriculum.

This analysis leads to a few conclusions: applied sciences and the scientific underpinning of these applied sciences that is provided by the basic sciences should be learned and taught as much as possible in combination with one another. Furthermore, measures should be taken that knowledge from different domains is integrated in such a way that it fits the real-life problems it will be later applied in. And finally, knowledge should be as much as possible restructured into problem-solving schemas that coordinate the application of knowledge and solution of the problem, which can only be done by solving relevant problems.

This is the moment to return to the delicate balance between science and pragmatics or between basic and applied sciences and to our question about giving first priority to learning instead of teaching in medical education. Medical education is again only an example.

Formal medical education has a very long tradition in Europe, going back to the middle ages in which we had two streams of training: university study and a sort of apprenticeship system supervised by the guild masters. The apprenticeship system was very pragmatic though not without theoretical training, while the university training was very scientific without much practical work with patients. Actually, only a few universities featured practical medical education in the form of bed-side teaching. In other schools students only learned the sciences of anatomy, physiology, botany and something like signs and symptoms of disease. This dual system remained unaffected until the beginning of this century, at least in The Netherlands. Talking about a balance between pragmatics and science, we see that one method of teaching and learning (the guild method) favoured pragmatics over science, while in the universities the balance was tipped toward science. Even in those times the unfavorable consequences of such imbalances were felt. Guild doctors often lacked a solid theoretical background that could help them to arrive at rational decisions in difficult, non-routine cases, while university doctors, especially those who had recently graduated, lacked practical knowledge.

These mismatches between pragmatics and science were partly due to the structure of the curricula. The lack of scientific knowledge and systematic description of diseases was another factor, which is of diminishing importance nowadays. Yet, there still remains a great deal of symptoms of diseases that science cannot explain or has competing theoretical explanations for. Students have to learn to live with that, although they may find that difficult to handle.

All these years medical teachers and medical schools have struggled with the question of how to organize their curricula, and many variants of sequenced or integrated courses have been tried out. I hope that I have made clear what kind of problems are associated with the solutions tried out.

Recently another approach has been tried that may remind you vaguely of the guild method, i.e., problem-based learning. The point of departure of all learning in this system is a problem. An example could be our alcoholic lawyer and his liver problems. The choice of the problem will depend on the goals one has. In this case, the goal will probably be that students will study all these subjects we have mentioned before, like anatomy and physiology of the liver, destruction of liver cells by an infectious process and its anatomical and physiological consequences. Students may also want to know whether this process is reversible, and if not what the consequences are in the long run. Another question may be whether this disease can be treated and if not, whether its symptoms can be relieved or whether later complications can be prevented. By studying these subjects in the context of a problem, basic and applied sciences are integrated automatically and the knowledge acquired is linked to a real-life situation, i.e. the context of a patient with alcoholic liver cirrhosis.

The advantage of using problems as a starting point of learning over the principles of basic and applied sciences is of course that it is based on an analysis of the kind of problems that graduates will have to solve in later practice. A different outcome of the analysis will result in a different selection of problems presented to the students and hence different learning activities. Hence the knowledge and skills of graduates will better match with the situation they will have to deal with. For that reason the World Health Organisation has advised that all continuing medical education would be problem based. A disadvantage is of course that the outcome of the analysis of problems students should be able to deal with is in a way uncertain, while the state of the art of basic science X or applied science Y is very certain. Yet, the certainty that most students will not need that knowledge and that if they ever did need it, the knowledge would be completely forgotten by that time, is reason enough to dismiss that argument.

I started this chapter with an analysis of the uncertainty of the daily practice our graduates should be trained for. There is no easy and no certain solution to this problem. Elsewhere, I have expressed the opinion that the lessons of expertise can also apply in these uncertain domains. However, our aim cannot be that students acquire a large set of relevant problem solutions schemas that can be applied immediately and quickly lead to a solution. This is not only due to the uncertainty we have talked about, but also because policy problems, and probably engineering problems as well, are quite extensive. They require far more time for analysis and solution than a typical medical problem. Instead we could think of using a few prototypical problems that students in a specific domain should be able to deal with anyway. Although a few problems are not enough for developing a rich base of problem solution scripts, there is no reason to refrain from including such experiences in a curriculum. Students will at gain at least two valuable things from such experiences: concrete memory episodes of the solution of a problem and of what went right and what went wrong (and maybe why), and general ideas about how such a problem (probably in a totally different domain) can be solved: the abstract structure of a script.

References

Boshuizen, H. P. A. (1993). Hoe verwerven studenten wetenschappelijke expertise? [How do students acquire scientific expertise?] Keynote speech at the first lustrum seminar 'Wetenschappelijk opleiden voor beleid' [Scientific education for policy making] of the Faculty of Policy Studies of the Catholic University Nijmegen. Nijmegen, May 14 1993.

Boshuizen, H. P. A. and Schmidt, H. G. (1994). The development of clinical reasoning expertise. In J. Higgs and M. A. Jones (eds.). *Clinical reasoning skills.* Oxford: Heinemann-Butterworth.

Feltovich, P. J. and Barrows, H. S. (1984). Issues of generality in medical problem solving. In H. G. Schmidt and M. L. De Volder (eds.), *Tutorials in problem-based learning; A new direction in teaching the health professions.* Assen: Van Gorcum.

Mandl, H., Grube, H. and Renkl, A. (1994). Problems of knowledge utilization. In W. J. Nijhof and J. Streumer (eds.). *Flexibility and cognitive structure in vocational education.* Utrecht: Lemma.

Mandl, H., Grube, H. and Renkl, A. Learning to apply: From 'school garden instruction' to technology-based learning environments. In S. Vosniadou, E. de Corte, R. Glaser and H. Mandl (eds.), *International perspectives of the psychological foundations of technology-based learning environments.* Hillsdale, NJ: Erlbaum.

Schmidt, H. G., Norman, G. R. and Boshuizen, H. P. A. (1990). A cognitive perspective on medical expertise: Theory and implications. *Academic Medicine, 65,* 611–621.

14

Mathematics (Grades 7–12)

Steven R. Williams

Introduction

[. . .] I wish to construct an understanding of how outstanding secondary mathematics classrooms work and how to encourage their development. I am interested primarily in assisting efforts to improve student learning in secondary mathematics classrooms and not so much in transmitting the results of individual studies of learning algebra or geometry as offering a lens by which to view both the purposes and processes of these classrooms. In doing so, I hope to avoid the mistake of concentrating on individual bricks at the expense of the buildings themselves. Excellent reviews of the literature are readily available (Grouws, 1992; Putnam *et al.*, 1990; Wagner and Kieran, 1989, are some starting points), so this chapter will not exhaustively review the research literature. Instead, I hope to bring to light a few of the major issues that drive the current reform movement, and suggest directions for implementing reforms in classrooms.

Three complementary movements in mathematics education have informed the writing of this chapter: (1) emerging views of what mathematics is, (2) the movement toward constructivism as a framework for explaining teaching and learning in mathematics, and (3) the reform movement in mathematics education as represented by the three documents, the *Curriculum and Evaluation Standards for School Mathematics* (National Council of Teachers of Mathematics [NCTM], 1989), the *Professional Standards for Teaching Mathematics* (NCTM, 1991), and the *Assessment Standards for School Mathematics* (NCTM, 1995), known in what follows as the *Curriculum Standards*, the *Teaching Standards*, and the *Assessment Standards*, respectively. Drawing on these movements, I begin with a critical took at both traditional and newly emerging views of mathematics, and what they imply for teaching and learning in the secondary mathematics classroom. Next, I review constructivist thought as interpreted in the scholarly literature of mathematics education, providing brief descriptions of several complementary branches of the constructivist family tree. I then elaborate on how views of mathematics and constructivist theory relate to the reform movement and how all three combine to suggest specific instructional

---

This chapter has been edited.

practices. I next provide a few examples of blueprints for success – studies of student learning and classroom life that illustrate constructivist principles in the spirit of the reform movement. Finally, I provide some cautionary tales of reform and summary comments.

A New Look at Mathematics

Beginning a discussion of teaching and learning mathematics from within mathematical philosophy might seem to be a largely academic exercise, especially to those interested primarily in improving instruction. Increasingly, however, it is recognized that the nature of mathematics itself is a fundamental issue affecting teaching and learning. Any serious discussion of students' construction of mathematical knowledge must address what it means to know mathematics, and all scholarly work that attempts to address students learning mathematics must make assumptions about this issue, whether or not they are made explicit. As Reuben Hersh reminds us, 'Ideas have consequences. One's conception of what mathematics is affects one's conception of how it should be presented. One's manner of presenting it is an indication of what one believes to be most essential in it' (1986, p. 13). In this passage, Hersh was pointing out the plausibility of a connection between a formalist philosophy of mathematics and the formal expository style prevalent in mathematics journals. However, the point is equally well taken as it applies to pedagogical exposition. One's beliefs about what mathematics is, about what is essential to mathematics, must certainly be reflected in pedagogical choices about what to teach and how to teach it (for a discussion of research on how teachers' knowledge and beliefs affect instruction, see Fennema and Franke, 1992; Thompson, 1992).

It is important to understand that this careful examination of beliefs about mathematics is more than an academic exercise. As an example, consider the discussions that take place in a school where any new approach to teaching mathematics is being attempted side by side with more traditional approaches. Sides are taken quickly, and discussions about what can and cannot be done by students from the other course make their way into the workroom and sometimes into the classroom. Students and parents quickly become aware that something different is being taught. The debate that takes place is not really about whether students can perform a trigonometric substitution or a partial fraction decomposition, or perform three-digit by three-digit multiplications on paper. The argument is about what is basic to mathematical learning: whether, for example, conceptual understanding, in the face of altered procedural competence, should really 'count' as legitimate mathematical knowledge Beliefs about what counts as legitimate mathematical knowledge are based directly on views of what mathematics is all about.

Still, working mathematicians tend to ignore such philosophical issues, choosing instead to simply do mathematics. Cannot practicing teachers do the same? After all, we have fairly well-defined curricular responsibilities: algebra, geometry, trigonometry, calculus. Surely these can be taught, and taught well, without concern for philosophical foundations. Unfortunately, ignoring foundational beliefs does not mean adopting a neutral stance. Rather, it means that those beliefs go unexamined, and pedagogical possibilities become limited to what has always been done. If those who choose to ignore history are doomed to repeat it, those who choose not to examine their views of mathematics are doomed to replicate those views in their classrooms.

The Contrast between Knowing and Doing Mathematics

Work in mathematics education brings this issue into sharp focus. Welch (1978) describes typical instruction in mathematics classrooms two decades ago:

> In all math classes I visited, the sequence of activities was the same. First, answers were given for the previous day's assignment The more difficult problems were worked by a teacher or a student at the chalkboard. A brief explanation, sometimes none at all, was given of the new material, and problems were assigned for the next day The remainder of class was devoted to working on the homework while the teacher moved about the room answering questions. The most noticeable thing about math classes was the repetition of this routine. (p. 6).

Romberg and Carpenter (1986) point out that such routine is symptomatic of a belief that mathematics is a 'static, bounded discipline' (p. 851), divorced from inquiry and largely divorced from reality. They go on to suggest that mathematics has been fragmented into concepts, facts, skills, and procedures, which are then arranged into courses, topics, and lessons, and that knowledge of these isolated facts and concepts has become a replacement for knowledge of flow to *do* mathematics. Hence, knowledge of facts and procedures are valued, even though by themselves they may not provide students with the ability to deal mathematically with problems that they confront. This has been the case, with few exceptions, for the better part of a century (see Stanic, 1986, for a review of how our current mathematics curriculum has developed).

The *Curriculum Standards* (NCTM, 1989) argues that this view does justice neither to mathematics, nor to the idea of understanding mathematics:

> First, 'knowing' mathematics is 'doing' mathematics A person gathers, discovers, or creates knowledge in the course of some activity having a purpose This active process is different front mastering concepts and procedures. We do not assert that informational knowledge has no value, only that its value lies in the extent to which it is useful In the course of some purposeful activity. (p. 7)

Thus, the measure of students' mathematical understanding is their ability to engage in mathematical behavior, to have what the *Curriculum*

Standards call *mathematical power*, 'the ability to explore, conjecture, and reason logically, as well as the ability to use a variety of mathematical methods effectively to solve nonroutine problems' (NCTM, 1989, p. 5).

A starting point, then, is to focus on the doing of mathematics, as opposed to the learning of mathematics as a collection of distinct facts and procedures, to be applied at some future date. This leads directly to the question of what 'doing' mathematics entails. It is here that modern philosophy of mathematics can be of use. The directions we explore in the philosophy of mathematics will lead us naturally to constructivism as a philosophy of learning.

Mathematics as Practice

Traditional philosophies of mathematics have in common a search for a *foundation* on which mathematics can be built. Doing mathematics has been seen, on the one hand, as discovering the truths of an immutable, rational, and consistent mathematical reality 'out there' somewhere. This *Platonist* view explains why mathematics is useful (because it uncovers truth about the world) but traditionally has problems explaining how we gain access to these truths. On the other hand, mathematics has also been seen as essentially a mental game, using logic to arrive at mathematical results from agreed-on axioms with no necessary connection to the real world. This view avoids the problems of how humans gain access to mathematical truth (they create it), but has more problem explaining why mathematics is so useful in solving real-world problems, of these two views, the second, *formalist* position has had the greater impact on school mathematics as we know it. It is exactly this formalist view of mathematics that Hersh (1986) discusses as undergirding secondary mathematics instruction tie makes a strong case that changes in classroom teaching depend on directly confronting the formalist viewpoint;

> The criticism of formalism in the high schools has been primarily on pedagogic grounds; 'This is the wrong thing to teach, or the wrong way to teach.' But all such arguments are inconclusive if they leave unanswered the dogma that real mathematics is precisely formal derivations from formally stated axioms. . . . The real issue is not, What is the best way to teach? But, What is mathematics really about? To discredit formalism in pedagogy, one must challenge its philosophical base . . . Controversies about high school teaching cannot be resolved without confronting problems about nature of mathematics. (p. 13)

Formalism is often supported by an implicit theory of mathematics learning, what Skovesmose (1993) has called a *monological* view. This view suggests that gaining knowledge is essentially an individual activity, involving one's senses: Interaction with others is not a necessary feature of learning. Although Skovesmose does not see these two views as strictly compatible, both views have been used to justify much of traditional mathematics instruction: teachers impart formal rules and procedures to students, who are largely responsible for making sense of them (or just memorizing them) and being able to demonstrate individually that they can apply those procedures properly. Mathematics becomes memorizing rules and procedures and knowing when to apply them.

Various authors in philosophy, education, and sociology have recently outlined new approaches to the philosophy of mathematics (cf. Restivo, Van Bendegem, and Fischer, 1993; Tymoczko, 1986). These new approaches contrast with the more traditional views lust outlined and have in common a concern for the social aspects of mathematics. These new philosophers of mathematics argue against a view of mathematics as a static, bounded discipline or as a body of canonized truths to be mastered. Rather, they emphasize the way in which mathematical knowledge is arrived at in practice: conjecture, discussion, justification, refutation, and modification, all in a social arena. In doing so, they argue for a *fallibilist* view of mathematics, giving up the search for a metaphysical foundation and suggesting that mathematical truth, like scientific truth, is subject to revision. Moreover, they insist that the production of knowledge is inherently social. As Restivo (1993) suggests, individual mathematicians do not create mathematics. Rather, *math worlds* – 'networks of human being communicating in arenas of conflict and cooperation, domination and subordination' (p. 249) – actually create mathematics. Nicholas Goodman describes it this way:

> Mathematical truth, unlike a mathematical construction, is not something I can hope to find by introspection. It does not exist In my mind. A mathematical theory, like any other Scientific theory, is a social product. It is created and developed by the dialectical interplay of many minds, not just one mind . . . Each generation of mathematicians rethinks the mathematics of the previous generation, discarding what was faddish or superficial or false and recasting what is still fertile into new and sharper focus. (1986, p. 87)

Thus, mathematics is a human creation, developed to serve human ends, and modified as needed to meet those ends. This explains mathematics' usefulness In describing our world, and why mathematical truth needs to be judged not only formally, that is, from the point of view of logical consistency, but from empirical grounds as well.

Freudenthal (1987) supports this view when he calls for a *realistic* view of mathematics. He argues that

> mathematics, from both the historical and individual perspectives, starts in reality. Mathematical structures are not presented to the learner so that they might be filled with realities (or rather, pseudo-realities). They arise, instead, from reality itself, which is not a fixed datum, but expands continuously In man's individual and collective learning process. (p. 280)

This view of mathematics has served as a foundation for curriculum development in the Netherlands as well as the United States (Romberg *et al.*, 1993).

Summary

This brief introduction to modern philosophy of mathematics is not sufficient to describe a complete, consistent Philosophy of mathematics. These emerging philosophies are in their infancy, and a good deal of work remains ahead. Nor has my treatment been exhaustive. Other reasonable and useful frameworks exist for discussing the nature of mathematical knowledge. My major intention is to bring to light the implied criticism of traditional views, particularly as they relate to learning and teaching school mathematics. Traditional mathematics instruction is based on views of mathematics that are increasingly untenable. This includes viewing mathematics (1) as something done long ago or far away, transmitted through teacher and text to students; (2) as involving formal rules requiring memorization and a good deal of individual mental work; and (3) as absolute and infallible, not open to debate, discussion, or modification. On the other hand, basing instruction on fallibilist views of mathematics underscores the importance of the social construction of mathematical knowledge and suggests that mathematics is best learned within a community of discourse and best viewed as a quasi-empirical science, subject to hypotheses, conjecture, refutation, and revision.

In any attempt to deal with mathematics learning, beliefs about what we are teaching are critical. Choosing not to teach traditional mathematics may have as profound an affect as choosing not to teach mathematics traditionally. As I will argue, beliefs about mathematics weave together with beliefs about learning to inform practice. To change practice requires a change in the mathematics we teach.

Constructivism and Reform in Mathematics Education

A Brief Overview of Constructivist Thought in Mathematics Education

Constructivism in various forms has become what might be called the 'state religion' of mathematics education. It would be very difficult to find a mathematics educator who did not claim to be a constructivist. This is not to say that all those who claim to be constructivists would agree on what constructivism is or even on how mathematics should be taught. A wide range of beliefs fall under the general label of *constructivism,* and it seems important to examine briefly these beliefs and what they mean for instruction.

Steffe and Kieren (1994) trace the roots of constructivism in mathematics education most directly to the work of Jean Piaget and the interpretation given his work by Ernst von Glasersfeld. Constructivism emerged in the context of efforts to account both for behaviorism's apparent failure and the epistemological problems of how knowledge of the outside world (e.g., mathematical structures) could be gained internally. Von Glasersfeld's is a two-pronged attack. He asserts that 'a) knowledge is not passively received but actively built up by the cognizing subject, [and] b) the function of cognition is adaptive and serves the organization of the experiential world, not the discovery of ontological reality' (von Glasersfeld, 1989, p. 162). Those who accept both of these propositions are called *radical* constructivists, while those who accept only the first are called (by their radical siblings) *trivial* constructivists. Specifically, radical constructivists reject the flow of anything like 'information' between a teacher and a student, insisting that 'knowledge cannot be *transferred* to the student by linguistic communication,' but instead 'language can be used as a tool in a process of guiding the student's construction' (von Glasersfeld, 1989, p. 163). By way of analogy to evolutionary processes, radical constructivists suggest that cognitive structures are molded by testing their viability against the world. Therefore, they speak of a cognitive construction *fitting* with the world if it works well enough for the cognizing subject to achieve its goals. By contrast, they categorically deny any match between a cognitive construction and what it is supposed to represent. This contrast between a construction *fitting* the world, in the sense of providing a viable organization and predictive ability, and a construction *matching* some ontological reality, is central to radical constructivism. To quote von Glasersfeld (1983), 'From an explorer who is condemned to seek "structural properties" of an inaccessible reality, the experiencing organism now turns·into a builder of cognitive structures intended to solve such problems as the organism perceives or conceives' (p. 50).

In many ways, trivial constructivism is less problematic and less controversial than radical constructivism. Probably the majority of those who say they are constructivists, or that their teaching is constructivist, have in mind the first of von Glasersfeld's two propositions but not necessarily the second. For many whose primary concern is day-to-day classroom life, the finer philosophical nuances of radical constructivism may not seem to matter. Indeed, a wide range of beliefs that can be called *constructivist* take no hard stand on von Glasersfeld's second proposition. Lyddon and McLaughlin (1992) discuss four essentially different kinds of constructivist thought, two of which are radical constructivism and theories like Piaget's that depend on dialectic interplay between person and environment. In addition, they discuss two other constructivist schools of thought that have wide acceptance in the mathematics education community.

The first includes various cybernetic theories of cognition. Such theories typically assume the existence of some sort of mental representation of knowledge and equate understanding with the quality or integrity of these representations. In mathematics education, attempts to describe understanding have attended in large part to the organization of knowledge representations, and are hence constructivist in this sense. Heibert and Carpenter (1992) describe this viewpoint well.

> A mathematical idea or procedure or fact is understood if it is part of an internal network. More specifically, the mathematics is understood if its mental representation is part of a network of representations. The degree of understanding is determined by the number and the strength of the connections (p. 67)

Understanding, then, is characterized by robust representations that are rich in connections. A good deal of work in mathematics education is done with this general view of understanding in mind.

Lyddon and McLaughlin's fourth general school of constructivism has also had broad acceptance in mathematics education, where it is usually called *social constructivism* (Ernst, 1991). The fundamental proposition underlying social constructivism is that knowledge is a product of social processes and not solely an individual construction. Lyddon and McLaughlin, for example, describe Gergen's (1985) social constructionist views as seeking 'to place knowledge not exclusively in the minds of single individuals . . . or in the environment . . but rather in the processes of social exchange and linguistic construction that set conceptual parameters on personal categories of understanding' (p. 95). From this view, social processes cannot be divorced from knowledge production.

It should be clear that social constructivism is in harmony with the fallibilist views of mathematics discussed earlier. Ernst (1991) makes these connections explicit, taking social constructivism as a philosophy of knowledge production in mathematics and suggesting that accounts of learning, teaching, and mathematical practice could be developed in parallel ways. As I will argue, social constructivism, both as a philosophy of learning and as a philosophy of knowledge production in mathematics, is compatible with much of the current reform movement in mathematics education. [. . .]

Constructivism, Mathematics, and the Reform Movement

The reform movement in mathematics education, as represented by the *Standards* documents, resonates both with constructivist ideas and with emerging views of mathematics. As discussed previously, the *Curriculum Standards* (NCTM, 1989) focus on *doing* mathematics as the fundamental aspect of knowing mathematics. They also discuss at length the historical changes in mathematics that have taken place with the advent of computing technology. They call for more attention to mathematics as a way of quantifying problems in many disciplines, and suggest that 'students need to experience genuine problems regularly' (p. 10). This supports both Freudenthal's focus on realistic mathematics and a view of mathematics as a tool to better understand and manage our world. Finally, the *Curriculum Standards* suggest that 'individuals approach a new task with prior knowledge, assimilate new information, and construct their own meanings' (p. 10) and supports understanding as connected knowledge in the sense of Heibert and Carpenter (1992). Clearly, there is a strong constructivist undercurrent in reform.

Social constructivist ideas can also be seen in the reform documents. The Standards for Teaching, in *Professional Standards for Teaching Mathematics* (NCTM, 1991), for example, emphasize task selection and structuring mathematical discourse about those tasks as a major part of describing instructional practice. The document explores at length the teachers' role in discourse, the students' role in discourse, and ways of enhancing discourse. This focus on knowledge production through discourse (which includes questioning conjecturing, and providing and evaluating evidence) is closely aligned with both the theories of mathematics we discussed earlier and social constructivist views of how mathematical understanding is produced.

Although constructivist theories and new views of mathematics are not the sole driving forces behind the reform movement, it seems clear that major threads from the recommendations of the reform documents the basic tenets of constructivism, and the emerging views of mathematics all intertwine to produce a set of common recommendations for mathematics instruction. In the next few sections, I briefly discuss some of these recommendations.

Recommendations for Reform

Intellectual Authority

One issue that pervades reform efforts in mathematics education is the idea of intellectual authority; that is, who validates mathematical knowledge produced in the classroom. At one time, of course, this was exclusively the teacher's job and in some sense it still is. The teacher has the responsibility to guide knowledge production in useful ways. The *Teaching Standards* (NCTM, 1991) state it well:

> For the discourse to promote student learning, teachers must orchestrate it carefully. Because many more ideas will come up than are fruitful to pursue at the moment, teachers must filter and direct the students' explorations by picking up on some points and by leaving others behind. Doing this prevents student activity and talk from becoming too diffused and unfocused . . . Beyond asking clarifying or provocative questions, teachers should also, at times, provide information and lead students. (p. 36)

To a much greater degree, however, the responsibility for validation of correct mathematics is being turned over to students or at least shared between teacher and students. Validation of mathematical reasoning is given by the community of scholars in which the construction is taking place, so that when a student provides an answer to a mathematical problem, the answer is not just checked by the teacher but subjected to questioning by the class. Reasoned explanation, justification, and argument are increasingly expected of students when they do mathematics. Not surprisingly, this parallels the process of knowledge production in mathematics as a discipline. Proofs are produced and subjected to the scrutiny of others in the field and decisions are made regarding their usefulness, appropriateness, generalizability, and so forth.

Rich Mathematical Tasks

Another aspect of reform teaching that seems closely linked to constructivist ideas is the importance of task selection. The *Teaching Standards* make it clear that the environment in which students work, the kinds of tasks they work on, should be chosen to facilitate students' construction of useful knowledge. Tasks must be chosen that are rich mathematically, and time must be given to explore the mathematics in those tasks. Discourse among students and teachers, as appropriate, can facilitate the exploration. In general, it is also assumed that sufficiently rich tasks facilitate connections between mathematical topics, and so lead to the building of more connected knowledge, in the sense that Heibert and Carpenter (1992) discuss.

A Focus on Student Understanding

A fundamental aspect of constructivist theory that applies to instruction is the importance of forming models of students' understanding. Confrey (1990) states:

> When one applies constructivism to the issue of teaching one must reject the assumption that one can simply pass on information to a set of learners and expect that understanding will result. Communication is a far more complex process than this. When teaching concepts, as a form of communication, the teacher must form an adequate model of the students' ways of viewing an idea and s/he then must assist the student in restructuring those views to be more adequate from the students' and from the teachers' perspective. (p. 109)

This is the core idea behind the constructivist teaching experiment, in which a teacher bases instructional decisions on his or her understanding of students' constructions. Knowledge of students' thinking becomes a critical factor in constructivist teaching of any kind.

The focus on student understanding implies a need for teachers to gain reliable information on students' understandings as a basis for instructional decisions. Thus, constructivist teachers rely on a wide range of information, verbal and nonverbal, to assess student's conceptions. To the extent that teachers can be provided with information on students' thinking, they can successfully use it to plan instruction (see Franke and Grouws, 1997; Carpenter *et al.*, 1988).

Balancing Conceptual and Procedural Knowledge

A final important aspect of the reform movement that seems tied to constructivist ideas is a concern for conceptual as opposed to procedural knowledge. The epistemological question 'What counts as mathematical knowledge?' has for some time been answered by mathematical formalists, who had a very strong affect on curriculum and practice. For example, Kleiner and Movshovitz-Hadar (1990) discuss how what we know as modern symbolic algebra grew out of a formalist philosophy of mathematics. Today, it is touch more accepted that formalisms are of less importance than the ability to apply mathematics to real-world situations. Although the tensions between formalism and practicality have been present to some extent for decades (Kleibard, 1992; Kleiner and Movshovitz-Hadar, 1990; Stanic, 1986), it is now widely accepted that it is important for all students to make mathematical connections, not only between different areas of mathematics but between mathematics and areas of application. With this comes an emphasis on conceptual knowledge as opposed to procedural knowledge (Heibert and Lefevre, 1986).

Summary

The constructivist zeitgeist in mathematics education merges nicely with emerging philosophies of mathematics to support reform in mathematics classrooms. In general, the reform movement calls for classrooms in which students construct mathematical knowledge through engaging in rich mathematical tasks and discourse about those tasks. The teachers' role in these classrooms shifts from an authoritative dispenser of information to facilitator of discourse and construction, concerned with individual students' understanding. Finally, the focus shifts to students' conceptual understanding and away from disconnected procedural knowledge. In what follows, I examine a few examples of such classrooms and instructional practice commensurate with the reform movement.

A Few Exemplary Studies

A great deal of work at the elementary level has been done in support of these reform goals (see Franke and Grouws, 1997). Much of the foundational work that helps us understand social construction of knowledge in mathematics seems to be taking place prior to the middle school years (Cobb *et al.*, 1991; Lampert, 1990). Indeed, indications are that, although secondary school teachers claim to be well aware of the Standards documents, their use of pedagogical practices is much less aligned with the Standards than those of elementary school teachers (Weiss *et al.*, 1994). Stories of reform in secondary classrooms have only begun to reach the literature. However, I can point to some studies that discuss the kinds of classes and instructional practices discussed here.

Healy's Build-a-Book Geometry

Healy (1993) reports on a high school geometry course he developed in 1987. The class used no textbook, but instead built their own geometry book by starting with three 'given facts' (the only geometric knowledge ever provided by the teacher) and compiling 'discovered truths,' definitions, and so forth on which the class agreed. On the first day of class, students were randomly assigned to small groups. The groups were given sheets that contained only a statement at the top, one of three given facts: parallel lines never meet, a triangle contains 180 degrees, a linear pair contains 180 degrees. They were instructed to write on the sheets the comments of group members about the given statements. Following each class period, the teacher would read the comments of the groups, and choose some to be the statements for discussion on the next day. Over time, the statements emerging from the groups would be brought before the class, who would vote on whether they should be included in the geometry book.

When students had questions about the meaning of terms, groups would be given the task of coming up with a class definition for the terms. These were debated (sometimes hotly) among the whole class and, when consensus was achieved, became part of the class book. Students were allowed to use any sources they wished, provided they were able to explain and support what they found. They also used the Geometric Supposer (Schwartz and Yerushalmy, 1985–1988) software to test conjectures. Students were evaluated using questions from the geometry book they built, and the tests were corrected using definitions and discovered truths from the book.

Healy reports considerable success, including increased passing rates for geometry and increased student interest. He also notes that grades and SAT preparation were not sacrificed. However, the real story to be told is from the students themselves, and he offers several excerpts from students writing about the class. The students' reactions range from shock, disbelief, and anger at the first of the year to gradual acceptance and on to enjoyment at the end. As one student put it, 'You actually have to use a part of your brain you don't use very often in school. The thinking part. The class questions and situations force you to think . . . . I love it. I love being forced to think' (p. 103).

The description of build-a-book geometry illustrates several of the aspects of constructivist theory discussed earlier. Most obviously, perhaps, it illustrates that individual students' mathematical knowledge can be constructed in a social arena, where ideas are subjected to public scrutiny. In this class, mathematical knowledge was (tautologically) social knowledge. Determining the usefulness of ideas, the validity of arguments, and the value of concepts, each involved social processes. This gave the students a different view of mathematics: 'I think our book will be better (than other books) because ours was made by normal humans' (p. 104). Mathematics becomes something normal humans can do, rather than something only geniuses do (see Schoenfeld, 1989). It is not surprising that, in this context, several worthwhile goals beyond mathematical knowledge were achieved. Students learned a good deal about their own capabilities and to express themselves, as one student said, 'keeping our personal feelings to ourselves'.

A second aspect of social constructivist thought illustrated by Healy's course is the importance of teachers surrendering intellectual authority. Healy noted that it takes 'from 1 to 3 months for the mystique surrounding the teacher to be minimized by the discoveries students make' (p. 87), during which time the teacher is unable to ask questions or participate in class activities. In this case, Healy is radically departing from his traditional role and giving responsibility for the class to the students. He concludes: '1. Students need to have ways of assuming authority and responsibility for their own learning. 2. If one permits students to exercise authority and responsibility, many of them learn to do so' (p. 104). [. . .]

A Case Study from the QUASAR Project

[. . .] Another example of a successful classroom comes from a report of the QUASAR project by Williams and Baxter (1996). This project, funded by the Ford Foundation and centered at the Learning Research and Development Center at the University of Pittsburgh, has as its goal the demonstration that it is 'both feasible and responsible to implement instructional programs that foster the acquisition of mathematical thinking and reasoning skills by students attending middle schools in economically disadvantaged communities' (Silver and Lane, 1993, p. 12). The project selected schools in various cities and established a partnership between school personnel and resource partners from local colleges and universities. These partners worked together to develop and implement programs of instruction that addressed the particular needs of their students.

As part of their efforts, QUASAR project staff documented how classroom instruction occurred at each school (cf. Stein *et al.*, 1991). [. . .] These data provided the basis for Williams and Baxter's analysis.

As part of their analysis they describe a typical day in the classroom of one exceptional teacher they call Ms. H. [. . .]

> In a typical lesson Ms. H presented a problem from the curriculum on the overhead projector. Her problem presentation was usually lean, with little elaboration. Students then worked on the problem in small groups, using manipulatives and calculators as needed. They were encouraged to talk the problem over, share ideas and possible solution strategies, and explain their thinking to one another. Finally, the whole class discussed the problem, with several students going to the overhead projector and using it to explain their thinking with drawings or manipulatives. This sequence of problem presentation, small-group work and whole-class discussion was often repeated a number of times during a lesson. (p. 29)
>
> There was more student talk in this classroom than one would expect in a traditional mathematics classroom where the teacher is the center of conversation. In addition, we saw important developments in *what* students said. Ms. H's students contributed substantively to class discussions, their responses to teacher questions were thoughtful and at times original, reflecting their efforts to understand mathematical ideas. In addition, students talked to each other in meaningful ways. They built on each other's ideas and questioned each other's thinking rather than merely supplying right answers. (p. 32)

As in the previous study, it is clear that intellectual authority became shared among members of the class. Students were expected to justify their work and to ask questions of other students. They were expected to explore and discuss numerous paths through the problem. They were expected and encouraged to make connections. A very strong sense was gleaned from both interviews with Ms. H and from observations of classroom practice of the importance of constructing understanding.

Williams and Baxter (1996) coined the term *discourse-oriented teaching* to describe the teaching they saw in Ms. H's classroom, although they contend that hers is a reasonable interpretation of the reform movement and of constructivist principles. Williams and Baxter noted that Ms. H spent a good deal of time discussing and modeling expected social behaviors, setting up the norms for mathematical discussions in class. They referred to this as building a *social scaffolding,* which helps students to direct their mathematical discourse in productive ways. With the social scaffolding in place, the hope was that student discussions about rich mathematical tasks would build an *analytic scaffolding* to support the construction of useful mathematical knowledge. Ms H tended to spend a lot of time on social scaffolding, helping students learn to act as their own support when discussing mathematical ideas.

Summary

It seems safe to draw a few general conclusions from the examples just discussed. These generalization are my own, but I believe they are in keeping with the best knowledge we have of building successful constructivist classrooms at the secondary level.

1. Students' constructions are important, meaningful, and need to be taken seriously. Successful teachers are those who gather information on how their students think and use it as a basis for selection of mathematical tasks. In all three cases, teachers gathered information on a daily basis and used it to decide when to go on and how to select tasks.
2. Mathematical understanding can be constructed within a social context where teachers and students share responsibility for validating mathematical ideas and concepts. This provides students with a more reasonable view of the social nature of mathematical knowledge, and supports the belief that knowing mathematics involves their *doing* mathematics, including subjecting their mathematical ideas to public scrutiny.
3. Mathematically rich tasks that are designed to require time, effort, and exploration provide an excellent context for mathematical discussion, and hence knowledge production. This is contrasted with the traditional use of procedural exercises from textbooks or worksheets.
4. Teachers need the opportunity to reflect on their own understanding of mathematics, teaching, and learning. In all three cases discussed, the teachers reflected frequently on their own knowledge of mathematics, how to deal with specific mathematical concepts, their goals for instruction, and their practice. In the absence of such reflection, attempts to alter a classroom culture are extremely difficult. Moreover, making the changes discussed in the examples – leaving behind textbooks, withdrawing from traditional leadership roles in the classroom, focusing on individual under-

standing of students in a large class – can be an overwhelming burden. Without support, many of us will become discouraged and fall back on our traditional ways of doing things. [. . .]

Some Cautionary Tales

In this final section I consider some cautionary tales that come from attempts to change mathematics instruction and other aspects of classroom culture in ways consistent with the general constructivist philosophy of the reform movement. My purpose here is to alert those who attempt such changes to a few blockades that might be encountered so that they can be better prepared or, at least, know they are not alone.

Dilemmas of Discourse-Oriented Teaching

In the example from the QUASAR project, Williams and Baxter (1996) argued that real changes had taken place in Ms. H's classroom. However, they also note 'trade-offs' involved in Ms. H's decisions to engage in discourse-oriented teaching. Classroom conversations showed genuine frustration by the students and the teacher. Williams and Baxter pointed out that Ms. H was a strong believer in her interpretation of constructivist theory: she believed she needed to take a hands-off, noninterventive role in her students' learning of mathematics. Through selections of good tasks from a reform-oriented curriculum, orchestrating the discourse, and setting expectations for what was expected in small-group and whole-class discourse among students, Ms. H believed that she was assisting students in building a scaffold for the creation of mathematical knowledge. Part of this scaffold was social and part was analytic, and the responsibility for building it was shared among the teacher, the student, and the curriculum and tasks. However, having set up this scaffold did not mean that the instruction always flowed smoothly to desired ends. Williams and Baxter focus on two kinds of situations in which problems arose.

Among the problems that Williams and Baxter (1996) point out are the ritualizing of discourse and the radical contextualizing of discourse. Some students' explanations suggested that they viewed the discourse as a ritual; that is, as an end in itself rather than a means to an end. In one example, Ms. H asked students to explain how they had arrived at an answer. Eventually, after extended questioning, one student told Ms. H that they 'worked in groups'. The student knew that working together was required, and they had indeed worked in groups, but had not arrived at a group understanding. The work as a group and the discourse among group members was a ritual they performed with no real purpose. In other cases, students would seem to ask questions of one another when they already knew the answer, apparently to fulfil the expectation that they ask questions. The questions were not genuine but were part of a ritual of the classroom.

Students would also radically contextualize discourse. Students are very good at finding out what the teacher expects, and when those expectations shift from procedural mathematical knowledge to conceptual knowledge within a social realm, students may still use the discourse only to please the teacher and not to build legitimate knowledge. Williams and Baxter (1996) give an example of a group of students who, over the course of a class period, were able to go through the motions of group discourse about problems while still operating on a largely procedural level. They aimed only at accomplishing the task as they saw it and not on letting their discussion promote understanding. Setting up excellent tasks and norms for engagement did not necessarily communicate to students what was expected and what they should be gaining, nor did it guarantee their cooperation (see Edwards and Mercer, 1987, for a discussion of these issues in 'discovery' classrooms).

Classroom Interactions

A second kind of cautionary tale comes from a two-year project on classroom communication in middle school classrooms funded by the National Science Foundation. Two different reports from that project point to the importance of attending to beliefs of the students in the reform process. The first report, by Walen (1993), deals specifically with the role of teachers' questions and answers. Walen spent most of a year in two algebra classes of a teacher who was attempting to initiate reforms. The teacher hoped to encourage class discussions, sense making, and the construction of understanding by her students. Walen studied this process through extensive classroom observations, journal exchanges and interviews with six students who acted as key informants, and whole-class questionnaires based on interviews and observations.

Walen points out that traditional classroom interaction follows what Mehan (1979) calls the initiation–response–evaluation (IRE) pattern of classroom instruction. Here, teachers initiate a verbal interaction, typically by asking a question. A student or students will give a response, and the teacher will evaluate that response (e.g., say it is correct) before initiating another interaction. In the past, teachers' questions have been largely rhetorical, they knew the answers and were using the questions to test students' knowledge of facts or sometimes as attention-getting or disciplinary devices. As teachers adopt the philosophy of reform and attempt to create communities of learners in which they play a legitimate role, they will tend to ask questions that are actually questions to them; that is, broader questions for which discussion and exploration are necessary.

During these early phases of reform, students are still used to more traditional kinds of questions. Walen reports that in the classrooms she studied, both kinds of questions were used, and students had a difficult time deciding when questions were legitimate and when they were largely part of an IRE pattern. Students in her study overwhelmingly believed that teachers ask questions to which they already know the answer, to find out if students know the answer or if students are listening or to determine whether it is time to move on to a new topic.

Walen reports on one memorable incident, where the class was exploring the generalization of a rule for multiplying two-digit numbers by 11 (add the two digits together and place the result between the two digits to get the three-digit answer). This was a genuine problem for the teacher, who had not before considered how to generalize the rule. The class struggled for some time with conjectures and attempted justifications that students' methods would work every time. The teacher encouraged students to persevere, explored connections between algorithms, and facilitated the search for patterns. At one point, the following dialogue occurred (from Walen, 1993, p. 192):

> Pat: I don't think there is a pattern.
> Teacher: I bet there is.
> Fred: She knows how (confidently, to the other students).
> Teacher: No, I don't. I've never done this before. I'm learning just like you are.
> Fred: Liar (challenging tone followed by nervous laughter).
> Teacher: I have *never* done this before.

The teacher's last line was spoken with obvious irritation, which almost immediately dissolved as she reinterpreted Fred's statement. At this point, however, the classroom discussion took on a different character. Increasingly, the class and teacher fell back on the IRE pattern that they were used to. By way of explanation, Walen suggests that Fred, and other students in the class, had trouble negotiating rules for discussions when the familiar IRE pattern was displaced. In this example, Fred fell back on the informal patterns he would use with other students as a model for discourse. Moreover, he failed to understand that the teacher was playing a different role; she really did not have the answer, but this was outside his realm of experience. When these expectations led to conflict, both teacher and student returned to more comfortable and established patterns of discourse.

For Walen, the message is that students and teachers together need to work toward a joint understanding of new discourse patterns. 'Both the teacher and students had difficulty in knowing how to modify the existing classroom structure, how to maintain existing changes during problematic episodes, and how to evaluate their progress.' (p. 219). More explicit attention needs to be paid to the changes we are asking students to make, and how students' beliefs and social needs combine to make those changes difficult. Walen concludes, 'Ultimately, without addressing student concerns for changing the classroom environment, reform movements in mathematics education have little chance of continued success.' (p. 226)

Conflicting Worldviews

A study by Ivey (1994) explored students' *worldviews* as one way of getting at the idea of students' concerns. She uses the work of Pepper (1942, 1982) to discuss how students' basic worldviews affect their participation in mathematics class. Pepper argues that humans rely on root metaphors, such as machines or living organisms, to understand their experience and that such metaphors affect the way they view the world in general. Hence, worldviews are strong internal belief systems that can affect many areas of students' lives.

Ivey (1994) tells the stories of students in a prealgebra class of one teacher who was attempting to implement reforms in his teaching. Ivey combined extensive classroom observations with interviews of 10 key student informants to describe how traditional and emerging classroom cultures clashed. In addition, she evaluated the worldviews of two of her informants in detail, demonstrating how worldviews interact with the classroom culture to either inhibit or enhance movement toward reform.

One student, Urissa, is described as having a consistently *mechanistic* worldview. This worldview has as its root metaphor the machine. Those with this worldview tend to see the world in terms of cause and effect. Descriptions of truth tend to be quantitative, focusing on measurables (how much, how often, when, where), and explanations have the flavor of descriptions of how the machine – the causes, effects, actions, and reactions – works.

A second student, Lisa, was described as having a *contextual* worldview. The root metaphor for this worldview is an act in context. Descriptions of truth involve interpretations of actions and experiences as they unfold in context and explanation often consists of anecdotes, stories told of experiences that bring out pertinent connections. Lisa's responses to interview questions were frequently grounded in the context of her everyday experience, the narrative of her life.

Ivey (1994) also uses the work of Misshauk (1979) to identify two cultures in the classroom she studied and describes how these students reacted to the different cultures. One was a traditional, mechanistic culture described by Ivey as one in which 'the teacher is the sole authority, the teacher allocates time and space, and the teacher questions students in order to evaluate them' (p. 105). The second was an organic culture that reflected the teacher's desire for change. In this new culture, students' roles were less distinctive, they were given more freedom and authority in deciding how to work and when they were on the right track. The teacher's management style was more permissive, allowing movement around the class, more noise and confusion. He delegated more authority. Finally, the teacher and students relied more on oral, rather than written, communication.

Ivey argues that these two students acted in ways consistent with their worldviews and that their actions were dramatically different. On one occasion, when the class was discussing divisibility rules, Urissa volunteered the rule for divisibility by four. The teacher, Mr. Scott, validated the rule by restating it and showing a few examples. At this point, Lisa conjectured a different rule for divisibility by four, involving multiplying the first and last digits together. In this case, Mr. Scott responded differently. Even when Lisa found that the rule did not work for some two-digit numbers, Mr. Scott searched for counter examples among three- and four-digit numbers. In the midst of this searching, the class considered the number 320, and the product of 3 and 0, which is 0. Mr. Scott asked if 0 was a multiple of 4, and Lisa argued that it was, because '0 times any number is 0.' Eventually, a counter-example was found, and the class moved on, Ivey (1994) concludes:

> The important point, for this analysis, was the difference between the effect of Urissa's actions on the class and the effect of Lisa's actions. Even in what was primarily a mechanistic lesson – rules were stated with no justification, and examples were given of their uses – Lisa was able to act in a contextual way. Her search of connections between the examples listed on the board led to a much richer class discussion. (p. 123)

Ivey also discusses the roles Urissa and Lisa played in small group work, in which the culture of the classroom was more organic. Urissa was successful in turning small group work into the kind of work she was used to. When compelled to work in groups, she would work individually and only compare answers with other group members. She refrained from participating in group discussions, except on rare occasions when she would explain her solution by describing the algorithm she had used to obtain it. Lisa, on the other hand, was eager to engage in group discussion. Even when doing individual seatwork, Lisa would engage in informal group discussions whenever Mr. Scott would allow it. She sometimes worked as a liaison between groups. In an effort to connect more students' ideas with hers. Justification was a normal part of her working in groups, to the extent that she provided it as part of her normal discourse in groups.

The point, for Ivey, is that 'both Lisa and Urissa were able to substantively change the course of particular classroom activities to make them more consistent with their particular world views' (p. 137). When confronted with a new culture at odds with her worldview, Urissa modified the new culture to make it conform more with her expectations. On the other hand, Lisa was able to adopt the new culture at a high level of expertise, because it was consistent with her worldview. Ivey concludes,

> Students' world views are powerful influences on their responses to new cultural expectations. As current reform efforts are tantamount to cultural change, students' world views have important consequences for reform efforts. Failure to address new expectations for students in explicit ways will lead to classroom

difficulties. What must be done . . . is to recognize the power of a student's world view to shape her or his actions in the classroom and even to partially shape instruction itself, and to consider ways of dealing with differing world views in the classroom. (p. 142).

Summary

The cautionary tales of this section point to one aspect of the complexity of change. Other problems might include lack of administrative support, incompatible teachers' beliefs, or parental expectations. My intention is to point to the students as important but frequently overlooked players in the reform process and to the ways in which their views of reform can have a profound effect on individual teachers' success.

Conclusion

In this chapter I attempted to provide a rationale for recommendations on improving secondary mathematics instruction. While I attempted to ground my recommendations in solid research, I also attempted to show the philosophical background that informs both the recommendations and the research. In part, this is due to my conviction that individual teachers, given time and support, will find good ways to teach, provided they have clear visions of *what teaching and learning mathematics means.* I have tried to provide a window to the best current thinking on these issues.

One critical point remains to be made. In *Wrestling with Change*, Lew Romagnano (1994) reports on a collaborative project with a first year teacher in which they worked together in two ninth grade general math classes to implement the kinds of reforms we have discussed in this chapter. Some but not all of Romagnano's recommendations parallel those brought to light in this chapter; the need for teachers to develop their own understanding of mathematical ideas, the need for rich mathematical tasks, the need to negotiate new classroom traditions with students, and the need to work through traditional practices such as grading and tracking in light of these new classroom traditions, however, the message that emerges most strongly for me from Romagnano's work is the idea that teaching involves managing dilemmas and that changing teaching will bring to light a new set of dilemmas to manage (see also Lampert, 1985). Such dilemmas as when and how much to tell students (as opposed to letting them discover), how best to assess and assign grades to students, and how to make reforms in the context of pressures from school policy must be managed, and many may not be solvable. Romagnano argues that teachers need to reconsider their roles as teachers to include managing these dilemmas. 'They can then apply the same knowledge, judgement, and creativity they bring to other aspects of their work to the task of coping with the dilemmas of change' (p. 174).

Returning to the metaphor with which I began, I feel that the individual bricks needed to build a reformed classroom are becoming increasingly easy to come by. As teachers, we gather facts about students and classroom life all the time. What I have attempted to provide is a scaffold on which to stand as we attempt to build from that information a better classroom. With that scaffold in place, good teachers can successfully build the kinds of classrooms that are equal to the vision of reform.

References

Carpenter, T. P., Fennema, E., Peterson, P. L., and Carey, D. A. (1988). Teachers' pedagogical content knowledge of students' problem solving in elementary arithmetic. *Journal for Research in Mathematics Education*, 19(5), 385–401.

Cobb, P., Wood, T., and Yackel, E. (1991). A constructivist approach to second grade mathematics. In E. von Glasersfeld (Ed.), *Radical constructivism in mathematics education* (pp. 157–176). Boston: Kluwer Academic Publishers.

Confrey, J. (1990). What constructivism implies for teaching. In R. B. Davis, C. A. Maher, and N. Noddings (Eds.), *Constructivist views on the teaching and learning of mathematics* (Journal for Research in Mathematics Education Monograph Series, No. 4, pp. 107–122). Reston, VA: National Council of Teachers of Mathematics.

Edwards, D., and Mercer, N. (1987). *Common knowledge: The development of understanding in the classroom*. London: Routledge.

Ernst, P. (1991). *The philosophy of mathematics education*. New York: Falmer Press.

Fennema, E., and Franke, M. L. (1992). Teachers' knowledge and its impact. In D. A. Grouws (Ed.), *Handbook of research on mathematics teaching and learning* (pp. 147–164). New York: Macmillan.

Franke, M. L. and Grouws, D. A. (1997). Developing student understanding in elementary school mathematics: a cognitive perspective. In G. A. Phye (Ed.) *Handbook of academic learning: construction of knowledge*. San Diego: Academic Press.

Freudenthal, H. (1987). Mathematics starting and staying in reality. In I. Wirszup and R. Streit (Eds.), *Developments in school mathematics around the world. Proceedings of the UCSMP International Conference on Mathematics Education*, 28–30 March 1985 (pp. 279–295). Reston, VA: National Council of Teachers of Mathematics.

Gergen, K. I. (1985). The social constructionist movement in modern psychology. *American Psychologist*, 40, 266–275.

Goodman, N. (1986). Mathematics as an objective science. In T. Tymoczko (Ed.), *New directions in the philosophy of mathematics* (pp. 79–94). Boston: Birkhauser.

Grouws, D. A. (Ed.), (1992). *Handbook of research on mathematics teaching and learning*. New York: Macmillan.

Healy, C. C. (1993). Discovery courses are great in theory, but . . . . In J. I. Schwartz, M. Yerushalmy, and B. Wilson (Eds.), *The geometric supposor: What is it a case of?* (pp. 85–104). Hillsdale, NJ: Erlbaum.

Heibert, J., and Carpenter, T. P. (1992). Learning and teaching with understanding. In D. A. Grouws (Ed.), *Handbook of research on mathematics teaching and learning* (pp. 65–97). New York: Macmillan.

Heibert, J., and Lefevre, P. (1986). Conceptual and procedural knowledge in mathematics: An introductory analysis. In J. Heibert (Ed.), *Conceptual and procedural knowledge: The case of mathematics* (pp. 1–27). Hillsdale, NJ: Erlbaum.

Hersh, R. (1986). Some proposals for reviving the philosophy of mathematics. In T. Tymoczko (Ed.), *New directions in the philosophy of mathematics* (pp. 9–28). Boston: Birkhäuser.

Ivey, K. M. C. (1994). *World views in the mathematics classroom: Students translating beliefs into actions.* Unpublished doctoral dissertation, Washington State University. Pullman.

Kleibard, H. M. (1992). *Forging the American curriculum: Essays in curriculum theory and history.* New York: Routledge.

Kleiner, I., and Movshovitz-Hadar, N. (1990). Aspects of the pluralistic nature of mathematics. *Interchange*, 21(1), 28–35.

Lampert, M. (1985). How do teachers manage to teach? Perspectives on problems in practice. *Harvard Educational Review*, 55(2), 178–194.

Lampert, M. (1990). When the problem is not the question and the solution is not the answer: Mathematical knowing and teaching. *American Educational Research Journal*, 27, 29–63.

Lyddon, W. J., and McLaughlin, J. T. (1992). Constructivist psychology: A heuristic framework. *Journal of Mind and Behavior*, 13(1), 89–108.

Misshauk, M. J. (1979). *Management: Theory and practice.* Boston: Little, Brown.

National Council of Teachers of Mathematics (NCTM). (1989). *Curriculum and evaluation standards for school mathematics.* Reston, VA: Author.

National Council of Teachers of Mathematics (NCTM). (1991). *Professional standards for teaching mathematics.* Reston, VA: Author.

National Council of Teachers of Mathematics (NCTM). (1995). *Assessment standards for school mathematics.* Reston, VA: Author.

Pepper, S. C. (1942). *World hypotheses: A study in evidence.* Berkeley: University of California Press.

Pepper, S. C. (1982). Metaphor in philosophy. *Journal of Mind and Behavior*, 3, 197–205.

Putnam, R. T., Lampert, M., and Peterson, P. L. (1990). Alternative perspectives on knowing mathematics in elementary schools. In C. B. Cazden (Ed.), *Review of research in education* (Vol. 16, pp. 57–150). Washington, DC: American Educational Research Association.

Restivo, S. (1993). The social life of mathematics. In S. Restivo, J. P. Van Bendegem, and R. Fischer (Eds.), *Math worlds: Philosophical and social studies of mathematics and mathematics education* (pp. 247–278). Albany: State University of New York Press.

Restivo, S., Van Bendegem, J. P., and Fischer, R. (Eds.) (1993). *Math worlds: Philosophical and social studies of mathematics and mathematics education.* Albany: State University of New York Press.

Romagnano, L. (1994). *Wrestling with change: The dilemmas of teaching real mathematics.* Portsmouth, NH: Heinemann.

Romberg, T. A., Allison, J. L., Clarke, B. A., Clarke, D. M., Middleton, J. A., Pedro, J. D., Smith, M. E., and Spence, M. (1993). *A blueprint for maths in context: A connected curriculum for grades 5–8* (Revised). Madison, WI: Wisconsin Center for Education Research.

Romberg, T. A., and Carpenter, T. P. (1986) Research on teaching and learning mathematics: Two disciplines of scientific inquiry. In M. C. Wittrock (Ed.), *Handbook of research on teaching* (3rd ed., pp. 850–873). New York: Macmillan.

Schoenfeld, A. (1989). Explorations of students' mathematical beliefs and behavior. *Journal for Research in Mathematics Education*, 20, 338–355.

Schwartz, J., and Yerushalmy, M. (1985–1988). *The geometric supposer.* Pleasantville, NY: Sunburst.

Silver, E. A., and Lane, S. (1993). Balancing considerations of equity, content quality, and technical excellence in designing, validating and implementing performance assessments in the context of mathematics instructional reform: The experience of the QUASAR project. Pittsburgh, PA: Learning Research and

Development Center, University of Pittsburgh. (ERIC Document Reproduction Service No. ED 361 370).

Skovesmose, O. (1993). The dialogical nature of reflective knowledge. In S. Restivo J. P. Van Bendegem, and R. Fischer (Eds.), *Maths worlds: Philosophical and social studies of mathematics and mathematics education* (pp. 162–181). Albany: State University or New York Press.

Slife, B. D., and Williams, R. N. (1995). *What's behind the research? Discovering hidden assumptions in the behavioral sciences.* Thousand Oaks, CA: Sage Publications.

Stanic, G. M. A. (1986). The growing crisis in mathematics education in the early twentieth century. *Journal for Research in Mathematics Education*, 17, 190–205.

Steffe, L. P., and Kieren, T. (1994). Radical constructivism and mathematics education. *Journal for Research in Mathematics Education*, 25(6), 711–733.

Stein, M. K., Grover, B. W., and Silver, E. A. (1991). Changing instructional practice: A conceptual framework for capturing the details. In R. Underhill (Ed.), *Proceedings of the thirteenth annual meeting of the North American Chapter of the International Group for the Psychology of Mathematics Education* (pp. 36–42). Blacksburg: Virginia Tech Department of Curriculum and Instruction.

Thompson, A. (1992). Teachers' beliefs and conceptions: A synthesis of research. In D. A. Grouws (Ed.), *Handbook of research on mathematics teaching and learning* (pp. 127–146). New York: Macmillan.

Tymoczko, T. (1986). *New directions in the philosophy of mathematics.* Boston: Birkhauser.

von Glasersfeld, E. (1983). Learning as a constructive activity. In J. C. Bergeron, and N. Herscovics (Eds.), *Proceedings on the fifth annual meeting of the North American Chapter of the International Group for the Psychology of Mathematics Education* (pp. 41–68). PME-NA: Montreal.

von Glasersfeld, E. (1989). Constructivism in education. In T. Husen, and T. N. Postlethwaite (Eds.), *The International Encyclopedia of Education, Supplementary Volume* (pp. 162–163). Oxford, England: Pergamon.

Wagner, S., and Kieran, C. (Eds.), (1989). *Research issues in the learning and teaching of algebra.* Reston, VA: National Council of Teachers of Mathematics; Hillsdale, NJ: Erlbaum.

Walen, S. B. (1993). *An analysis of students' knowledge of the mathematics classroom.* Unpublished doctoral dissertation, Washington State University: Pullman.

Weiss, I. R., Matti, M. C., and Smith, P. S. (1994). *Report of the 1993 national survey of science and mathematics education.* Chapel Hill, NC: Horizon Research.

Welch, W. (1978). Science Education in Urbanville: A case study. In R. Stake and J. Easley (Eds.), *Case studies in science education* (pp. 5–1 – 5–33). Urbana: University of Illinois.

Williams, S. R., and Baxter, J. A. (1996). Dilemmas of discourse-oriented teaching in one middle school mathematics class. *The Elementary School Journal*, 97 (1), 21–28.

15

Some Voices are More Equal than Others: Subject and Other in the School Curriculum

Carrie Paechter

Editors' Introduction

*In the book from which this chapter is taken Carrie Paechter uses the con-
cept of woman as Other, of the female seen as deviating from the 'normal'
male Subject of discourse, to question much of what is taken for granted in
the education of girls. Examining who or what is treated in this way can be a
useful tool in unpacking social (and in this case educational) structures and
hierarchies, by forcing us to look at who and what are excluded, as well as
those whose inclusion is taken for granted. Thus, in this context, the Other is
those students and teachers who are treated as abnormal, as deviations in the
school setting. In this chapter the notion of Other is extended to include those
individuals and subjects which have not been central in the conception of the
school curriculum.*

> If knowledge is power, then some forms of knowledge are more powerful than
> others. It is no accident that the least powerful forms of knowledge are those
> taught to the least valued groups of pupils.
>
> (Attar, 1990 p. 22)

In schools there is a wide range of voices, reflecting differences not just of
gender but of 'race', social class and 'ability'. Some are powerful and more
easily heard, some are positioned as Other, and, again, this is due to more
than just gender. Gender is, however, an important structuring factor in the
way schools operate, and in particular in determining who has power, and
for whom the official curriculum is intended. In this chapter I am going to
consider how gender roles and gendered subject forms are used to position
some subjects, teachers and students as Others within the education
system.

One way we can examine the complex nature and interplay of inequalities within schools is to look in detail at who are the Others in this
setting, and how their Othering comes about. In this chapter I want to
·consider the Others of the curriculum: those subjects and students seen as
'exceptions' when the purposes and content of education are discussed. By

exploring which subjects are Other to the dominant school curriculum, and by looking at who studies them, we can see how academic Otherness is constructed within schools, which teachers and which students are in powerful positions in this arena, and how this affects schooling as a whole.

In this chapter I shall mainly focus on secondary education, though I will refer to other sectors from time to time. Although in recent years the UK has seen increasing subject specialism in the primary phase, the issue of differential subject status remains most clearly exemplified at secondary level. As curriculum specialisation increases as students get older, it is comparatively easy to see which areas are intended for which groups of students. Tertiary education is only intended for a relatively elite group, so at this stage the differences between curriculum areas are exemplified mainly through what is included and what excluded. At the same time, it should be noted that there is also a hierarchy of sectors in the education system as a whole, in which primary education is itself positioned as Other in several ways. In England and Wales, for example, less state funding is provided for the education of younger children, and the English and Welsh National Curriculum is structured around the discrete subject areas found in secondary schools, rather than around the integrated approach still favoured by many primary school teachers.

A useful way of approaching an examination of the dominant is to focus on that which is subordinate. By looking at what is common to people and systems positioned as Other we are able to bring to light what is usually taken for granted as normal. That is not to say that we should not put the 'normal' explicitly under examination, and in some contexts (for example, in the area of sexuality and sexual orientation (Richardson, 1996; Wilkinson and Kitzinger, 1993)) this has become an important tool in redressing the balance between Subject and Other. In the school context, however, there has been a longstanding tendency for researchers to focus on high status curriculum areas, ignoring those associated with less powerful forms of knowledge. It is therefore illuminating to look instead at what it means for a school subject, and those who study it, to be marginal within the curriculum.

Design and Technology and Physical Education: Life in a Marginal Subject

> I expect that the status that [D&T] holds in other teachers' opinions is quite the same as it was 20 years ago . . . I still feel that people probably feel the same way towards us as they do towards, say, PE. I never minded that, it was never a problem for me. I actually think that technology is of a lower academic status anyway . . . As far as academic status is concerned, I rate it low compared with more important things like English, maths and science.
> (Ravi Korde, CDT teacher, Bursley School, 21/2/94)

Design and technology (D&T) and physical education (PE) are almost paradigmatic in their positioning as marginal subjects, and both have deeply gendered histories whose legacies remain today. PE is unusual for a low status curriculum area in that it has been the focus of a number of studies, on which I draw for my discussion in this chapter. In examining D&T I shall be citing evidence from my own research,[1] coupled with a number of studies of its contributor/predecessor subjects: craft, design and technology (CDT) and home economics (HE). These studies suggest that the condition of subject marginality is bound up not only with issues of the comparative status of different kinds of knowledge, but also with images of masculinity and femininity that involve ideas about the body, about social class and about the relationship between power, knowledge and the self.

Both D&T and PE are comparatively recent combinations of what were, explicitly or by default, separate subjects for girls and boys. In the case of D&T, the introduction of the National Curriculum in England and Wales included an attempt to replace CDT, HE and business studies (BS), all of which, while officially open to students of both genders, contained heavy gender imbalances, with a gender-neutral subject originally focused around the design process. PE has, until recently, had separate male and female forms, which emphasised different skills and qualities and required different sorts of training for the teachers involved (Fletcher, 1984; Flintoff, 1993). Of course, sport, especially for boys, has always been important to the ethos of fee-paying and other elite schools. In the state sector, however, where both D&T and PE have been taught for more than 100 years, working class students have been seen as an important client group; in the case of HE and PE the subjects were made compulsory with the intention of improving the health of the poor (Fletcher, 1984; Hunt, 1987; Manthorpe, 1986). It is notable, in this context, that the aim for boys was the improvement of their own health, while that for girls was that they should be better wives and mothers, presumably in order that they might improve the fitness (for military service, among other things) of their husbands and sons (Dyhouse, 1976, 1977).

Gendered Subject Ideologies and the Social Control of the Working Classes

Both CDT[2] and its predecessors, the manual crafts (mainly woodwork and metalwork), and the various forms of HE[3] were explicitly used, throughout this century, as agents of social control. In the mid nineteenth century a concern for the morals and health of the poor, particularly in the cities (Hunt, 1987; Manthorpe, 1986) led to the introduction of domestic subjects, for girls only, in elementary schools. The finding that in Manchester 800 out of 11000 volunteers for the Boer War were unfit for active service raised fears about 'national degeneracy', and the high infant mortality rate was blamed on the ignorance and carelessness of mothers, particularly those working outside the home (a belief that was not borne out by the official figures) (Dyhouse, 1977). A general fear of the potential of the working classes to spread both disease and dissent was combined with the belief that the family would act as a stabilising force, centred around women as home-makers; the domestic training of young girls was designed to counteract what was seen as a worrying trend in the industrial centres (Dyhouse, 1976). Poverty and malnutrition were attributed to a lack of domestic management skills on the part of working-class women; it was believed that this might be remedied by the introduction of classes in cookery, needle-work, cleaning and laundrywork (Porter, 1991; Purvis, 1985), even though the schemes of work employed often had little relevance to the actual living conditions of working-class families (Attar, 1990; Turnbull, 1987). The teaching of domestic tasks in ways that failed to take account of the real-ities of students' lives not only positioned them as Other with respect to presumed social norms, but was combined with an image of family life to which they were expected to aspire. This regarded poverty as an individual issue, amenable to individual thrift, and the maintenance of a 'respectable' home as an entirely female responsibility.

> The development in schools of what in 1910 one educationalist called 'the domes-tic arts – *cooking, cleaning* and *clothing*' reveals how persuasive and persistent an ideology of domesticity was in influencing girls' schooling. This ideology sug-gested that domestic work and love of the home should be the focus of women's lives . . . the progress of domestic subjects shows how the curriculum was moulded to encourage working-class girls to see their primary role as members of society to lie in serving others by sewing, cooking and cleaning, both in their own households, and, as a result of society's 'servant problem', in the homes of others.
>
> (Turnbull, 1987 p. 87, emphasis in original)

For working-class males, a parallel ideology underlay the introduction of craft subjects into boys' state education. Although there was a belief that crafts were an essential part of a liberal education (Penfold, 1988), CDT and its predecessors were also associated with the inculcation of moral training and industrious habits. Part of the attempt to control the poor through the hegemony of bourgeois family values was a stress on the importance of regular labour to a respectable life; while the dependent wife remained at home, the husband was expected to labour cheerfully at the tasks that were his lot. Manual training was intended to promote this.

> Manual labour and moral training give an impulse to industrious habits which is not given without them. I have carefully watched the influence such training has on some of the most degraded of society . . . Therefore, I conclude that any system of education unconnected with the manual labour is yet imperfect, and I believe this to be the opinion of most experienced people.
>
> (Forss, C. (1835) *Practical Remarks upon the Education of the Working Classes*, quoted in Penfold, 1988 p. 3)

Along with the introduction of universal elementary schooling came a concern that educating working-class children might cause some to aspire beyond their station. Both manual crafts and the HE subjects had a part to play in counteracting this by encouraging young people to be satisfied with their lot:

> the great thing is to show to the working class the real dignity of labour . . . and to let them feel that it is a far nobler thing to be the head of an engineers shop, or to be a first-rate joiner, or a good mason, than it is to be a poor clerk who has to contend against the frightful competition which exists in that class, and who must appear respectable on the narrowest possible means.
>
> ('Technical Teaching'. *The Health Education Literature* 14 (1884), quoted in Penfold, 1988 p. 6)

> Amongst girls . . . great mistakes are made by their longing to 'better themselves' as they say. And in one sense it is quite right that they should have such a wish. But first let them be sure that it is bettering themselves to change merely for higher wages, or to get into a higher family. When the girl who is only fitted for housework thinks that because she has been well educated at school, she ought to be a lady's maid, when the lady's maids wish to be governesses, depend upon it they are not getting on in life . . .
>
> (Grant, A. R. (1871) *School Managers' Series of Reading Books, V*, London, Weale, quoted in Davin, 1987 p. 147)

The use of HE and 'boys' craft subjects as instruments of social reform and control, through the direction of different messages towards male and female working-class students, reinforced the ideology of separate spheres for men and women throughout life. Similar ideologies and effects are inherent in the separate forms of boys' and girls' PE. Male and female forms of PE have continued until very recently, and there remains an ideological split between those (mainly male) teachers who see as their main purpose the fostering of the sporting success of the elite, and those (mainly female) interested in promoting the personal and social development of all students through self-paced individual activities (Sparkes, 1991a). The justification for the introduction of PE into elementary schools in the nineteenth century was, again, a perceived need to improve the health both of military recruits and of future mothers (Fletcher, 1984). Sparkes (1991b) argues that this traditional focus on persuading the individual to adopt a particular lifestyle, with the aim of reducing mortality and morbidity in the population as a whole, remains a major impetus behind health-related fitness programmes. This, he suggests, ignores social structural issues in the health of different social groups, and equates concepts of morality with questions of lifestyle. In a way that parallels nineteenth-century ruling-class perceptions of the causes of poverty, those who lead 'unhealthy lives' are seen as morally lax.

PE and CDT both also have a role in promoting and perpetuating forms of working-class masculinity that are associated with working with, and on, the body. Although gender is primarily a social construct, it is attributed on the basis of physical signs and forms. Sherlock (1987) notes that there is social pressure on male PE teachers to demonstrate their masculinity by being big and strong physically, while Sparkes (1991a) points out that the possession of a high level of physical skill is a central aspect of the professional identity of many male PE teachers. Similarly, I found that many male CDT teachers saw excellence at craft skills as fundamental to their identities; this was reflected not only in remarks about their current roles but in reflecting on their schooldays. This teacher, for example, explicitly links his youthful pride in his work to his current curriculum focus:

> My mum's house was filled with stuff that I'd made at school. I enjoyed it and it's there forever. That may be just me being very much centred on hand skills.
>
> (Ravi Korde, Bursley School, 21/2/94)

D&T and PE as Low Status Subjects

Of course, the association of both PE and the D&T subjects with the body and manual labour contribute considerably to their low status in the curriculum. Both areas have traditionally been targeted at 'less academic', often working-class and disaffected students, partly because such curriculum divisions keep these groups apart from higher achievers, whose progress might be undermined by the former's distracting presence. In England and Wales, for example, the 1944 Education Act introduced a tripartite system which differentiated between the 'academic' student, who would have a traditional liberal education at a grammar school, those who were considered more suited to the study of science and technology, who would go to technical schools, and the rest, who were considered to be more able to deal with concrete things than with ideas (Thom, 1987) and went to the secondary moderns which were formed (along with primary schools) from the former elementary schools (Penfold, 1988). However, few technical schools were established, leaving most of the secondary-age population, as was in practice the case before the Act, split between the largely middle-class grammar school elite and the largely working-class remainder.

Within this system, the low status of CDT and HE was demonstrated as much by their absence from some parts of the system as by their presence in others. Neither CDT nor HE ever became well established in the universities, despite concerted efforts from practitioners (Attar, 1990; Manthorpe, 1986; Penfold, 1988), and, indeed, teacher education in home economics was generally carried out in separate colleges until the 1970s (Attar, 1990). Before it became a requirement for receiving grants in 1905, the higher status girls' schools in England often did not teach HE at all, their headmistresses arguing that such skills were better learned at home (Dyhouse, 1976). Even when forced to introduce them, these schools often gave domestic subjects low status and inferior facilities, preferring to model their curricula on those of the boys' grammar schools. Only those considered not able enough for more academic studies took practical subjects to examination level. A student at the Park School for Girls in Preston in the 1930s, for example, explained that:

she 'made bread and marmalade and cakes' for only about twelve months, 'because we were streamed you see, and I wasn't in the cookery stream after the first two years. I went in the Science form, and the Domestic Science was more for the – well when I say lower form, I'm not being derogatory, but some are better with working with their hands and they were streamed accordingly.'

(Summerfield, 1987 p. 156)

Meanwhile, housecraft and other domestic subjects were seen as central to the education of girls in secondary moderns (Attar, 1990). A similar differentiation took place regarding boys' craft subjects, and, indeed, the boys' grammar schools continued to resist them long after HE had become compulsory for girls.

Deep seated prejudices against practical work and long memories of the pattern and provision for workshop teaching within the old elementary school system meant that practical subjects were relegated predominantly to the domain of the lowest stratum – the secondary moderns. In Grammar schools they were never more than a peripheral activity.

(Penfold, 1988 p. 112)

With the introduction of comprehensive education, with its ideals of equal access to all, it might have been expected that there would be an end to this division between those whose education was academic and those whose was practical. However, what happened in practice was that some students were encouraged to spend a considerable proportion of their time studying CDT and HE, while others were not. Riddell (1992), for example, notes that, even as recently as the 1980s, the high-achieving boys in her study were channelled out of applied science and technology subjects. Meanwhile, those considered to be 'less able' have been encouraged, particularly after age 14, to spend as much time as possible in the CDT and HE areas. One teacher, for example, explains the reluctance of the former head of her school to move from CDT and HE to the less practical D&T:

in this school, that whole area certainly gave him the best results in examination level. It also kept him out of an awful lot of trouble because a large number of the less able children for example were pushed into that area because it was practical.

(Sue Pennington, Turnhill Community School, 6/1/93)

In largely working-class schools like Turnhill, such differential curriculum access did have some advantages for the 'less able' students, some of whom had their only examination successes in these subjects. There were other benefits for both schools and staff. Craft subjects continue to make an important contribution to the public face of many schools, with graphic design work and completed artefacts being displayed in public areas and at parents' evenings. The concentration of the 'less able' and disaffected in the domestic and CDT subjects also provided one source of status for the teachers, who, because of the practical nature of the work, its perceived relevance to the world outside school, and the less formal relationships possible in a kitchen or workshop, were often able to succeed with students considered to be difficult to teach elsewhere in the school. Those students seen as Other to the dominant model of the academically able, white and often male norm were successfully contained in subject areas also seen as Other to the dominant academic curriculum.

The move to the less practical D&T, with its greater design focus and whole-school clientele, while, in theory at least, raising the status of the contributing subjects, reduced this source of success and prestige. D&T was intended to be a gender-neutral amalgam of the best of HE and CDT, with a stronger and more rigorous focus on the design process to systematize the subject and stretch the more able students. However, not only did the amalgamation between two very gendered subject areas prove difficult in practice, particularly for the staff involved, but the attempt to raise the new subject's status by making it a compulsory 16+ examination subject had a number of unforeseen results. The new subject became increasingly 'masculine' in orientation, in the sense that there was an emphasis on those aspects, originally taught in CDT, that were traditionally associated with males. This was paralleled by increasing male domination of the teaching staff, particularly in terms of promotional opportunities (Paechter, 1993; Paechter and Head, 1996). At the same time, the increased academic content marginalized the traditional constituency of 'less able' students, who found themselves no better able to cope with this subject than with the rest of the curriculum (Paechter, 1993). The thinking behind the National Curriculum, because it focused on the 'more able' and 'average' students as Subject, failed to deal with the loss, for the less academically successful, of a curriculum area in which they could do reasonably well. As one teacher put it:

> Another subject has been removed from the curriculum that kids look forward to, if they do look forward to it, for enjoyment and pleasure. And now the underachievers in academic subjects underachieve in technology as well . . . And I find that the kids that achieve well in the other subjects achieve well in this one.
> (Ravi Korde, CDT teacher, Bursley Comprehensive School, 22/4/93)

With the revisions of the National Curriculum introduced in 1995, D&T, while remaining compulsory, is no longer an examination subject for all, and its content has moved once again towards having a more practical orientation. This is likely to mean a move back to a situation similar to that in most schools before the National Curriculum, with 'more able' students being counselled into taking only a 'short course' in the subject after age 14, and the 'less able' being encouraged, once again, to spend more of their time there. Furthermore, those students who do take 'long' courses at this stage are given a choice of specialism, which has resulted in similar gender divisions to those prior to the introduction of D&T. These changes, coupled with the development of associated vocational courses and the flexibility in school timetables to offer subjects such as child development as a GCSE option, is likely to reinstate the position of the D&T subjects as a potential gendered ghetto for working-class and disaffected students. The effect of this is two-edged. While it has some advantages for the students, giving them a space in which they can be successful with teachers who enjoy teaching them, at the same time it means that they have fewer opportunities to study higher status subjects. It also perpetuates the positioning both of these subjects and of those who teach and learn them as marginal to the dominant purposes of the school.

This differential counselling of the 'more able' out of and the 'less able' and disaffected into lower status subjects also takes place with respect to PE, which, again partly because of its informal nature, can be the only aspect of school that some students enjoy (Templin, *et al.*, 1988). It is suggested by some researchers that this is particularly true of young black males. Carrington and Wood (1983), for example, point to the 'colonisation' of school sports teams by black students already 'cooled out' of the academic mainstream. They argue that in the school they studied this process was encouraged by teachers, who overlooked poor behaviour from students who were playing in school teams, and was reinforced, through their influence on team membership, by the black students themselves. The importance of PE, and particularly inter-school sporting success, to the school's public image meant that disciplinary concessions were made to keep good athletes committed to playing in school teams. Carrington and Wood note some of the problems associated with this way of dealing with disaffected students:

> The shortcomings of this coping strategy are self evident: (1) It serves to reinforce both academic failure and unacceptable behaviour. (2) Insofar as the opportunities for success in school sport are restricted, it also denies many non-academic pupils even the consolation of an alternative to academic failure! (3) It can result in an intensification of interracial rivalries and conflict.
>
> (Carrington and Wood, 1983 p. 38)

This use of PE as a place to keep the disaffected out of trouble has recently become more difficult because of the rise of PE as an examination subject with an academic component. At the same time, the prevalence, among male PE teachers working with such groups, of a perspective on the subject centred around sporting prowess, encourages the development within some schools of a dominant, often partially resistant, masculinity which gives status to those individuals with certain bodily forms and behaviours. The hegemony of such masculinities can position as Other boys who do not conform to this image (Parker, 1996), and keeps girls firmly on the margins of the subject.

Because being able to work successfully with disaffected and 'less able' students has been a source of pride for D&T and PE teachers, there has been a tendency for them to stress the specific importance of their subjects for these groups. This HE teacher, for example, explicitly locates the value of her subject in its ability to develop students' self esteem:

> I think it's a really important subject. I mean, there's a case, one of my pupils last year. A real little scrap in the second year[4] and he came in and made chocolate chip cookies. He went out and his head was five times the size it was when he arrived and he was smiling from ear to ear. His sense of achievement in that lesson was probably the highest sense of achievement he's had all year. And I think that it's a pity that they can't . . . do more of that. You know, just the straightforward cooking, because it does their self respect so much good.
>
> (Anita Crawford, Turnhill Community School, 17/9/93).

While of course it is important for non-academic students to have access to sources of success and self-validation within the school setting, this approach positions the 'less academic' and less interested as Other in terms of curriculum provision; they are the abnormal, for whom the 'normal', academic, diet is considered unsuitable. The emphasis on the particular needs of such groups and the requirement to preserve non-academic options to cater for them consolidates their marginalization while perpetuating the low status of these curriculum areas and ensuring that the 'more able' continue to be counselled out of spending more than the minimum time in them.

Furthermore, the existence in the curriculum of subjects that appeal directly to images of masculinity (Parker, 1996; Connell, 1987; Willis, 1977) and femininity (McRobbie, 1991) held by working-class teenagers may lead these students to make curriculum choices that not only have conservative social structures as part of their overt and covert content, but also, by taking up their school time, exclude them from pursuing subjects with more value in the academic and employment marketplaces (Riddell, 1992). It also perpetuates a gendered and classed Otherness within the curriculum, as some students are encouraged to take these lower status, gendered subjects, while others are counselled to avoid them.

Students and Subjects as Parallel Others

It seems to me that there is a parallel between the Otherness of marginal subjects in the curriculum, the Otherness of specialists in these subjects and the Otherness of the students that study them. PE is so Other to the dominant academic image of a school subject that it is ignored in otherwise important studies (for example, Riddell, 1992; Arnot *et al.*, 1996). Teachers of D&T and PE, because they are not seen as contributing much to the education of the 'high value', 'more able' students, have relatively weak voices in whole school curriculum negotiation. Sparkes *et al.*, (1990), for example, noted that not only were PE staff regarded by others as having little to contribute to general curriculum debate, but that young PE teachers in particular tended to be unaware of the importance of being able to operate as professionals in the wider school arena. Similarly, many discussions of the school curriculum treat girls, black boys and less able students as Others, outside of the normal scope of the curriculum, and for whom it has to be modified. It is not considered strange that what is supposed to be a curriculum for all is at the same time perceived as being unsuitable for more than half of the students. Where the curriculum is seen to fail certain groups, it is not modified for all students, but just for these special cases.

There is a close relationship between the way that some groups are constructed as Other and attempts to exclude them from particular areas of the curriculum. This can be illustrated by the debates early in the twentieth century about whether domestic science should be promoted as an alternative science curriculum for girls. At this time the formal and academic nature of school science meant that it was seen as unsuited to the needs of most girls, who were being educated by and large either for household labour or its supervision. Manthorpe (1986) argues that, while some of those proposing an alternative, 'female' science curriculum had the need to reform an over-academic subject as their prime motivation, the move to replace, rather than supplement, science with domestic science was seen by teachers as threatening the newly-won right for girls and young women to study science as equals to men. Although there was a clear need to make school science more relevant to everyday life, to do this for one gender alone clearly placed that gender as an Other for whom the unchanged, high-status male curriculum had to be modified, while at the same time excluding girls from the wider scientific community, as was already happening in the USA (Manthorpe, 1986). This was clearly understood by those working in the middle-class girls' schools, who aspired to provide an education for girls equal, in both intellectual rigour and academic status, to that experienced by their brothers:

> The woman science teachers in the early twentieth century believed, as had their predecessors, that a *different* science education for girls would be regarded as an *inferior* science education. Furthermore, an alternative science for girls based on domestic examples was evidently bound up with particular assumptions about women's place and role in society . . . Thus a 'domestic science' could not be accepted by women science teachers or many headmistresses because it intended to create a separate school science for girls. This would have explicit consequences for the future of those girls who intended to go to university . . . As in the late nineteenth century the dilemma was between taking the same courses as boys – and thus maintaining the same traditions of science education which had been developed in a male education system – or making science more relevant, which at that time meant linking girls' interests to naturalistic assumptions about their future role.   (Manthorpe, 1986 pp. 212–213)

This example brings to the fore an interesting and important aspect of the relationship between gender, status and curriculum subjects. The cases of D&T and PE make it clear that it is quite possible for alternative male and female forms of a subject to develop and flourish more or less independently for decades, even in mixed schools. The subjects where this has happened, however, are those that are themselves Other within the school curriculum; they are of low status, and generally aimed at those, often working-class, students who are seen as 'less able'. Higher status subjects only come in one main form; there are no gendered alternatives. The forms and structures of these subjects, with some modifications, are based on the liberal curriculum originally developed for boys and taken up by the middle-class girls' schools aiming to provide equal access to an academic education. In other words, they are the male conceptions of these disciplines. It is only in subjects that are themselves Other that alternative female forms have been allowed to succeed. Conversely, attempts to establish female forms of higher status subjects, such as the development of domestic science as a genuinely alternative science, were bound to fail. Given the hegemonic nature of the male forms of the academic disciplines, alternative conceptions would not have been given equivalent status with the already established male forms. It has therefore not been in the interests of those working with girls, particularly with those of academic aspirations, to mount a challenge to the dominance of particular subject cultures. In the struggle to allow at least some girls to become Subjects rather than Others in the academic world, it has been necessary to maintain a parallel male domination of school knowledge forms.

Notes

1 I shall be using evidence from two studies. The first, for my Ph.D, (Paechter, 1993) was carried out during the academic year 1990–91, the first year of the introduction of D&T. The second study took place between 1992 and 1994, and was funded by the Economic and Social Research Council (ESRC number R000233548), was based at the School of Education, King's College, London, and co-directed by John Head and myself. In both studies, the names of teachers, advisory staff and schools have been replaced by pseudonyms.

2 Although CDT is a relatively recent configuration, I am using it as a convenient shorthand for a variety of 'boys' craft subjects, including its predecessor subjects, woodwork and metalwork.

3 I am using 'HE' here to refer to all the domestic subjects (food, textiles, child development, housecraft, laundrywork, etc.), although they have singly and as a group been referred to by a number of names since the nineteenth century. Throughout this period, though the content has changed from time to time, their association with women's work has not, and the teaching staff remains overwhelmingly female.

4 Year 8, age 12–13.

References

Attar, D. (1990) *Wasting Girls' Time: the history and politics of home economics* (London, Virago Press).

Arnot, M., David, M. and Weiner, G. (1996) *Educational Reform and Gender Equality in Schools* (Manchester, Equal Opportunities Commission).

Carrington, B. and Wood, E. (1983) Body talk: images of sport in a multi-racial school, *Multiracial Education*, 11: 2, pp 29–38.

Connell, R.W. (1987) *Gender and Power* (Cambridge, Polity Press).

Davin, A. (1987) Mind That You Do As You Are Told: reading books for Board School girls, 1870–1902, in: M. Arnot and G. Weiner (Eds) *Gender Under Scrutiny* (London, Hutchinson).

Dyhouse, C. (1976) Social Darwinistic ideas and the development of women's education 1880–1920, *History of Education*, 5: 1, pp 41–58.

Dyhouse, C. (1977) Good wives and little mothers: social anxieties and the school-girl's curriculum 1890–1920, *Oxford Review of Education*, 3: 1, pp 21–35.

Fletcher, S. (1984) *Women First* (London, The Athlone Press).

Flintoff, A. (1993) Gender, physical education and initial teacher education, in: J. Evans (Ed) *Equality, Education and Physical Education* (London, Falmer Press).

Hunt, F. (1987) Divided aims: the educational implications of opposing ideologies in girls' secondary schooling 1850–1940, in: F. Hunt (Ed) *Lessons for Life* (Oxford, Basil Blackwell).

Manthorpe, C. (1986) Science or domestic science? The struggle to define an appropriate science education for girls in early twentieth-century England, *History of Education*, 15: 3, pp 195–213.

McRobbie, A. (1991) *Feminism and Youth Culture* (Basingstoke, Macmillan Education).

Paechter, C.F. (1993) What happens when a school subject undergoes a sudden change of status?, *Curriculum Studies*, 1: 3, pp 349–364.

Paechter, C.F. and Head, J.O. (1996) Power and gender in the staffroom, *British Educational Research Journal*, 22: 1, pp 57–69.

Parker, A. (1996) The construction of masculinity within boys' physical education, *Gender and Education*, 8: 2, pp 141–157.

Penfold, J. (1988) *Craft, Design and Technology: Past, Present and Future* (Stoke on Trent, Trentham Books).

Porter, P. (1991) The state-family-workplace intersection: hegemony, contradictions and counter-hegemony in education, in: D. Dawkins (Ed) *Power and Politics in Education* (London, Falmer Press).

Purvis, J. (1985) Domestic subjects since 1870, in: I. F. Goodson (Ed) *Social Histories of the Secondary Curriculum* (Lewes, Falmer Press).

Richardson, D. (1996) (Ed) *Theorising Heterosexuality* (Buckingham, Open University Press).

Riddell, S. (1992) *Gender and the Politics of the Curriculum* (London, Routledge).

Sherlock, J. (1987) Issues of masculinity and femininity in British physical education, *Women's Studies International Forum*, 10: 4, pp 443–451.

Sparkes, A., Templin, T.J. and Schempp, P.G. (1990) The problematic nature of a career in a marginal subject: some implications for teacher education, *Journal of Education for Teaching*, 16: 1, pp 3–28.

Sparkes, A.C. (1991a) Alternative visions of health-related fitness: an exploration of problem-setting and its consequences, in: N. Armstrong and A. Sparkes (Eds) *Issues in Physical Education* (London, Cassell).

Sparkes, A.C. (1991b) Exploring the subjective dimension of curriculum change, in: N. Armstrong and A. Sparkes (Eds) *Issues in Physical Education* (London, Cassell).

Summerfield, P. (1987) Cultural reproduction in the education of girls: a study of girls' secondary schooling in two Lancashire towns 1900–50, in: F. Hunt (Ed) *Lessons for Life* (Oxford, Basil Blackwell).

Templin, T.J., Bruce, K. and Hart, L. (1988) Settling down: an examination of two women physical education teachers, in: J. Evans (Ed) *Teachers, Teaching and Control in Physical Education* (Lewes, Falmer Press).

Thom, D. (1987) Better a teacher than a hairdresser? A mad passion for equality, or, keeping Molly and Betty down, in: F. Hunt (Ed) *Lessons for Life* (Oxford, Basil Blackwell).

Turnbull, A. (1987) Learning her womanly work: the elementary school curriculum 1870–1914, in: F. Hunt (Ed) *Lessons for Life* (Oxford, Basil Blackwell).

Wilkinson, S. and Kitzinger, C. (1993) (Eds) *Heterosexuality: a feminism and psychology reader* (London, Sage)

Willis, P. (1977) *Learning to Labour* (Aldershot, Gower).

16

Content as Context: The Role of School Subjects in Secondary School Teaching

Pamela L. Grossman and Susan S. Stodolsky

Editors' Introduction

This chapter is drawn from a review of literature and a survey of teacher views of their subjects. (The detailed statistical results have been omitted here.) It generalises some of the ideas Williams (Chapter 14) indicated, about how teachers' views on the nature of the subject are related to views on teaching and learning. But it goes further than Williams in identifying important subject differences among teachers that create the idea of a subject subculture.

For too long, research and policy in the United States have treated teaching as a generic activity and teachers as more or less interchangeable parts within a school system.[1] Seen through the lens of subject matter, high school teachers and the subject-specific contexts in which they work are far from interchangeable. If we are to be successful in restructuring high schools or reforming the nature of curriculum and instruction within secondary classrooms, we must sharpen our understanding of how the subject matters to secondary school teachers. Through undergraduate majors, subject-specific methods courses, and professional organizations, subject matter permeates the professional identity and much of the career-long professional development of high school teachers. Subject matter also undergirds the organizational structure of most American high schools in the form of academic departments. Though all of this may seem obvious to anyone connected with high schools, the most obvious features of schooling often have the most far-reaching consequences, as Jackson (1990) illustrated in his work on elementary school teaching.

Despite, or perhaps because of, the centrality of school subjects in high school teaching, subject matter has a taken-for-granted quality in much research on secondary teaching. Research on high schools has tended to look at features of the school as a whole (Boyer, 1983; Cusick, 1983; Lightfoot, 1983; Powell *et al.*, 1985) or aspects of teaching and learning within a particular subject matter. In this chapter we contend that taking a

---

This chapter has been edited.

comparative approach toward understanding subject-matter *differences* among high school teachers is crucial for the analysis and reform of secondary school teaching. We argue that the nature of the parent discipline and features of the school subject, as well as teachers' beliefs regarding the subject, help create a conceptual context within which teachers work. Throughout this discussion of content as context, our central interest is in how subject-matter differences among secondary school teachers help explain curricular and instructional patterns in high schools and responses to reform efforts. Shared beliefs about the possibilities and constraints offered by different school subjects help contribute to the 'grammar of schooling' in high schools (Tyack and Tobin, 1994) and complicate efforts to restructure schools or redesign curriculum.

After first defining what we mean by context, we describe features of disciplines and school subjects that differentiate among subject matters and give rise to distinct subject subcultures. In arguing that these subcultures are characterized by differing beliefs, norms, and practices that affect teachers' work and responses to reform efforts, we present illustrative research findings from our own empirical research as well as that of other researchers. In conclusion, we discuss a variety of implications for research, policy and high school reform efforts based on this understanding of subject-matter differences.

Definitions of Context

In this analysis, we focus on *school subjects* as specific contexts within which secondary teachers teach.[2] Throughout this discussion, we assume that contexts are socially constructed, located frequently but not necessarily within institutions, and individually interpreted. Lave (1988) makes a helpful distinction between arenas and settings in her description of context. She defines arenas as the larger institutions, which, though socially constructed, have a given set of features that both enable and constrain certain activities. A setting, in Lave's framework, is the individually constructed and represented version of the arena. The construct of setting helps us understand why individuals can experience the same arena so differently. In our framework, teachers of a specific school subject share a common arena for practice, though they may differ in their specific interpretations of the subject.

The organizational context of high schools also explicitly interacts with subject matter (Talbert and McLaughlin, 1993); most secondary schools reify subject-matter distinctions through the existence of subject-based departments. Departments can be a powerful feature of secondary teachers' lives, as the work of Ball (1981), Johnson (1990), Siskin (1991, 1994), Siskin and Little (1995), and Talbert (1995) demonstrates.

School subjects, as arenas for practice, possess different features, histories, and status that affect teachers' work (Goodson, 1985; Stodolsky, 1993). These features of school subjects pose implications for the nature of teaching within the subject and may mediate reform efforts. A comparative perspective focuses attention on the normative views of the subject shared by many teachers who teach it. These shared beliefs may help define the possibilities and constraints teachers perceive as they do their daily work and respond to innovations. The shared beliefs and norms of teachers who share a common school subject can usefully be characterized as a subject subculture (Ball, 1981; Ball and Lacey, 1984).

Content as Context: The Origin and Features of Subject Subcultures

The disciplinary socialization of prospective teachers contributes to the origin of subject subcultures. The parent disciplines from which many school subjects derive may exert an important, if often invisible, influence on secondary school curriculum and instruction. Academic disciplines differ in their histories, their epistemologies, and the degree of theoretical consensus existing within the field (e.g. Bernstein, 1971; Schwab, 1978). Bernstein (1971), for example, distinguishes between disciplines that form strong boundaries around their subject matter and offer fewer curricular electives and disciplines that blur the boundaries among subjects and offer students more choice. These features of the discipline affect high school teachers, particularly because secondary teachers receive a significant portion of their education within the discipline they will later teach. However, school subjects, the locus of secondary school teaching, differ in important ways from the traditional academic disciplines (Goodson, 1985).

We now turn to certain features of school subjects, such as status, perceived sequentiality, and scope, which help shape the subject-matter arena within which teachers work. School subjects differ in their degree of status within the school and larger community. Higher status subjects, such as math or science, may be able to claim greater resources and power within the school than lower status subjects, such as art or music (Ball, 1987; Ball and Lacey, 1984; Goodson, 1985). Higher status subjects are more likely to count for college entrance or to be considered part of the core curriculum. Subjects also differ with regard to their relationship to state and district assessment programs; while subjects such as math or English are regularly included in mandated testing programs, other subjects such as foreign language or art are not.

School subjects also differ with regard to the perceived or inherent sequentiality of the subject and curriculum (Stodolsky, 1993). A school subject such as foreign language has a fairly rigid sequential curriculum – French I, French II, French III French IV and AP French. Teachers of French II depend on their colleagues in French I to have taught particular grammar skills and vocabulary to their students. Without having mastered the content of French I, students may find it difficult to move on to the next level. Social studies, as a school subject, would seem to possess less sequential dependency with regard to content. Students who were baffled by Ancient Civilization in the 9th grade go on to study American History in the 11th without noticeable consequence. Teachers' perceptions of the inherent hierarchy or sequentiality of a subject relate to their beliefs and actions regarding the importance of content coverage (Stodolsky and Grossman, 1995). Department policies regarding curriculum coordination may also reflect the degree of sequentiality related to the school subject.

School subjects also differ with regard to their scope and coherence. Some subjects, such as English or social studies, include a number of different disciplinary areas, resulting in a broad curricular scope with relatively less coherence than subjects such as math or chemistry. Social studies, for example, draws on the disciplines of history, anthropology, geography, political science, economics, psychology, and sociology. The extent to which departments are composed of teachers from diverse disciplines may contribute to the degree of cohesiveness of the department. Departments that draw together teachers from diverse disciplinary backgrounds, such as social studies, may find it more difficult to develop consensus about curriculum. Alternatively, struggles to develop consensus in social studies might be amplified by the differing perspectives, values, and theoretical orientations at issue in the school subject itself.

Because teachers work in subject-specific contexts and hold a number of subject-specific beliefs related to teaching and learning, the particular issues and policies that high school teachers view as problematic may vary. We argue that these conceptions of subject matter create a 'conceptual context' that helps frame the work of high school teachers and mediates their responses to reform proposals. For example, teachers of broad, less well-defined subjects, such as English or social studies, may feel a greater sense of curricular autonomy than do teachers of more defined and more sequential school subjects. Because the subjects they teach are so broad, they may feel they need to make individual choices about what to include and what not to include (Grossman, 1993; Protherough and Atkinson, 1992; Stodolsky, 1988).[3] Even a change in how the school day is structured might be perceived differently by teachers of different subjects. Teachers of subjects perceived as more sequential, such as foreign language or math, may worry over schedules that have them meet students only two or three times a week, whereas teachers of science or art might welcome such a schedule.

Research Findings

Before reporting findings from our own research, we review the few studies of secondary teaching that have taken a comparative subject-matter approach. These studies seem to confirm the existence of specific subject subcultures.[4] For example, Siskin's (1994) study of math and English departments suggested that the departments were characterized by different cultures and norms, and that math departments at different schools shared more common features than the math and English departments at the same school. Ball's (1981) study of a British secondary school that was considering multi-ability grouping found that math and foreign language teachers were most resistant to such a change, in large part because of their beliefs about the nature of their subject matter. These departments argued successfully for an exemption from the policy on multi-ability grouping on the grounds that their subject matter would not allow it. An earlier British study (Hayes, 1976) found similar differences between math and foreign language teachers, who supported tracking or streaming, and English teachers, who supported mixed-ability classes. Similar results are reported by Wheelock (1992), Gamoran and Weinstein (1995), and for middle-school teachers by Loveless (1994).

Other studies have tried to delineate differences in patterns of belief among teachers of different subjects. In a study of Dutch teachers, de Brabander (1993) found that teachers contrasted school subjects in relation to the nature of knowledge (hard versus soft) and on the emphasis on 'work' or 'play' in the subject matter. The teacher-generated contrasts were consistent with those postulated by Bernstein (1971). In a survey of Israeli teachers, Yaakobi and Sharan (1985) found that humanities teachers differed significantly from language teachers in their attitudes toward academic knowledge, with humanities teachers adopting a more 'progressive' perspective on knowledge and teaching. A somewhat similar British study tried to distinguish between high school teachers who held transmission orientations toward writing and those who believed that writing involved interpretation (Barnes and Shemilt, 1974). Teachers of biology, physics, chemistry, and language agreed more often with the transmission perspective, whereas teachers of English and religion adhered to an interpretation perspective.

In our own comparative study of subject matter, we have relied upon a number of data sources to study the ways in which subject matter serves as a context for the work of high school teachers.[5] Here, we briefly describe some ways in which teachers from different fields vary in their conceptions of subject matter, instructional beliefs, and curricular coordination and control.

Teachers seem to regard conceptions of school subjects as one of the commonplaces of their daily work lives. In interviews not specifically connected to subject matter conducted with teachers from 16 schools as part of a study on the contexts of secondary school teaching, teachers spontaneously spoke of what their subjects did and did not 'permit' them to do. English teachers, for example, talked about the 'permissive' nature of the subject matter,[6] whereas math teachers spoke of what they perceived to be the constraints of the content. Math teachers commented frequently on the demands for coverage of a well-established curriculum, of having 'to get to a certain point by a certain time,' as one informant described. They also spoke of their sense of the sequential nature of the subject matter and the ways in which it affected their teaching. As one math teacher commented, 'Math is the type of subject where [the students] just can't skip it. There's no point in saying "You missed that, you get a zero." They need it, they have to do it 'til they are ready to go on to the next section.' Another math teacher echoed a belief in the linearity of learning. 'The outline of the topics you can't change too much because so much of Algebra depends on what you do previously. You can't do a lot of problem solving until you've had positive and negative numbers. The same thing with factoring and things like that. You can't solve quadratics until after you've factored.' In contrast, English teachers described English as broad in scope; 'English is the basis for all communication at the school.' They also described the negotiability of the curriculum; as two teachers commented, not all students have to read the same text or even the same genre, as long as they are learning to read and to write. Said one teacher, 'My goal is to have a student read. If they are going to read a fantasy book – and I don't like fantasy – that's o.k. They're reading.' Finally, the permissive nature of English was mentioned by several teachers. A teacher who taught both German and English at a public school commented, 'But I've always liked to do different things, and I can do that more in English than I can in German, of course.' Another English teacher stated that the reason you might find cooperative learning in his department is that 'our subject matter allows us to do that a lot.' These comments suggest that high school teachers explain their work partly in relation to the constraints and possibilities they perceive as offered by specific school subjects.

These perceptions are confirmed by survey data from 399 teachers of 5 academic subjects (math, English, science, social studies, and foreign language) in these same 16 high schools (Stodolsky and Grossman, 1995). Teachers completed survey items having to do with perceptions of the subjects they taught, beliefs about the extent to which they were free to decide the content of their classes, and perceptions of the extent to which they coordinated the content of their courses with other colleagues. (See Appendix for survey items used to report findings in this section). Confirming the reports of the perceived importance of sequence in mathematics found in interview data, math teachers, along with colleagues in foreign language, scored significantly higher on the *sequentiality* scale than did teachers of science, English, or social studies. [. . .] Math and foreign language teachers rated their subjects as significantly more *defined* than did teachers of science, English, and social studies. [. . .] Math teachers also rated their subjects as considerably more *static* than did teachers of the other 4 academic subjects [. . .], with English teachers most strongly rejecting the portrayal of their subject as static.

Along with different conceptions of their school subjects, teachers of the five academic subjects also reported varying levels of curricular autonomy and control. Elsewhere (Stodolsky and Grossman, 1995), we argue that these and other curricular consequences result from the degree of sequen-

tiality and definition associated with each subject. While all teachers felt
free to decide on the teaching techniques to use in their classes, math
teachers felt significantly less freedom to decide on the content of their
classes than did teachers of the other four academic subjects. [. . .] Math
teachers also stood out from their colleagues in their reports of coordinat-
ing course content with other members of their departments, with math
teachers reporting the most coordination and science and social studies
reporting the least. [. . .] Similarly, math teachers were most likely to develop common exams with other department members, with English and
social studies reporting the least likelihood. [. . .]

In addition to curricular coordination and control, instructional practices
and policies may also be affected by subject subcultures. For example,
tracking or student differentiation is a practice with important consequences for students. Beliefs about tracking [setting] may be associated
in part with conceptions of subject matter, particularly with the perceived
importance of sequentiality. (Beliefs about the advantages and disadvantages of tracking may also represent value positions with respect to equity
and the social distribution of opportunity.) The survey responses from
teachers of five academic subjects showed significant group differences in
beliefs about tracking. Math teachers believe most strongly that 'instruction in my subject is most beneficial when students are grouped by
prior academic achievement' while social studies teachers reject this statement most strongly. [. . .][7]

Though far from complete, when taken together, our research and the
research of other scholars suggest that subject subcultures may be characterized by both beliefs about the subject matter that bind teachers together
and by norms regarding teaching practice, curricular autonomy, and coordination. These studies provide support for the idea that high school
teachers work in somewhat separate arenas, defined by the subject matter
they teach. The issues and concerns of the typical math teacher are not the
same as those of the typical English or social studies teacher, nor do they
work under the same constraints. While norms of specific departments,
regardless of subject matter, can also affect the practices of an individual
department, an important point made by Gutiérrez (1995), Talbert (1995),
and Talbert and Perry (1994) in their analysis of departments, teachers of
different subjects, in general, may hold quite different beliefs about the
nature of the subject and the possibilities for curricular coordination. In the
next section, we develop some of the implications for policy and directions
for future research following from this perspective.

Toward Rethinking Research and Policy

We urge the research community to investigate the role of subject matter in
secondary school teaching more systematically in analyses of teaching and
to use a subject-matter lens in interpreting extant research. As we have

already indicated, teachers of different subjects bring differing frames of reference to their teaching; these subject-matter frames, which inform teachers' thought and actions, must be better understood. Pooled analyses of high school teachers, for example, mask the real differences that may exist among teachers of different subjects. Claims regarding secondary school teaching in general may be more true for some subject matters than for others. For example, Cusick's (1983) study of high schools describes the curricular electives created by high school teachers in their efforts to attract students. However, many of the examples he cites in his work are from social studies and English, two subject areas of broad scope, in which the subject subcultures may permit more content negotiation by teachers; in contrast, relatively few quotations come from math teachers.

Researchers might also investigate the origin of beliefs about subject matter. How are beginning high school teachers socialized into subject subcultures? To what extent does the organization and representation of subject matter in universities prepare prospective teachers to hold particular beliefs about school subjects? Lacey (1977) commented on the strong role that subject-matter played in the socialization of prospective teachers in Britain.[8] Researchers need to investigate the 'hidden curriculum' of subject-matter majors within higher education to understand how prospective teachers come to hold certain beliefs. While gaining the subject-matter knowledge required for teaching, prospective secondary school teachers are also being socialized into a particular view of the world, as seen through disciplinary lenses. In part, this socialization relates to disciplinary ways of thinking. However, students may also be absorbing beliefs about the subjects they will later teach from the ways in which majors are organized and the subject is institutionalized within higher education. For example, math and science courses designed to weed out all but the most serious students may teach those who remain that higher level math and science are not for everyone, a problematic lesson for prospective high school teachers if one wants to make higher level math available to a wide range of students. Similarly, academic departments that strongly differentiate the curriculum for majors and non-majors are implicitly providing prospective teachers with a model of tracking.[9] The number of prerequisites required for different courses within a major may also teach prospective teachers a lesson about the importance of sequence in learning a subject. Although research in higher education has documented the existence of strong subject subcultures within universities (Becher, 1989; Clark, 1987), relatively little research has investigated the effects of these subcultures on prospective teachers.

Research on teacher socialization has rarely investigated the high school department as a site for the socialization of new teachers. Studies of how departments socialize newcomers into their ranks might shed light on how beliefs about school subjects are maintained over time. Departments that deviate from normative views of the subject matter – for example, math departments that reject a view of mathematics as inherently sequential – provide a strategic research site for seeing how departmental culture can mediate subject subcultures (Gutierrez, 1995). Given the differences that can exist among departmental cultures within a single school (McLaughlin and Talbert, 1993), this analysis suggests that secondary teacher education programs consider placing student teachers with partner departments rather than with partner schools. Although less common, nondepartmentalized high schools offer a strategic counter case deserving of study. Finally, the importance of department chairs [heads] should be more carefully studied. To what extent does departmental leadership contribute to the maintenance of a distinct subject subculture? If chairs participate in hiring decisions, to what extent do they use this role to maintain departmental norms and prevailing beliefs about the subject matter? Can strong department chairs overcome commonly held beliefs about the subject matter when these beliefs run counter to reform efforts?

Policy Implications

Clearer insights regarding subject matter differences in secondary school teaching must also inform the formulation and implementation of educational policy. For example, policy implementation is certain to be mediated by the different subject-matter arenas in which teachers teach. Teachers' perceptions of subject matter may also mediate their response to reform proposals. As mentioned earlier, teachers of broad, less well-defined subjects such as English or social studies may feel a greater sense of curricular autonomy than teachers of more defined subjects and make less of an effort to coordinate the overall curriculum within their subject. If they perceive and value greater autonomy over the content to be taught as an inherent feature of the subject they teach, teachers may resent reforms that threaten to deprive them of this autonomy. At the same time, such policies may have the side-effect of encouraging more departmental coordination of curriculum, or at least discussion of what is being taught, than is likely to occur normally. For example, the English department at Esperanza High School, one of the schools we have studied over the past few years, responded to the California Assessment Program's new writing assessments by meeting to coordinate writing instruction across the curriculum. As a department, they divided up the writing prompts included in the CAP writing test by grade level, and committed to teaching students to respond to those prompts. The new assessment policy resulted in more curricular coordination within this particular department.

In contrast, teachers of well-defined, more sequential subjects such as math or foreign language may already make more of an effort to coordinate the vertical curriculum within their subject; however, they may respond cautiously to reforms that would affect the ways in which the curriculum is sequenced for learners. The math department at Rancho High School, another high school we have studied, believed strongly in the importance of sequence in math teaching and learning. When the state mandated that all students would study algebra and abolished many of the general math courses, the department responded by instituting a two-year sequence for students who were not seen as ready for the traditional Algebra 1 course – a year-long algebra course to cover the first half of the material in the standard Algebra I course and a second year-long algebra course to cover the remaining chapters of the course. In this manner, the Rancho faculty were able to hold on to their strong belief in student readiness, while conforming to the 'letter of the law' mandating that all students study algebra.

According to this analysis, efforts to restructure high schools will bump into the subject subcultures that currently exist in secondary schools. Without a better understanding of the patterns of belief and practice held by teachers of different subject matters, proposals to decompose departments, to detrack the curriculum, or to create interdisciplinary curricula may falter. Our analysis suggests that efforts to restructure the high school curriculum will run into resistance from math and foreign language departments if issues of sequence are not addressed, a pattern that seems to be confirmed by current research on restructuring schools. In a study of restructuring schools, Gamoran and Weinstein (1995) found that efforts to eliminate tracking posed more problems for math teachers than for social studies teachers. Even in the schools that claimed to be eliminating homogeneous grouping as part of their restructuring effort, most of the high schools continued to rely on homogeneous groups for math instruction; 'For the most part, especially in the middle and high schools, mathematics appears most resistant to the elimination of ability grouping' (p. 7).

In a study of departmental responses in high schools that are restructuring, Little (in press) found that math teachers at one school that had joined the Coalition of Essential Schools responded cautiously to the maxim 'less is more.' Little quotes one veteran math teacher who commented, 'I think you can do "less is more" in reading books; you can read three books instead of six books. But I don't think you can do "less is more" in math.' The chair of the math department at this school reinforced this view; 'You can't teach "less is more" in math. There isn't anything you can throw out.' At all three schools Little studied, teachers raised issues of subject integrity in questioning reform efforts.

Two kinds of difficulties have been detected in studies of schools trying to adopt the interdisciplinary approach of the Coalition of Essential Schools (Muncey and McQuillan, 1993). Members of core fields (English, social studies, math, and science) may have difficulty working out how to create an interdisciplinary program and still cover what they believe is essential to each area. In addition, teachers outside the core, such as teachers of foreign languages, express difficulty in trying to find both the means and justification for students to study their field. [. . .]

Policymakers also need to understand that instructional policy will always be mediated through individual teachers' own conceptions of subject matter (Cohen, 1990; Cohen and Ball 1990) – the specific subject-matter 'settings' in which they work. For example, math teachers who value problem solving and discourse within their subject are probably more likely to embrace current reform efforts of the NCTM (1991) or those introduced through the Urban Math Collaborative (Romberg and Middleton, 1994) than are those teachers who strongly believe in a more sequential, skill-oriented approach to mathematics. New curricular guidelines will also be interpreted differently by teachers, depending on their specific beliefs about the subject matter. Policy implementation, then, must take into account the role of teachers' existing conceptions of subject matter and how they fit with the intentions of curricular or instructional policies and guidelines. Instructional policies are often introduced as new actions to be taken or curriculum to be covered and do not explicitly incorporate the conceptual base teachers need to think through the proposed policy (Cohen and Barnes, 1993). We believe that explicit attention to the fit between teachers' existing conceptions and goals regarding subject matter and the subject-matter conceptions of proposed reforms is needed for successful introduction of educational reforms. [. . .]

This analysis suggests that departments, rather than whole schools, may represent an alternative initial site for reform efforts aimed at large comprehensive secondary schools. Though this strategy runs the risk of reifying subject-matter differences, it offers an opportunity to build from commonalities shared within a subject subculture and move toward more understanding and collaboration across departments. Investing in department chairs as brokers of reform takes advantage of subject-specific leadership already available at the school site, while providing a career path for expert teachers who wish to move beyond the classroom. If provided with appropriate release time and opportunities for professional development aimed at leadership of adults, department chairs can work with their colleagues to develop new curricula and experiment with new forms of classroom teaching (Hill, in press). Alternatively, department chairs can also defend the status quo and resist efforts to integrate the curriculum or to blur the boundaries of their departments (Ball and Bowe, 1992). If reformers choose instead to create interdisciplinary structures that replace departments, they will need to acknowledge explicitly the subject-specific backgrounds and concerns of the participants (Ladwig and King, 1992; Little, 1995).

Responses to policy, implementation of various reform efforts, and classroom practice all depend upon the complex interweaving of the contexts in which teachers teach. Subject matter represents a critical strand in this intricate web, one we ignore at our peril in our efforts to understand and reform secondary school teaching.

Notes

1   This may reflect the larger issue of subject matter as a 'missing paradigm' in research on teaching until very recently (Shulman, 1986).
2   Our understanding of content as a central context for teaching has emerged from our work with the Center for Research on the Context of Secondary School

Teaching (McLaughlin and Talbert, 1993). Subject matter is clearly not the only arena within which teachers work, nor is it necessarily the most important. As McLaughlin and Talbert (1993) demonstrate, secondary teachers' work is profoundly influenced by the multiple and embedded contexts of department, school, district, and state. Part of our interest has also been in studying how content interacts with other contexts that define teaching. For example, the mission of the school may add a different twist to the status and role of school subjects. A performing arts magnet [specialist] school will give a preference to the arts that is missing in most comprehensive high schools. The kinds of students served by a particular school serves as a crucial context for teachers, as much of teachers' work involves adapting subject matter for specific students.

3   Alternatively, different kinds of personalities may be attracted to different subjects, which may account for subject-matter differences among teachers. Certain individual characteristics may be associated with teachers' choices of their college majors and the subjects they teach. Some of the norms, beliefs, and preferences shared by teachers of a given school subject may emanate from shared proclivities, orientations, and values, in addition to, or in tandem with, specific features of the school subjects themselves.

4   See Grossman and Stodolsky (1994) for a complete review of related research. [. . .]

5   As part of a smaller project within the Center for Research on the Context of Secondary School Teaching, we have had access to the large body of data collected by the Center over a 3-year period on issues related to school context (McLaughlin and Talbert, 1993). Both qualitative and quantitative data were collected from teachers, administrators, and students at 16 different schools in two states. Surveys over a 3-year period inquired into teachers' goals for instruction, perceptions of subject matter, their professional roles and responsibilities, the role of state and district resources and reform efforts, professional development activities, reports of instructional practice, and department and school climate. In addition, core interviews were conducted with teachers and administrators at all 16 schools on issues related to school context, instructional practice, and professional roles and responsibilities. Finally, we conducted a set of 12 case studies of math and English teachers at 3 of the 16 high schools. We selected English and math as they possess both similarities with regard to their importance within the high school curriculum, and differences with regard to the nature of the school subjects and parent disciplines. These case studies were designed around issues central to our own investigation of content as context. Data for these case studies included two to three interviews with each of the 12 teachers, classroom observations, and survey data.

6   See also Protherough and Atkinson (1992) for discussion regarding teachers' beliefs about the permissive nature of English.

7   We have just replicated these findings (with the exception of one item on coordination) regarding differences among teachers' conceptions of subject matter and curricular activity in a national sample of over 600 high school teachers.

8   As many of the studies that have investigated and found subject subcultures are British, it is possible that there are cross-national differences in the strength of disciplinary socialization that account for the research findings.

9   One of the authors took 'Physics for Poets' and 'Biology and Human Affairs' in college, but nowhere in her English courses did she encounter courses entitled 'Poetry for Physicists' or 'Books for Biologists!' We suspect that more specialized courses for nonmajors exist within math and sciences than they do in the humanities.

Appendix

Scale Items[a]

Scales
Defined Subject Matter: α = .55
  There is a well-defined body of knowledge and skills to be taught in my subject area.
  There is little disagreement about what should be taught in my subject area.
  There is a clearly defined body of knowledge that guides my work.

Static Subject Matter: α = .57
  Thinking creatively is an important part of the subject matter I teach. (scored in reverse)
  Knowledge in my subject area is always changing. (scored in reverse)
  The subject I teach is rather cut and dry.

Sequential View of Learning: α = .47
  Students must practice basic skills within my subject area before tackling more complex tasks.
  If I do not cover my curriculum, students' future learning in this subject will be jeopardized.

Student Differentiation: α = .46
  Curriculum materials (textbooks, books, a.v., etc.) for a given course should be different for classes with different achievement levels.
  Instruction in my subject is most beneficial when students are grouped by prior academic achievement.

[a]Items are from the 1991 CRC survey.

References

Ball, S. (1981). *Beachside comprehensive: A case study of secondary schooling.* New York: Cambridge University Press.

Ball, S. (1987). *The micropolitics of the school: Towards a theory of school organization.* London: Metheun.

Ball, S. J., and Bowe, R. (1992). Subject departments and the 'implementation' of national curriculum policy: An overview of the issues. *Journal of Curriculum Studies, 24,* 97–115.

Ball, S., and Lacey, C. (1984). Subject disciplines as the opportunity for group action: A measured critique of subject subcultures. In A. Hargreaves and P. Woods (Eds.), *Classrooms and staffrooms.* Milton Keynes, England: Open University Press.

Barnes, D., and Shemilt, D. (1974). Transmission and interpretation. *Education Review, 26,* 213–228.

Becher, T. (1989). *Academic tribes and territories: Intellectual enquiry and the cultures of disciplines.* Milton Keynes, England: Open University Press.

Bernstein, B. (1971). On the classification of educational knowledge. In M. F. Young (Ed.), *Knowledge and control: New directions for the sociology of education* (pp. 47–69). New York: Collier Macmillan.

Boyer, E. (1983). *High school: A report on secondary education in America.* New York: Harper and Row.

Clark, B. R. (1987). *The academic life: Small worlds, different worlds.* Princeton, NJ: Carnegie Foundation for the Advancement of Teaching.

Cohen, D. K. (1990). A revolution in one classroom: The case of Mrs. Oublier. *Educational Evaluation and Policy Analysis, 12,* 327–345.

Cohen, D. K., and Ball, D. L. (1990). Relations between policy and practice: A commentary *Educational Evaluation and Policy Analysis, 12,* 249–256.

Cohen, D. K., and Barnes, C. A. (1993). Pedagogy and policy. In D. K. Cohen, M. W. McLaughlin, and J. E. Talbert (Eds.), *Teaching for understanding: Challenges for policy and practice.* San Francisco, CA: Jossey Bass.

Cusick, P. A. (1983). *The egalitarian ideal and the American high school.* New York: Longman.

de Brabander, C. J. (1993). Subject conceptions of teachers and school culture. In F. K. Kieviet and R. Vandenberghe (Eds.), *School culture, school improvement, and teacher development* (pp. 77–105). Leiden University, The Netherlands: DSWO Press.

Gamoran, A., and Weinstein, M. (1995, August). *Differentiation and opportunity in restructured schools.* Paper presented at the annual meeting of the American Sociological Association, Washington, DC.

Goodson, I. (Ed.). (1985). *Social histories of the secondary curriculum: Subjects for study.* London: Falmer Press.

Grossman, P. L. (1993). *English as context: English in context* (Tech. Rep. No. S93–2). Stanford, CA: Stanford University, Center for Research on the Context of Secondary School Teaching.

Grossman, P. L., and Stodolsky, S. S. (1994). Considerations of content and the circumstances of secondary school teaching. In L. Darling-Hammond (Ed.), *Review of Research in Education: Vol. 20.* Washington, DC: American Educational Research Association.

Gutiérrez, R. (1995, April). *Practices, beliefs, and cultures of high school math departments: Understanding their impact on student advancement.* Paper presented at the Annual Meeting of the American Educational Research Association, San Francisco, CA.

Hayes, K. (1976). Which subjects can be taught in mixed-ability classes – Teachers' views. *Cambridge Journal of Education, 6,* 32–38.

Hill, D. (1995) The strong department: Building the department as a learning community. In L. S. Siskin and J. W. Little (Eds.), *The subjects in question: Departmental organization and the high school.* New York: Teachers College Press.

Jackson, P. W. (1990). *Life in classrooms.* New York: Teachers College Press.

Johnson, S. M. (1990). The primacy and potential of high school departments. In M. W. McLaughlin, J. E. Talbert, and N. Bascia (Eds.), *The contexts of teaching in secondary schools: Teachers' realities* (pp. 167–184). New York: Teachers College Press.

Lacey, C. (1977). *The socialization of teachers.* London: Meuthen.

Ladwig, J. G., and King, M. B. (1992). Restructuring secondary social studies: The association of organizational features and classroom thoughtfulness. *American Educational Research Journal, 29,* 695–714.

Lave, J. (1988). *Cognition in practice.* Cambridge: Cambridge University Press.

Lightfoot, S. L. (1983). *The good high school: Portraits of character and culture.* New York: Basic Books, Inc.

Little, J. W. (1995). Subject affiliation in high schools that restructure. In L. S. Siskin and J. W. Little (Eds.), *The subjects in question: Departmental organization and the high school.* New York: Teachers College Press.

Loveless, T. S. (1994). The influence of subject areas on middle school tracking policies. In A. Pallas (Ed.), *Research in sociology of education and socialization* (pp. 147–175). Greenwich, CT: JAI Press.

McLaughlin, M. W., and Talbert, J. E. (1993). *Contexts that matter for teaching and learning: Strategic opportunities for meeting the nation's educational goals.* Stanford, CA: Stanford University: Center for Research on the Context of Secondary Teaching.

Muncey, D. E., and McQuillan, P. J. (1993). Preliminary findings from a five-year study of the Coalition for Essential Schools. *Phi Delta Kappan, 74*(6), 486–489.

National Council of Teachers of Mathematics. (1991). *Professional standards for teaching mathematics.* Reston, VA: Author.

Powell, A. G., Farrar E. and Cohen, D. K. (1985). *The shopping mall high schools: winners and losers in the educational marketplace.* Boston: Hougton-Mifflin.

Protherough, R. and Atkinson, J. (1992). How English teachers see English teaching. *Research in the Teaching of English, 26,* 385–407.

Romberg, T. A., and Middleton, J. A. (1994). Conceptions of mathematics and mathematics education held by teachers. In N. L. Webb and T. A. Romberg (Eds.), *Reforming mathematics education in America's cities: The urban mathematics collaborative project* (pp. 83–104). New York: Teachers College Press.

Schwab, J. J. (1978). Education and the structure of the disciplines. In I. Westbury and N. J. Wilkof (Eds.), *Science, curriculum, and liberal education* (pp. 229–272). Chicago: University of Chicago Press.

Shulman, L. (1986). Those who understand: Knowledge growth in teaching. *Educational Researcher, 15*(2), 4–14.

Siskin, L. S. (1991). Departments as different worlds: Subject subcultures in secondary schools. *Educational Administration Quarterly, 27,* 134–160.

Siskin, L. S. (1994). *Realms of knowledge: Academic departments in secondary schools.* Washington DC: Falmer Press.

Siskin, L. S., and Little, J. W. (Eds.). (1995). *The subjects in question: Departmental organization and the high school.* New York: Teachers College Press.

Stodolsky, S. S. (1988). *The subject matters.* Chicago: University of Chicago Press.

Stodolsky, S. S. (1993). A framework for subject matter comparisons in high school. *Teaching and Teacher Education, 9,* 333–346.

Stodolsky, S. S., and Grossman, P. L. (1995). The impact of subject matter on curricular activity: An analysis of five academic subjects. *American Educational Research Journal, 32,* 227–249.

Talbert, J. E. (1995). Boundaries of teachers' professional communities in U.S. high schools: Power and precariousness of the subject department. In L. S. Siskin and J. W. Little (Eds.), *The subjects in question: Departmental Organisation and the High School.* New York: Teachers College Press.

Talbert, J. E., and McLaughlin, M. W. (1993). Understanding teaching in context. In D. K. Cohen, M. W. McLaughlin, and J. E. Talbert (Eds.), *Teaching for understanding: Challenges for policy and practice* (pp. 167–206). San Francisco: Jossey Bass.

Talbert, J. E., and Perry, R. (1994, April). *How department communities mediate mathematics and science education reforms.* Paper presented at the Annual Meeting of the American Educational Research Association, New Orleans.

Tyack, D., and Tobin, W. (1994). The 'grammar' of schooling: Why has it been so hard to change? *American Educational Research Journal, 31,* 453–479.

Wheelock, A. (1992). *Crossing the tracks: How 'untracking' can save America's schools.* New York: New Press.

Yaakobi, D., and Sharan, S. (1985). Teacher beliefs and practices: The discipline carries the message. *Journal of Education for Teaching, 11*(2), 187–199.

Index